WH S

STUDY AND REVISE

AS/A2 Level

Government & Politics

First published 2002
exclusively for WHSmith by
Hodder & Stoughton Educational
338 Euston Road
London NW1 3BH

Reprinted 2003, 2004

Impression number   10   9   8   7   6   5   4   3
Year   2007   2006   2005   2004

Typeset by Fakenham Photosetting, Norfolk

Printed and bound in Great Britain by
The Bath Press, Bath

A CIP record for this book is available from the British Library.

ISBN 0 340 84857 X

CONTENTS

- **This book has been written as a study and revision aid for students taking A2 Level and AS Level examinations in British Government and Politics and as an up-to-date supplement to any text books used throughout a course. It should help you bring together this mass of information into an easily digestable form.**

- **The Labour Prime Minister Harold Wilson is credited with the saying 'A week is a long time in politics', meaning that you cannot predict future political events and that everything can and usually does happen quickly in politics.**

- **Factual information gained in this subject will therefore quickly date. The obvious way round this problem is to keep abreast of political events as and when they occur.**

- **This does not mean that the basic arguments in British Government and Politics continually change – there is a body of academic knowledge built up in Political Science as in all other social sciences that needs to be acquired and there is no simple short cut to the hard work of studying to gain this knowledge.**

Studying Government and Politics

Besides using this book and your mainstream course text books I hope you will read a newspaper on a regular basis – it can but does not have to be a heavyweight broadsheet, there are plenty of adequate popular tabloids that give sufficient political information. Cut out and keep any particular articles that you think add to your knowledge and file them for later use. Television (news, current affairs and discussion programmes) is now well established as a major source of information for Politics students and little needs to be said about content or bias in presentation. Most students are aware that newspapers are more partisan in their reporting of politics than television, which is subject to greater controls over objectivity.

I am often asked by students about the historical content of modern politics as they are worried that their lack of specialised knowledge of this subject will penalise them in the examination. I always reply that the current examination boards do not expect a detailed academic knowledge of the interpretation of modern British history but obviously politics cannot be studied in a vacuum. British politics is rich in history – it informs our understanding of the institutions in the State and you will be expected to have some appreciation of post-1945 events for all the syllabuses.

Approaches to the study of Government and Politics

As the sources of information open to today's students of Government and Politics are greater than at any previous time, they are expected to be able to produce answers of a higher quality. One way to do this is to attempt to see politics in the round – to take each topic and see how it fits into the greater order of things. This will aid your organisational and analytical skills which are now tested in the examination.

Some obvious topics like Voting Behaviour and Culture will relate closely to sociological descriptions of political activity. Others like Parliament, Prime Minister and Cabinet will examine historical inputs but only as they contribute to our understanding of current concepts.

FACTFILE

There are three broad approaches to the study of British Government and Politics that you will encounter in your AS and A2 Level work:

- **The institutional** Here the focus is on the institutions of the state including Parliament, the constitution and administration.

- **Policy cycle** The main attention here is on policy-making and the processes that accompany it. The executive including the Prime Minister and Cabinet and other policy influencers are examined.

- **Socio-political** The socio-political approach is concerned with the sociological context of politics and focuses on the aspects of class, power and structures in British government that inform the wider perspective.

Using this book

Each chapter in this book provides succinct and up-to-date coverage of one of the major topics contained in the Common Core of the A2 Level and AS Level Government and Politics syllabuses of the examining boards – AQA (Assessment and Qualifications Alliance), OCR (Oxford, Cambridge; RSA) and EDEXCEL (London). The first half of the chapter identifies the current academic debate in the topic, then breaks this down using theoretical and empirical studies so it can be easily assimilated. Diagrams are used where relevant as a descriptive aid to learning. Academic sources have been extensively identified throughout these chapters as well as in the textual references to each section.

Each chapter contains a sample of different types of examination questions provided with answers. Look at them critically, try to improve them and test your analytical powers. Remember there is no right or wrong answer in politics. What examiners are looking for in A-level Politics answers are quality of thought, a good range of knowledge, and demonstration of understanding and evaluative skills – in other words, the ability to advance good arguments on paper.

Finally, do try to work through the sets of questions in each chapter. These are based on key areas and should act as aids to learning.

Units and syllabuses

All the units in this book relate to the AS common core for all the examination boards. They also have relevance to the full A2 Level examination (AS+A2) and all A2 work where indicated in the table below. British Government and Politics is embedded in all AS and A2 examination papers either as stand alone knowledge or on conjunction with comparative government knowledge usually contrasted with the Politics of the USA. In the synoptic element of A2 papers students are expected to draw together knowledge and understanding gained in both AS and A2 work.

Syllabuses

All the syllabuses of AQA, Edexcel and OCR follow a format whereby students are introduced to a fairly basic understanding of British Government and Politics at AS (Advanced Subsidiary) level taken after 1 year of study – sometimes called A1. The A2 second year of study follows naturally from the first year and leads to the award of the full Advanced or A Level (AS+A2) GCE (General Certificate of Education award). A Levels cannot be achieved without passing the AS first or concurrently with A2 at the same sitting if you are taking the full course in one year. A2 work is more intellectually challenging and builds on the foundations laid in AS work. At A2 most of the syllabuses include comparative work either with USA government or more theoretical work looking at the ideologies of the respective political parties, or in greater depth at political culture or some other aspect of politics, political issues or the problems of governing the political state.

The breakdown of the syllabuses below is only given for outline guidance. For more detail you must consult the relevant documents available from the respective Examination Boards.

Chapters and Units		AQA		EDEXCEL		OCR	
		AS	A2	AS	A2	AS	A2
1	Political Culture	✓	✓	✓			✓
2	Constitution		✓	✓	✓	✓	✓
3	Prime Minister	✓	✓	✓	✓	✓	✓
4	Cabinet	✓	✓	✓	✓	✓	✓
5	Parliament	✓	✓	✓	✓	✓	✓
6	Civil Service	✓	✓	✓	✓	✓	✓
7	Political Parties	✓	✓	✓	✓	✓	✓
8	Pressure Groups	✓		✓	✓	✓	✓
9	Public Opinion/Elections	✓		✓		✓	✓
10	Voting Behaviour	✓		✓		✓	✓
11	Local Government	✓		✓			✓
12	Europe	✓		✓	✓	✓	✓

AQA

AS Modules	1	Electoral Systems and Voting Behaviour
	2	Parties and Pressure Groups
	3	Features of Representative Democracy
A2 Modules	4	Comparative UK/USA Government
	5	The Politics of the USA (Option)
	6	The Politics of Northern Ireland, Scotland and Wales (Option)
	7	Ideas in Contemporary British Politics (Option)
	8	Government and Politics Synoptic Module

Edexcel

AS Modules	Unit 1	People and Politics
	Unit 2	Governing the UK
	Unit 3	The changing UK System
A2 Modules	Route A	Key political issues
One of routes	Route B	Political ideologies
A, B, C or D	Route C	Politics in the USA
	Route D	International politics

OCR

AS Modules	1	Elections, Electoral Systems and Voting Behaviour in the UK
	2	Politics of the UK
	3	Government of the UK
A2 Modules	1	US Government and Politics (Option)
	2	Political Ideas and Concepts (Option)
	3	Government and Politics Research Essay (Option)
	4	Government and Politics (US Option) synoptic
		or
	5	Government and Politics (Political Ideas and Concepts Option) synoptic.

Assessment

Most papers contain essay questions A2 or A Level plus a combination of short answer and data/stimulus response questions, AS Level.

Short answer questions are designed to test factual knowledge together with the ability to analyse and differentiate between ideas and concepts. Data response questions test understanding and interpretation of data based on selected passages or simple statistics. Questions are usually stepped. Those with the lowest mark can be answered from the text. Those with the middle range mark demand a textual response supported with understanding acquired in your studies. Those with the highest mark test analytical skills and demand a more complex response. Finally stimulus response questions demand the combination of all three skills found in data response as the student is expected to display the three levels of understanding, description, explanation and analysis.

All the A Level Government and Politics syllabuses variously test skills, knowledge and understanding. More emphasis is now placed on understanding and skills than on knowledge – it is no longer possible (if it ever was) to score high marks in a Politics A Level paper by simply presenting facts. The various skills objectives tested in the examination are as follows:

AQA Edexcel and OCR	1	Recall, select and deploy knowledge
	2	Analyse and evaluate
	3	Communicate

With **Objective 1** examiners look for a knowledge of the facts, they require an understanding of how conflicts are resolved. For **Objective 2** students must display evidence of ability to unpick and identify the components of a proposition bringing them together in a refocused way that answers the question. Finally **Objective 3** tests synthesis, relevance, structure/ organisation and reasoned conclusion. The point is made that examiners now like to see outlines of conclusions at the beginning of the answer as an aid to the development of that answer. Obviously the ability to communicate is crucial to this objective.

Revision and examination

Keep your revision **active and organised**. You will be given plenty of advice by your teachers or tutors. If you are working alone, consult one of the many books written on this subject from your local library.

Revising for an examination is like preparing for a race – you must gradually build up your stamina, skills and speed for the day when all will be brought into action. Treat it like a long campaign – always think of your studies over a nine month period and plan accordingly, for the second half of the academic year will involve you in taking the examination.

Try to **get organised** at the outset in your studies using file cards or other ways of keeping your notes in order – this will help in revision. If you have been studying effectively throughout the year, you will be surprised at the amount of material you have retained. A revision period should enable you to bring your material to the forefront of your mind. Practise answering examination questions at home within the time limits and gradually improve on your performance each time. **Use your memory and recall powers** to good effect – practise strengthening them whenever you can. Do this orally or in writing. Take a topic – say voting behaviour – and attempt to reproduce all the associated themes, ideas and writers on this subject on one side of A4 paper. Do this for all the topics in this book and rework and reread your file notes, lecture notes and relevant sections in books and articles. Finally make sure you know the syllabus and examination requirement (rubric) of your particular Board. You will then know exactly the type of questions you have to answer.

The examination

CHECKLIST

✓ **Make sure you know the time available to answer the paper and allocate it to questions accordingly.**

✓ **Read the paper carefully and select only those questions you plan to answer. Avoid panicking at this stage.**

✓ **Carefully plan each answer on the examination paper sheet at the head of each question on your paper. Leave the answer plan for the examiner to see and give credit for if necessary.**

✓ **Time each answer carefully – do not write longer than the allocated time on one answer. If you squander time on one answer the others will suffer.**

✓ **Remember the skills examiners are looking for – essays must be analytical and well answered.**

✓ **If you make a mistake, cross it through neatly and carry on, or select a new question if time.**

✓ **At the end of the examination – if you have spaced your answers carefully you should have a little time left to read through what you have written and make any last minute corrections. That is why you should leave plenty of space between each answer and always start a new question on a fresh page of the answer book.**

Definitions of political culture

- A political culture describes the **values, beliefs, attitudes and emotions** that people display towards their political system. According to *Moran* (*1994*), it covers the political culture of a community focusing on both procedural aspects of how we are governed and the substantive questions of what the government should do. People will therefore adopt attitudes to the political system which are dependent very much on upbringing and political socialisation, occupation and other sectoral cleavages like consumption which cut across social class divisions.

- Attitudes to the conduct of politics through parliamentary channels as opposed to violence are still prevalent. Generally speaking the British people believe in parliamentary as opposed to anti-parliamentary politics (street demonstrations, direct action protests and extremist or terrorist violence) and this belief has become a **cultural norm**. Although British political culture has never been totally quiet (*Pimlott 1989*), there is widespread support for the institutions of the state and for the idea that elections and the ballot box rather than the bomb and the bullet are the accepted way of transmitting opinions to the politicians.

FACTFILE

- **Attitudes to the British monarchy have changed but they are still supportive of the institution.**
- **The concept of a civic culture is used to explain the passivity of British politics.**

Different approaches to political culture

The following are the main approaches to British political culture.

Civility or civic culture model

Pioneering work on British political culture was carried out as early as 1963 by the Americans *G Almond and S Verba* using a functionalist perspective. Puzzled as to why British participatory democracy exhibited considerable degrees of subservience to established authority in comparison with other European democracies, they introduced the idea of a civility model. British political culture was neither completely parochial, subject or participant, all of which exhibit variations of involvement or subjection by people to ruling elites. British political culture had a **mix of participant and subject characteristics**. There was a degree of participation through elections transmitting authority to ruling elites, but it was not particularly active.

Deferential perspective

In his classic work on the English constitution first published in 1867, *Bagehot* drew attention to the deferential attitudes of the British people manifested in respect for law and order and reverence for the monarchy.

During the 1960s there was a tendency for functionalist writers to approach British political culture from this deferential perspective, the only substantive evidence of political attitude towards the state. Studies of voting behaviour had shown how deferential to the Conservative Party certain sections of the working class were (*Parkin 1967, Butler and Stokes 1969*).

Dominant ruling class model

Marxist writers developed counter theories of **hegemony** to explain continued passive working class adherence to the political and capitalist economic system. The ideas of the Italian writer *Antonio Gramsci, Miliband* (*1972*) showed how the ruling class dominated the value system by control of the ideological institutions – the media, education and political parties in the state. Such a view presupposes the working class suffer from a false consciousness in the sense that they cannot see that the political institutions and ideas in the state (which they absorb) are the product of a dominant class ideology.

Instrumental/ambivalent approaches

Modern sociologists have refined these ideas to take account of more sophisticated explanations of working class cultural attitudes. According to *Marshall* (*1988*) working class people's attitudes can fall into either **instrumentalism** (acceptance that capitalism works in their interests) or **ambivalence** (neither fully committed to capitalism nor wholeheartedly opposed to it). If either of these positions is accurate, working class attitudes to a dominant ruling class cultural model are no longer capable of simplistic interpretations.

WORKING CLASS ATTITUDES

INSTRUMENTALIST
Accept capitalist economic/political system. Try to improve living standards

AMBIVALENCE
Changing attitudes – switching; accept/reject capitalism and political systems. Implies (a) and (b)

Working class cultural attitudes to the state and economic system

(a)
No dominant political ideology – ruling class have not brainwashed working class

(b)
Fatalism – acceptance of status quo; cannot change system

C H E C K L I S T

✓ **Sociologically the idea of a culture relates to descriptions of the norms and values that regulate the conduct of people's lives. These are transmitted from one generation to the next largely by the primary agencies of socialisation – families – and the secondary agencies of schools, institutions and the political system.**

✓ **Borrowing from the Functional School in sociology (*Emile Durkheim, Talcott Parsons*) a culture is therefore essential for the maintenance and survival of a social system – it serves to integrate members of society.**

Political continuity

The British have a long historical continuity for their political state. Although there was a civil war in the seventeenth century this was not the revolutionary break with the past experienced later in some countries.

According to *Madgwick* (*1994*), there was a circular development to British political history which passed through the following stages:

1 **Supreme monarch** – dominant executive to seventeenth century

2 **Dual power** – monarch and Parliament sharing power (eighteenth century)

3 **Dominant Parliament** – eighteenth to nineteenth century

4 **Dual power** – Parliamentary executive managing House of Commons

5 **Supreme executive** – dominant executive (Prime Minister and Cabinet) based on Parliament

The past therefore presses heavily on the present practice of British politics and its stability may explain conservative attachment to the institutions of the state (*Madgwick 1994*).

Cultural Diversity

Britain has become descriptively a culturally homogeneous society – the majority of the population have an English, Welsh or Scots ethnic background, the minority are descended from immigrants who entered the country at various times. In the nineteenth and early twentieth centuries the British host population absorbed immigrants from Ireland and Europe and from the 1950s from the Commonwealth, the West Indies and the Indian sub-continent. Britain has been painfully transformed into a multi-cultural society with both Labour and Conservative governments eventually forced to restrict immigration (in the hope that this would improve race relations) and pass race relations laws.

The majority of immigrants from the New Commonwealth have settled in areas of high population concentration, for example in London and the cities of the North and Midlands where they have been made welcome by other immigrants.

Cultural perspectives

There are a number of cultural perspectives applicable to an understanding of immigrant-host relations.

- **Assimilation**   Assimilationists tend to the view that ethnic communities should adapt to the British way of life. They argue that the problems faced by immigrants are cultural rather than racist and they can be overcome by conformity to the institutions of the host country (*Patterson 1965*).

- **Ethnic pluralism**   This view points to the wide variety of cultural groups in Britain. There is already a multi-cultural society in existence and it is easy to over-simplify by focusing on a single ethnic culture (*Gilroy 1987*). Pluralists tend to see the relationship between host majority and ethnic minority as one of coexistence rather than dominance by English cultural values.

- **Class culture**   Marxists tend to regard ethnic culture as less important than class culture for purposes of analysis. They believe the focus should be on dominant and subordinate class positions rather than minority – majority cultures. From this perspective migrant labourers constitute a fraction of the working class and share all the disadvantages of this group (*Westergaard and Resler 1976*).

FACTFILE

- **It is often claimed that ethnic minority voters are preponderantly Labour largely because that party has a softer image on race relations and immigration issues generally.**

- **The three Race Relations Acts were all passed under Labour governments (*Denver 1989*).**

- **Apart from ethnicity other facts put forward as explanations of the ethnic vote include class and political geography. If the majority of immigrants fall into a working class category then the same influences pressing on the host working class will operate. The difficulty with this simplistic view is that there is little evidence to support the notion of either a united ethnic or working class.**

- **The evidence for geographical concentrations of black Labour votes is stronger. As immigrants have tended to concentrate in areas of Britain where ethnic communities are preponderant, so this has increased the tie between the Labour Party and this category of voter.**

Self-government for Scotland, Wales and Northern Ireland

The cultural cohesion of Britain is further affected by celtic nationalism. Of the constituent parts of what *Rose (1971)* calls a multi-national state – comprising England, Scotland, Wales and Northern Ireland – all groups subordinate to the English Westminster Parliament were able to move towards a devolved form

of self-government in the late nineties. Fearing separatist demands and the development of a Federalist Britain, Tony Blair conceded the case for a separate **Scottish Parliament** and **Welsh Assembly** after positive referendums in those countries in 1998. Both bodies were established after elections in Scotland and Wales in May 1999 held under a form of proportional representation, AMS (Additional Member System). In Northern Ireland, Nationalist and Unionist paramilitary ceasefires from 1995 lead to All Party Peace Talks and the Peace Agreement of April 1998. This was formally ratified by separate referendums in both parts of Ireland simultaneously, Northern Ireland and the Irish Republic. Elections under STV (Single Transferable Vote) created the new Northern Ireland Assembly in June 1998 and Shadow Northern Ireland Executive with power transferred from London in 1999.

Class and sectoral divisions

The social fabric of Britain still exhibits class and sectoral divisions although there is a remarkable degree of self-control among the different groups. Some writers claim that the passivity of the British in the face of what is an unequal society economically rests on the acceptance of the status quo. Working class attitudes have come to terms with the capitalist economic system, partly through rising living standards and cultural change. The **embourgeoisement debate** may have been discredited in the sense that possession of a higher living standard did not change the Labour-voting working class into Conservative (*Goldthorpe, Lockwood, Bechofer and Platt 1969*) but it was the first to pick up the growing scepticism or development of instrumental political attitudes. Margaret Thatcher successfully attracted the skilled working class vote (the C2s) in the three Conservative election victories of 1979, 1983 and 1987, largely because of policy voting for issues which offered greater shares of wealth to that section (*Crewe 1992*). Popular capitalist measures of sales of council houses, privatisation of public utilities and lower taxation attracted large sections of the working class vote. However, the decisive 1997 General Election victory for New Labour proved that these effects were now less important as an electoral factor. C2 voters had begun to return to Labour in the 1992 General Election. By 1997 this process was complete. The 2001 General Election victory confirmed New Labour as the party identified with the successful management of the economy – a reversal of the earlier image which benefited the Conservative Party.

As **class** and **party dealignment** theories have been developed to show post war electoral volatility breaking monolithic Labour and Conservative support, so new explanations tend to focus on other cleavages in the populace. Class categories are no longer permanent. *Crewe (1985)* first distinguished between the more affluent new working class, who were predominantly owner occupiers and working in private industry, and the poorer northern traditional old working class, who were living in council houses and were still reliant on trade unions and the Labour Party. Changes in middle-class culture have opened new divisions between traditional and new professions and salariat and service classes so increasing contradictory class locations in these groups. This again makes pronouncements about political behaviour difficult *(Wright 1976)*.

The class structure of Britain is more fluid than at any time since 1945 due in large measure to changes in industrial and employment patterns, educational opportunities and increased social mobility. Vertical consumption patterns divide and cut horizontal class categories on the basis of those who are self-reliant and those who need the State – those with wealth and those without *(Dunleavy 1979)*. One consequence of this is that although talk of a classless society is premature, class is having less of an impact on British politics and culture generally.

Questions

1 Why did Tony Blair concede the argument for self-government in Scotland, Wales and Northern Ireland?

2 Explain what is meant by a C2 voter.

3 What does political continuity mean?

Consensus

Political consensus

Political consensus or agreement contradicts the idea that politics and political activity exist because of disagreements, that politics is the settlement of disputes. Clearly if politics ended, political society as we know it would cease. Yet party politicians make rhetorical public statements whilst privately agreeing on many policy issues *(Kavanagh 1992)*. Analysis of consensus demands that we separate the substantive from the procedural, since consensus about ends (policy) is clearly different from consensus over means (procedure). Some critics claim that substantive or policy consensus disappeared under the governments of Margaret Thatcher only to return in a different form with John Major. But discussion of consensus also involves an examination of the part played by the opposition reacting to government

policies. After the General Elections of 1997 and 2001 the defeated Conservative Party moved away from consensus again but was unsure of what position to adopt in opposition. The party remained divided even after the election of the new leader Iain Duncan Smith in late 2001.

Policy consensus

The classic period of substantive or policy consensus occurred after 1945 – the post war consensus – when there was broad agreement and no great ideological difference between the Conservative and Labour parties in certain areas. According to *Seldon* (*1994*) there were six features of continuity or overlap between Conservative and Labour policies where divisions between the two parties were insignificant:

- Commitment to full employment.

- Acceptance of a mixed economy of state and private enterprise.

- Support for the welfare state idea of providing state security in health and welfare for the majority.

- Close relationships maintained with trade unions as representatives of organised labour.

- Promotion of policies designed to reduce inequality in society through progressive taxation.

- Bilateral approach between Conservative and Labour Parties towards foreign and defence policies.

Origins of post-war consensus

It is not difficult to find the origins of the post war consensus for they lay in the general desire of politicians of all parties to improve the lot of the people of Britain immediately preceding and after the Second World War. Plans were laid for improvements to the welfare benefits system (**the Beveridge Report 1942**) which were acceptable to both sides together with positive steps to increase government intervention in regulation of the economy to ensure a better match between supply and demand. The moderate Conservative *Harold Macmillan* had argued as early as the 1930s for a better 'middle way' solution to the problem of mass unemployment and the party under *Winston Churchill* (Prime Minister 1940–45 and 1951–55) came to accept **Keynesian** monetary policy (after the economist *John Maynard Keynes*) which appeared to find the solution to managing inflation with full employment.

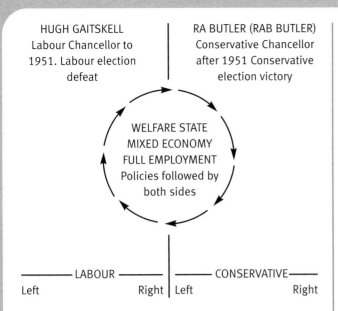

HUGH GAITSKELL
Labour Chancellor to
1951. Labour election
defeat

RA BUTLER (RAB BUTLER)
Conservative Chancellor
after 1951 Conservative
election victory

WELFARE STATE
MIXED ECONOMY
FULL EMPLOYMENT
Policies followed by
both sides

———— LABOUR ———— ———— CONSERVATIVE————
Left   Right | Left   Right

Consensus 1951–55.
Moderate Conservative economic and monetary policy (Butskellism)

The fairly short alternation in power of Labour and Conservative governments during the 1950s and the fact that the Conservative Party were returned to office in 1951 with a small majority contributed to feelings of policy consensus in the electorate with the result that governments did not depart too far from the centre ground. This was particularly evident in the field of economic and monetary policy where **Butskellite** policies of the moderate Conservative Chancellor, *R A Butler*, bore a striking resemblance to those of his predecessor in post, the moderate Labour Chancellor, *Hugh Gaitskell*.

Changing consensus

It is difficult to be precise over the date when the post war consensus or consensual policies between the two major parties began to diverge. Certainly government and opposition throughout the 1960s and 1970s were not widely different in their support for the status quo and consensus policies – Harold Macmillan, Alec Douglas Home, Harold Wilson, Edward Heath and finally James Callaghan all in their own ways followed middle ground substantive ideas. Despite party rhetoric (mainly for the benefit of party activists) Conservative and Labour governments to 1979 presided over or reached what came to be called the **high point of consensus** (*Holmes and Horsewood 1988*). From that point on consensus would become a term of abuse as the new radical Margaret Thatcher sought to lead the Conservative Party into a new direction.

Margaret Thatcher and the New Right

Consensus politics broke down under the Conservative governments from 1979 for a number of reasons – some practical, some ideological. Economically the policies of Keynesian money management were discredited as economic growth slowed and unemployment through the eighties rose. *Margaret Thatcher* turned to the economic philosophies of the 'New Right' to overcome the fiscal crises of the state whereby state incomes do not keep up with state expenditure. The removal of the commitment to full employment allowed tighter control over the money supply as advocated by the monetarist philosophies of *Milton Friedman*. In return this meant that state spending could be targeted on welfare benefits whilst maintaining a reduced form of welfare state system. In many policy areas, for example housing, privatisation, local government, education and the civil service, the intention was to drive down public expenditure by the introduction of market forces principles in line with new Conservative thinking on the advantages of free enterprise as opposed to state involvement. In this Margaret Thatcher was successful – British political culture was radically altered along with the cosy world of consensus politics.

FACTFILE

- Margaret Thatcher succeeded in one of her stated aims in changing the course of socialism for she compelled the Labour Party to move closer ideologically to the centre ground after a radical shake-up of policy first under Neil Kinnock (to 1992), then John Smith (to 1994) and finally Tony Blair (from 1994). In abandoning the more extremist socialist policies under Tony Blair, then accepting many of the policy changes of Margaret Thatcher and John Major, the Labour Party moved back to the right of the political spectrum raising the probability of an end to adversary politics.

- Although John Major continued with the broad drift of Thatcherite policies since 1990, he stamped his own personality on the party, after he was elected in his own right in the 1992 general election. Many Conservative policies were continued, such as those concerned with management of the economy, whilst there were initiatives in making state services more responsive to the public – the Citizens' Charter of 1991 could be seen in this light.

As the political divide began to open again there were those who felt the Conservative Party was pushing its radicalism to unpopular extremes. Yet the party was successful in three consecutive general elections under its radical leader. Paradoxically it was fear of losing a fourth general election that prompted the party to remove Margaret Thatcher and replace her by the more consensual John Major in 1990.

Consensus politics and the millennium

The Third Way of Tony Blair and the election of 2001

A major difficulty for William Hague in the 2001 General Election was to reassert Conservative Party identity in the face of New Labour and Liberal Democratic hold on the centre ground. If elections are traditionally won or lost on a government's record rather than on oppositional appeal then the events of 2001 confirmed the rejection of William Hague by an electorate grown tired of the worst excesses of Conservatism. A growing non-aligned electorate was another factor in the equation, demonstrated by tactical voting which helped the Liberal Democrats to 52 seats and Labour to a majority of 167 in the new Parliament. Most voters appeared to want moderate policies – the centrist **median voter** (neither left nor right) found Tony Blair's Third Way (neither Old Labour nor Old Conservative) attractive, reassured that the gains made would be safe with New Labour.

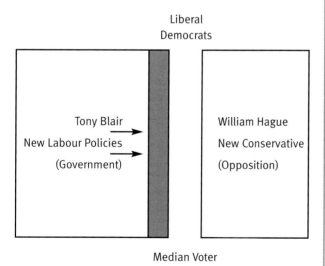

Liberal Democrats

Tony Blair
New Labour Policies
(Government)

William Hague
New Conservative
(Opposition)

Median Voter
Centre

The Realignment of New Labour and Problem of Conservative Party identification.
New Labour Government moves to the Right and makes it difficult for Conservatives to win 2001 Election.

In repositioning New Labour further to the right than any previous Labour government, Tony Blair in effect created a New Consensus and paradoxically may have ended two-party dominance of the political system (adversarial politics).

Procedural consensus

Procedural consensus implies that there is agreement about the means of conducting political debate even if there are substantive disputes over the content of political ideologies. There is still widespread acceptance of parliamentary channels or the law in settlement of grievances by the majority. A minority might be prepared to use violence against the state to achieve the replacement of laws they perceive as illegitimate as a last resort. This has occurred on relatively few occasions – discounting events in Northern Ireland – and includes opposition to industrial relations legislation and the Miners' Strike in 1984, inner city riots in the early eighties and nineties and demonstrations against the Community Charge or Poll Tax 1988–1990.

Violence and the state

Although criminal acts are clearly different to civil disobedience by virtue of motive – the one selfish, the other moral – demonstrations and anti-political activity are close to the dividing line between lawful and unlawful activity (*Heywood 1994*). Occasional outbreaks of violence also lead to claims of ungovernability, breakdown in law and order or support for the government. Marxist writers regard this as evidence of a **legitimation crisis** in the capitalist state – as people lose faith in the ability of government to reconcile conflicting demands so the state loses its legitimacy to govern. There is a corresponding lack of motivation to participate in the democratic processes with the result that citizens turn to other forms of political activity (*Habermas 1976*).

Moderate government

British governments usually command a majority in Parliament with the result that they can claim legitimate power or authority to rule. Although this legitimacy gives them authority over a vast governmental machine, they still depend on cooperation (consent willingly given) and acceptance from the electorate to achieve their programme. Little is to be gained in a democratic state from **coercion** and outright control over the people who have ultimate sovereignty to remove their rulers through parliamentary elections. Clearly there will be disputes in any political system and democratic governments usually display **toleration** towards the expression of political dissent.

Political culture since 2000

The following features in the new millennium have profoundly affected the British political culture.

A disillusioned electorate

Voter apathy has increased, measured by the fall in turnout in the 2001 general election and the fact that membership of all three main political parties, Labour, Conservative and Liberal Democrat, has fallen to record levels. Looking for explanations, The British Political Participation Survey (1992) found that the majority of respondents did not wish to be actively involved in politics. In 2004 the government floated the idea of compulsory postal voting as a potential solution to low turnout.

The role of the monarchy

After nearly a decade of media attention on the monarchy since the death of Diana, Princess of Wales, the public appears less certain of the role played by a constitutional monarch in the modern political system. Labour party MPs have focused on the Royal Prerogative powers and a Fabian Society Report of 2003 called for a clarification of the Queen's position with regard to the appointment of the Prime Minister and the opening of Parliament.

The war in Iraq and the fight against terrorism

The British involvement in the war in Iraq and its aftermath has damaged the credibility of the Blair government in terms of public support. And culturally the war on terrorism and the media response may have contributed to some Islamophobia over the loyalties of British Muslims. The March 2004 bombings in Madrid highlighted the necessity of the Labour government to become more aggressive in the fight against global terrorism.

Summary

1. **It is difficult to generalise about British political culture. Commentators saw the fifties as a time of restraint with quiet political activity and remarked on the acquiescent attitudes of the people towards their rulers (*Beer 1965*).**

2. **The high point for the post war consensus came during the sixties and seventies paradoxically during a period of pessimism when the survival of British parliamentary democracy was being questioned.**

3. **The eighties marked a retreat from consensus to conviction politics under the radical government of Margaret Thatcher with a noticeable change in public attitudes to the state. Some detected a move away from political movements, the so called 'end of ideology' debate; others detected a 'post material' outlook manifested in concerns for the environment and new social movements (*Inglehart 1977*).**

4. **The nineties witnessed consolidations in the cultural make-up of the United Kingdom and changed attitudes to the institutions of the state, for example the monarchy and electoral system lost the element of certainty they once had. The New Labour government of Tony Blair pushed elite attitudes to an acceptance of reform of these institutions including the House of Lords, House of Commons, Local Government and public perceptions of the monarchy. The death of Princess Diana in 1997 tested both the government and monarchy into a reassessment of public attitudes towards reform and demands for change.**

Sample questions and answers

AS Level questions

1. What is it about the British system of government that makes it parliamentary?
2. What is the difference between extra-parliamentary and anti-parliamentary political protest?

1. *This question demands a knowledge of the theoretical position of parliamentary government. An answer could discuss the idea of sovereignty of the people giving way to parliamentary sovereignty. It is important to show an understanding of the theory of the representative and the relationships to constituents prevailing in an indirect democracy.*

2. *Discuss the importance of extra-parliamentary activity as an adjunct to the legislature. This includes pressure groups and other organisations representing interests in the state usually working through democratic channels which may include protests. Anti-parliamentary actions may be political as opposed to criminal but they focus on public opinion as leverage over politicians. Some anti-parliamentary activity involves violence as a tool against government and is clearly anti-democratic. Other anti-parliamentary action (e.g. street demonstrations) is designed to draw political attention to a pressing issue demanding resolution.*

Describing the constitution

A constitution describes the relationships prevailing between the government and the governed within certain parameters, laws, customs and precedents (*Hood Phillips 1978*). It also regulates behaviour between the various branches of government: executive, legislative and judicial. The British constitution is generally regarded as **prescriptive** or informal because of the lack of a single written document to describe or formalise this arrangement. According to *Norton (1988)* it is this lack of abstract principles found in **descriptive** constitutions which has allowed the British constitution to work so effectively in the past.

Structures

Structurally the modern British constitution can be described as a constitutional monarchy governed by ministers in the name of the Queen. The executive includes these ministers and the Prime Minister who are responsible for policy formulation and implementation. The legislature involves Parliament where the laws are passed. The judiciary through judges and the courts operates the laws. Finally, the European Union makes legislation which is binding on the whole system.

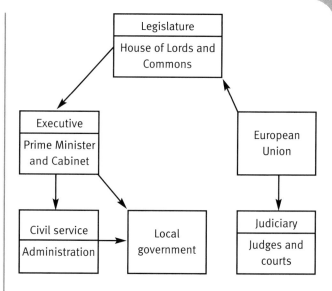

The structure of the British constitution

The separation of powers

The three branches of government – the executive, legislature and judiciary – are kept separate according to the principle of the separation of powers. The eighteenth-century political theorist Baron Montesquieu first observed that a **concentration of power** in a political system could best be avoided by separating government branches. This structure was adopted in the American constitution (1787), but has evolved differently in Britain. In the British constitution the principle is accepted in that the judicial branch is formally separated from the executive and legislature and functions without political interference. But for procedural reasons the personnel in the branches are not separated so there is an overlapping of power. The executive (Prime Minister and Cabinet Ministers) are drawn from and responsible to the legislature (the House of Commons and House of Lords). This has two implications:

- There is a lack of formal check and balance over the powers of the executive.
- The powers of the executive have grown at the expense of the legislature.

Both these features weaken the separated powers argument and lead to a concentration of authority in the hands of the executive. Early criticism of this overlapping power was made by the jurist *Lord Hewart* in his 'new despotism' arguments in 1929. This found an echo in *Lord Hailsham's* 'elective dictatorship' arguments of 1976.

Written or unwritten

Constitutions are often classified according to whether they are formally written down in a descriptive document or informally organised in a prescriptive arrangement. The fact that the British constitution is unwritten is no disadvantage in deciphering the political arrangement. It does not, as some claim, lead to uncertainty or a political vacuum because ideas and values are not clearly characterised (*Peele 1993*). The drawbacks of not having a written constitution in Britain have been overstated for **no** document can entirely encompass the political practices of a nation. The political reality is closer to the constitutional arrangements for both written and unwritten constitutions according to *Finer* (*1979*).

Flexible or inflexible

A similar simplistic comparison between constitutions is often applied to the mechanism for change and amendment. The British constitution is flexible in the sense that no special majorities or arrangements are needed to effect it. The **normal legislative** process of passing Acts through Parliament is sufficient to change the constitution and this can be done quickly, as in the case of the annual passage of the Prevention of Terrorism Act which has a bearing on a person's individual rights and freedoms. It can be argued that since the British constitution has a legal basis – various Acts of Parliament, for example Act of Union 1707, Parliament Acts 1911, 1949, have a bearing on the political system – careful thought would be given to any changes in the law which had a constitutional significance. This in turn introduces a

---

CHECKLIST

✓ **The British constitution has evolved over the centuries successfully adapting to changed political circumstances. This partly explains the lack of a written document.**

✓ **Parliament experimented with a republic after the overthrow of the monarchy in the seventeenth century.**

✓ **The Revolution Settlement of 1688 reformulated the rights of monarchy against Parliament.**

✓ **The nineteenth century introduced the beginning of democracy with a series of Reform Acts, each one increasing the size of the electorate.**

✓ **The early part of this century saw the completion of the constitution – votes were extended to women and the competing Conservatives and Liberals were joined by a Labour Party representing working class interests.**

---

degree of **inflexibility**, for governments would not repeal or change the above-mentioned Acts without all party **consultation**.

The comparisons with the inflexible American constitution are not productive either. Although special majorities are needed from the constituent States in the United States Congress to change the constitution, the inflexibility of this arrangement is balanced by the activity of the US Supreme Court. The Court has acted as a separate legislative branch on occasions, adding a degree of flexibility to the written document.

Theories of the constitution

The evolutionary nature of the British constitution can be tracked through theoretical descriptions which are grounded in history. There are three theoretical constructs that can be examined:

- **A balanced constitution**   The idea of a balanced constitution **emerged** in the seventeenth century and was classically described by Sir William Blackstone at that time. The Revolution Settlement of 1688 placed restrictions over royal power – now the King had to **accept** the authority of Parliament. The system was described as balanced because the powers of the monarch were **checked or balanced** by Parliament. Each House of Parliament (Lords and Commons) could **check the other** and the King's ministers were also restrained by the legislature.

- **A liberal constitution**   Using an historical framework, *Birch* (*1964*) described the nineteenth-century 'liberal' constitution as parliamentary. The middle classes were anxious to establish the supremacy or sovereignty of Parliament over the executive, and for a brief period (1830–40, the so-called **Golden Age**) this came into existence. Descriptions of the 'liberal' constitution tended to overlook the monarchy in their focus on Parliament. Writing in 1867, *Walter Bagehot* allocated a dignified constitutional role to the monarch, leaving Parliament as the efficient part – an accurate description of the situation prevailing at that time.

- **A Liberal Democratic constitution**   Descriptions of the current Liberal Democratic constitution include the influence of a mass electorate working through political parties choosing representatives for Parliament. We can detect two positions in this approach:

  - **The Whitehall view**   *Birch* (*1964*) produced a model of the constitution that focused on executive and administrative power. Parliament was now playing a subordinate role to the executive which decided on and implemented policy through the civil service. Parliamentary supremacy in this view has largely given way to executive dominance and control of both the House of Commons and the House of Lords.

- **An empirical view**   Some modern descriptions of the constitution go beyond the political institutions to include extra-parliamentary opinion formers. In an empirical view of the constitution, *Foreman* (*1985*) includes the media, industrial interests and pressure groups. Such a view is similar to the corporate model of the constitution popularised by the Labour governments during the seventies. These views may be descriptions of a pluralist political system rather than solely of a constitution.

Questions

1   What is the difference between a prescriptive and descriptive constitution?

2   What is the advantage of the separation of powers principle?

3   Give one advantage of a flexible constitution.

Sources of the constitution

Since the British constitution is unwritten and uncodified, there is no one single source where it can be found. This is not particularly advantageous or disadvantageous. Part of the constitution will have a legal basis; part will lie in the political arrangements of the state. The main sources are:

- Acts of Parliament;
- common law;
- conventions;
- European law;
- constitutional writings.

Acts of Parliament

Acts of Parliament as statute law constitute the most important source of the British constitution. They illustrate two important features:

1   Legislation gives a legal basis or footing to the constitution. Where so much is based on unwritten principles this is important.

2   They demonstrate the principle of parliamentary sovereignty.

Parliament is the supreme law-making body and can produce new laws and change existing ones as it pleases.

There are many examples of legislation having a political bearing and thus a constitutional significance. The important point is that all are capable of ordinary reversal (repeal) by the orthodox legislative process. Compared to a written constitution, this procedure has the greater flexibility.

FACTFILE

The following important Acts of Parliament all have a bearing on the constitution:

- **The Parliament Acts 1911 and 1949 regulate the relationship between the House of Lords and House of Commons.**

- **The Representation of the People Acts 1949 and 1969 regulate elections.**

- **The European Communities Act 1972 regulates relationships between the UK Parliament and the European Union.**

Common law

Common law has a number of ingredients. Rules made by judges form a customary basis on which many court decisions are made. Since parliamentary statutes need judicial interpretation in the courts, the case law which is built up over the years forms an important backdrop to the constitution.

The rules surrounding the monarchy also fall within the common law. Much of the royal prerogative power is protected by the courts on these grounds and can rarely be challenged. The residual powers of the monarch are now operated solely by ministers of the crown either directly (the prerogative of mercy, the granting of honours, the selection of the Cabinet) or indirectly by Prime Ministerial advice to the monarch (the decision when to dissolve Parliament, the content of the Queen's Speech opening a new session of Parliament).

Conventions

Conventions of the constitution are rules or understandings generally observed by politicians, but not enforceable at law. They add substance to the constitution by providing a framework against when politics can operate – 'the flesh on the bones of the constitution'. They are followed because it is expedient to do so; there would be political difficulties for a government if they were ignored or breached. The 1911 Parliament Act stipulates that general elections must be held every five years, but conventionally the selection of the date is left to the Prime Minister. Clearly this convention cannot be breached because it is sanctioned by an Act of Parliament.

This situation demonstrates the loss of flexibility if conventions are given the force of law. Sometimes this is necessary, as in the case of the Ministers of the Crown Act 1937 which statutorily recognised the leader of the opposition by the payment of a special salary. Prior to 1937 the opposition leader was only conventionally recognised. Conventions underpin the working of government; collective responsibility allows the Cabinet to operate with a degree of secrecy and accountability. They add flexibility to the constitution because they are easily discarded if no longer of use. By adjusting to the current political climate, they move the constitution forward.

Area of politics affected	Conventional behaviour	Why followed
MONARCH	The monarch keeps out of political controversy. Always acts on advice from Prime Minister/ ministers	To protect impartiality of constitutional monarchy
PRIME MINISTER	Since 1900 the Prime Minister has come from the House of Commons	Recognition of primacy of House of Commons as electorally accountable to the people

Examples of conventions of the constitution

European law

Since Britain joined the European Community in 1973 (now the European Union or EU) European law has been a source of the constitution because of its impact on Parliament and English law. European law and some EU rules take precedence over British law and are applied without further parliamentary debate. This in turn has consequences for parliamentary sovereignty – the UK Parliament has lost some of its **exclusivity in law-making** power over UK citizens. But a future government could always take Britain out of the EU by renouncing the Treaty of Rome. Such a step is now unlikely to happen, especially as the movement towards greater unity is quickening. The passing of the Maastricht Treaty and the Single European Act of 1986 together with the demands for European Monetary Union by the end of the decade are further areas where the British government's sovereignty is being reduced (*Nugent 1991*).

Constitutional writings

Constitutional writings are an important source of the constitution because they give guidance to politicians in the grey area where conventional practice operates. Much of the procedure surrounding the working of Parliament is unwritten in the sense of being contained in Acts. **Authoritative books** like *Erskine May's Parliamentary Practice* (*1844*) therefore become important in any confusion over **interpretation** of the rights and privileges of Parliament. A similar status has been conferred on the constitutional writer *A V Dicey* whose *Study of the Law of the Constitution* was first published in 1885. Dicey is now regarded as an authority on the rule of law.

Constitutional principles

Since there is no written British constitution, there will always be a dichotomy (division) between the **form** (description) and **function** (practice) of the constitution. This is particularly obvious in the operation of the three main characteristics or principles of the constitution: parliamentary sovereignty, the rule of law and the unitary state.

Parliamentary sovereignty

The legal supremacy of Parliament is the central characteristic of the constitution. In principle this translates into the following aspects:

- There are no limits to the authority of the Queen in Parliament expressed through an Act of Parliament.
- One Parliament cannot bind another since all legislation is repealable by Parliament.
- Parliament can extend its life as it did during the 1914–18 and 1939–45 wars.
- Judges apply the law but do not determine the constitutionality of statute law.

The political reality of parliamentary sovereignty qualifies many of the above features. Parliamentary sovereignty itself is now taken to mean electoral sovereignty expressed through a Parliament of representatives indirectly responsible to the people. Since Parliament must submit itself for periodic re-election by the people, the doctrine of a mandate acts as a real restraint on the government.

It has been argued that the use of **referendums** has undermined parliamentary sovereignty because they by-pass Parliament. The 1975 referendum on European Community membership actually passed the decision whether to accept renegotiated terms back to the electorate from a divided Cabinet. The referendum offered Prime Minister James Callaghan a lifeline from which to escape internal Labour party feuding on this issue.

From another perspective, referendums are beginning to appear less foreign to the constitution particularly where they reinforce parliamentary sovereignty as there are no clear rules governing their use. All require parliamentary approval before or after the event and will be included in Bills eventually as Statutes as with any other laws. Their large majority (179 seats) after the 1997 General Election gave Labour the impetus to push through Parliament devolution proposals based on referendum approval for a separate Parliament in Scotland and new Assemblies for Wales and Northern Ireland. Referendums were held in Scotland and Wales in September 1997 and in Northern Ireland in May 1998. Functionally these devolution referendums had different purposes – the Scots and Welsh were accepting the notion of a separate parliament and Assembly, the Northern Irish were voting for the acceptance of the Good Friday Peace Agreement which created the New Northern Ireland Assembly.

The British government is **obligated to other states** by two main treaties: the North Atlantic Treaty and the Treaty of Rome, which was incorporated into British law by the provisions of the European Communities Act 1972. Both of these commitments can be viewed over the long term and in this sense breach the sovereignty principle by **committing future Parliaments** to a course of action decided by their predecessors. Although Parliament retains the ultimate right to withdraw from the Rome Treaty and the EU (and this would have occurred if the 1975 referendum on continuing membership of the EC had been lost) it is at the present time not conceivable that a government will renege on these obligations. British parliamentary sovereignty is therefore affected but not destroyed by continuing membership of the EU.

FACTFILE

- **British subordination to the laws of the European Union is demonstrated by the 1991 Factortame case. By signing the 1986 Single European Act the British government committed itself to a European fisheries policy which could not be affected adversely by British fishing law.**

- **The European Court of Justice ruled in this case that the UK courts had the power to suspend Acts of Parliament that appeared to be in breach of European law. Sections of the British Merchant Shipping Act of 1988 were therefore held inoperative (*Peele 1993*).**

Rule of law

The rule of law was classically seen by *A V Dicey* as a second central feature of the constitution alongside parliamentary sovereignty. Described as equality before the law, procedural fairness and supremacy of the law in the courts, the rule of law has ensured that political life is governed by legal principles.

Although governments observe these principles and are not above the law themselves, the expansion of administrative and executive power has produced cases of conflict between the courts and the executive. In the **Pergau Dam Affair** of 1994 the Foreign Secretary, Douglas Hurd, was found to have broken the law in agreeing to a deal that linked part of an overseas budget to **arms** sales to Malaysia. This case and others demonstrate that the principle of **judicial review** ensures that the executive keeps within the law applied by an independent judiciary.

Challenges to the rule of law have been made by those who have refused to accept the law as impartial or just. Violence was used in protests against the Conservative government policy of reducing the coal industry during the eighties. The anti-poll tax movement of the early nineties refused to acknowledge the legality of the community charge as a replacement for council rates. And the Republican and Nationalist forces in Northern Ireland never accepted the authority of the British government over Ulster.

Unitary state

Centralisation is a key feature of British government with political power concentrated in the hands of the majority party at Westminster. Constitutionally this arrangement is supported by a unitary system of government. Although the United Kingdom comprises the three ancient kingdoms of England, Scotland and Wales together with the province of Northern Ireland, political power resides with England. Each constituent country has a different history and has retained a degree of local government vastly different to the powers enjoyed by the separate states in the truly federal United States of America.

Scotland has its own legal and educational system by virtue of its peaceful accession into the Union in 1707. Wales received different treatment from the English as a result of conquest and was brought into the Union in 1542. Northern Ireland was originally part of Ireland and joined the Union as a separate entity in 1921 with the partition of that country. From 1921 to 1972 Northern Ireland had its own form of self government with a separate Parliament at Belfast (the Stormont). The breakdown in the province's political institutions in 1972 caused the British government to impose direct rule with the closure of the Northern Irish parliament.

Devolution

Devolution of power to Wales and Scotland has never been far from the political agenda in the United Kingdom. Described as the transference of political power away from Westminster to geographically elected bodies (*Bogdanor 1979*), devolution as an issue in United Kingdom politics first surfaced in the modern period in the 1970s.

The debate surrounding devolutionary proposals is well documented (*Norton 1994*). The creation of a separate Scottish Parliament and Welsh Assembly in 2000, with some tax raising powers for Scotland, has increased pressure for a new constitutional arrangement for regional assemblies for England as another tier of government. The 1997 and 2001 Labour Manifestos included proposals for the establishment of Regional Chambers to coordinate transport, planning, European funding and land use planning. This was seen as the first stage of a process leading to a referendum for directly elected regional governments.

FACTFILE

- **The so called problem of the 'West Lothian' question whereby Scots and Welsh MPs can vote on English legislation at Westminster yet English have no voice in the opposite direction is capable of resolution.**

- **First, Scots representation at Westminster could be reduced from 72 to 54 MPs in proportion to population.**

- **Second, Scots MPs could be prevented from voting on English domestic policy but clearly not on United Kingdom policy that affects all four countries (England, Scotland, Wales and Northern Ireland).**

Devolution of legislative and executive power to Scotland and Wales is unusual in Britain with no experience of subordinate legislative assemblies excepting the failed Stormont Parliament in Northern Ireland closed in 1972. Any future relationship between the new Northern Irish and Welsh Assemblies and Scottish Parliament and the central government in the Westminster Parliament could produce difficulties but they are not insurmountable. As subordinate legislatures within a uniting state, they lack the powers of legislatures in federal systems like the United States. Central government could always repeal or remove the offending legislation or even the assemblies themselves – but this would prove more difficult in the long run.

CHECKLIST

✓ **The British constitution is never static – by its evolutionary nature it has accommodated to a variety of pressures which have had implications for the internal working of the state. The following developments have all had an impact on the distribution of power within the constitution, since they change the balance between the government and the governed:**

✓ **Membership of the European Union has added an additional tier of legislative authority above the United Kingdom Parliament. Parliamentary sovereignty has been affected as the laws and directives of the EU must be given effect.**

✓ **A growing trend towards centralisation of power into the hands of the executive. This has had consequences for traditional Cabinet government and policy-making with the increasing tendency for decisions to be taken by a Prime Minister working in smaller Cabinet committees or advisory groups.**

✓ **Executive dominance of the legislature by a party guaranteed a working majority through an electoral system that favours larger parties. The Houses of Parliament (Commons and Lords), despite procedural and organisational change in the select committee system, are not effective checks over what *Lord Hailsham (1976)* called 'elective dictatorship'.**

✓ **The balance of power in relationships between the centre and subnational government has shifted in favour of the executive. Local government powers and democracy (localism) have to some extent been replaced by a growing centralisation as reforming governments have sought to control the costs and function of localities.**

✓ **An expansion in the 'patronage stage', of Non-Governmental Organisations (QUANGOS) exercising devolved executive administrative powers. These various bodies (trusts, boards, regulatory and advisory councils and other agencies) are not elected and are theoretically accountable to the executive (government) which appointed them.**

✓ **Relationships between government and citizens have changed as the state has further clarified civil liberties by amending the laws on criminal justice and official secrets.**

Reform of the constitution

Approaching reform

Although the British constitution has successfully adapted to problems faced by it, there have always been demands to introduce a new structure along the lines of a written or **codified format**, on the grounds that this would be preferable to the existing arrangement. Demands for a new constitutional arrangement became very evident in the decade 1970–80. Both Labour and Conservative governments began to tackle problems of administrative structural reforms and this led inevitably to the constitution itself. Questions were raised about the nation's capacity to absorb the pressures of industrial society; resist demands for devolution; face problems of inflation/stagflation; deal with governmental overload and manage the impression of general ungovernability.

The long period of **Conservative rule** from 1979 excluding the Labour and Liberal Democratic Parties also gave the impression of a breakdown in the two party system, and highlighted defects in the electoral system. The Liberal Party (later the Liberal Democrats) felt more confident about arguments over electoral and constitutional reforms as their popularity increased during the eighties. The sudden return of a Labour government in 1997 after 18 years in opposition gave a fresh impetus to liberal ideas for constitutional reform.

Political attitudes to reform

The political parties' position on constitutional reform reflected their ideological attitudes to the state. *Norton (1994)* identified seven theoretical approaches to reform: **High Tory, Socialist, Marxist, Group, New Right, Liberal and Traditional**. Of these approaches the more important, Liberal and Traditionalist, have had greater impact on political debate in the nineties. The Liberals advocate a written constitution guaranteeing individual rights, proportional representation, a revised House of Lords and revitalised House of Commons. The Traditionalists recognise that the state must adapt if it is to survive. They tend to focus on the importance of reformed parliamentary institutions as a check against excessive executive powers. The most active pressure group in this area is **Charter 88** with 12 main proposals for constitutional reform centred on two goals: (a) a democratic written constitution and (b) a culture of citizenship which would empower citizens to take a greater part in the running of their country. These radical ideas go beyond any Traditionalist position but do find an echo in the Liberal view of a reformed constitution.

1   A Bill of Rights
2   Freedom of information
3   Accountable government
4   A fair voting system
5   A reformed House of Commons
6   A democratic House of Lords
7   Judicial reform
8   Redress for state abuses
9   Independence for local government
10   Parliaments for Scotland and Wales
11   Devolution of power
12   A written constitution

Charter 88 proposals for a new British constitution

New Labour changes to the constitution

Tony Blair moved closer to this position after the 1997 General Election when Labour passed the Human Rights Act which incorporated the **European Convention on Human Rights** into UK law from 1998. This together with other new constitutional changes including devolution, reform of the voting system, changes to House of Lords membership and the 2000 **Freedom of Information Act** all demonstrate a movement closer to the Liberal Democratic and Charter 88 position in this area – possibly encouraged by the desire to work closer with the centre to avoid a repetition of the 18 years spent by Labour in opposition, a prospect looking increasingly remote after Labour's second election victory in 2001.

Since the 2001 general election Labour has continued with changes to their 'new constitutional settlement'. Conservative critics of these reforms claim that Labour has damaged a centuries-old constitution without thinking through the long-term effects of the changes. Radicals feel that Labour has not gone far enough and should have introduced a full written constitution of the type advocated by the Charter 88 Reform Group.

Apart from the introduction of the 1998 Human Rights Act and the 2000 Freedom of Information Act, the other major constitutional changes in Labour's first term (1997/2001) were devolution of powers to the Scottish Parliament and Welsh Assembly; the elected mayor system including the London Mayor; completion of the stage one reforms for the House of Lords; and changes to electoral law through the passage of the 2000 Political Parties, Elections and Referendums Act, which affected election spending.

In their second term from 2001 the pace of constitutional reform slowed but was still impressive. Proposals were announced for the completion of the second stage of Lords reform with the removal of the

Study and Revise AS and A2 Level Government and Politics

remaining hereditary peers but no final agreement has been reached and the matter has been postponed until beyond the next general election.

Regional devolution has been prioritised but referendums have yet to be held in 2004 to test the popularity of another tier of local government.

A new department of Constitutional Affairs was created in 2003 which coincided with the abolition of the ancient post of Lord Chancellor. Lord Falconer was appointed the transitional Lord Chancellor and Minister for the new department with the brief to oversee the dismantling of the Chancellorship by the next election. The argument surrounding this change was to remove the Lord Chancellor from the executive and thus end the breach in the separation of powers principle where the head of the independent judiciary was also a member of the executive. Similar arguments were behind the proposal to remove the Law Lords from the House of Lords and place them in a new Supreme Court. This last suggestion has attracted considerable criticism from members of the senior judiciary.

Summary

1 The arguments for and against a new or reformed constitution are long and complex; apart from theoretical positions, there is the practicality of introducing changes or writing a new document incorporating existing patterns of governmental practice including statute law, common law, conventions, European law and numerous constitutional writings. Although statute law is easy to change, as the sweeping reforms by New Labour testify, *Norton (1988)* makes the point that it would be difficult to introduce a totally new constitution because the mechanism for enactment does not exist. Even if all party talks could produce a consensus over the form a new constitution should take, Parliament may not have the legitimacy to overturn the existing arrangements.

2 Assuming a written constitution could be produced perhaps starting with the 1998 Human Rights Act, would it be an improvement on the existing arrangement? From the focus of rights of citizens it would produce greater certainty under the law for redress of grievances against the state. However, such constitutional safeguards would need protection of entrenchment to prevent repeal from a future government opposed to such reforms. Here the role of the judiciary becomes important, for judges would have to assume a guardianship of the HRA.

3 It is difficult to see how unelected judges (they are not as unrepresentative of popular opinion as is often supposed according to *Zander* (*1998*)) can assume this role in the British Constitution if they are not to conflict with the Executive and Parliamentary Sovereignty. Judicial review of legislation in the UK does not, as in the USA, give judges power to rule executive acts unconstitutional. Indeed it was partly to maintain this tradition of an independent judiciary that the Blair government decided in the 1998 Bill of Rights to adopt the approach of New Zealand which does not give judges the power to declare government statutes as unconstitutional.

Sample question and answer

A2 Level question

1   What would be the difficulties in establishing a written constitution for Britain?

This essay expects the student to be familiar with the arguments surrounding the technical difficulty of Britain adopting a written constitution. Reference needs to be made to the changes introduced by Tony Blair and to *Phillip Norton's* points about the problems of enactment and parliamentary sovereignty. The following points could be used in an answer:

1   *Briefly say why you think Britain should have a written constitution – greater certainty in the law, protection of civil rights, checks and balances against an overpowerful executive.*

2   *Examine how this could be done. Start with a written Bill of Rights. Is this the Human Rights Act?*

3   *Look at the technical, legal and political problems.*
   (a) Technical   How would Parliament enact a constitution that would take away parliamentary sovereignty? (Phillip Norton's points)
   (b) Legal   How could an unelected judiciary become guardians of the constitution?
   (c) Political   What would be the political implications to successive governments restricted or bound by a written document?

4   *Make some evaluation of the above points and conclude with a definite argument.*

PREVIEW

In this chapter you will revise the following main themes:

- **Different theoretical explanations of Prime Ministerial power.**
- **Examination of the relationship between a Prime Minister and other members of the Cabinet.**
- **The central importance of the Prime Minister in the machinery of government.**

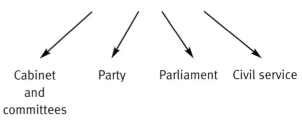

Prime Minister decides policy (monocratic power) which is implemented through

Cabinet and committees   Party   Parliament   Civil service

The prime ministerial government view

Explaining prime ministerial power

Prime Ministers today are vastly more powerful than their predecessors ever were. Government has expanded its activities over people's lives and this increasing centralisation of power has continued throughout the Conservative administrations of the eighties and nineties, and into the Blair government from 1997 and 2001. A number of different perspectives are used to analyse the position of the Prime Minister, some traditional, some modern.

The prime ministerial government debate (traditional)

The focus here is on how the powers of Prime Ministers are used at the expense of other branches of government – most noticeably the Cabinet and the House of Commons.

The principle arguments in this theory are:

- A **dominant** or **monocratic** style of premiership prevents the development of traditional **collegiate** or **group** policy deliberation within the Cabinet.
- Public policy decisions are now taken by the Prime Minister in **bilateral meetings** or small groups of advisers, ministers or officials before full Cabinet deliberations.

Secondary themes are:

- Successive Prime Ministers have expanded their powers over the core executive to the limits of what is constitutionally possible.
- The patronage system of rewards, honours and appointments in the gift of Prime Ministers has been personalised to the extent of devaluing or politicising its impartial nature.

The ideas of Crossman, Mackintosh and Benn

The starting point for this debate was *Crossman* (*1963*, *1977*). His observation that Britain was moving towards a presidential system of government was based on Cabinet experience in Harold Wilson's Labour government. Paraphrasing *Walter Bagehot's* analysis of English politics of 1874, Crossman relegated the Cabinet to the **dignified** or ceremonial side of the constitution alongside the monarch on the grounds that the Prime Minister had usurped the **efficient** role. The reasons given for this development were:

- Weakening of the independence of MPs who were now more reliant on their parties for their careers.
- Domination of the House of Commons by the executive which in effect meant the Prime Minister.
- Improvements in Cabinet support staff around the Prime Minister which increased the Prime Minister's powers of control over the executive.
- Creation of a unified civil service responsible to an official directly under the Prime Minister's authority made it easier for the Prime Minister to control the bureaucracy.

Mackintosh (*1962*) advanced similar ideas of a presidential style of prime ministership replacing traditional Cabinet government. The growth of the powers of Prime Ministers over the machinery of government made it impossible to remove or challenge them outside a general election.

In his *Case for a Constitutional Premiership, Benn* (*1980*) appeared to support the prime ministerial view by claiming that the powers of Prime Ministers were now so great that they affected the rights of the electorate, undermined the role of Parliament and usurped some of the functions of the Cabinet. His solution was to remove the electoral advantage conferred on Prime Ministers of calling general elections by the device of fixed term Parliaments.

FACTFILE

- **Chief executive** – a description of the Prime Minister as the head of government used in a non-evaluative way, not implying dominance or weakness.
- **Core executive** – refers to the grouping of institutions that are central to policy-making: Prime Minister, ministers, Cabinet, Cabinet committees, policy advisers and civil servants.
- **Machinery of government** – refers to the structures of government that make possible the art of public administration, for example the Cabinet and its committees, the civil service or bureaucracy, the system of local government and the agencies or quangos responsible for implementing aspects of central policy.

CHECKLIST

✓ *Crossman*, *Mackintosh* and *Benn* drew parallels between the British Prime Minister and the American President in order to demonstrate the dangers of the over centralisation of powers around a chief executive. Although these comparisons are historically useful in charting the gradual expansion of the office of Prime Minister, they must be used with care.

✓ Constitutionally a British Prime Minister's powers are limited by a different set of legislative arrangements to an American President's. Prime Ministers are members of the House of Commons and must operate successfully there. They are not elected in their own right but as a Member of Parliament.

✓ American Presidents face a more rigid separated power system of executive and Congress. They are elected directly – not as a result of party – and depend on strength of personality and a complex system of relationships for survival.

Margaret Thatcher and prime ministerial government

Margaret Thatcher's premiership (1979–90) is cited as evidence that the prime ministerial government thesis was an accurate description of the relationships prevailing between a Prime Minister and a Cabinet. She made less use of full Cabinet meetings for policy-making and gave the impression of governing through bilateral meetings of committees and ad hoc groups (*Hennessy 1986*). This inevitably reduced the role of the Cabinet to a committee with peripheral policy-making power. Matters came before Cabinet for final sanction, not full and frank discussion in the traditional sense. It is worth noting, however, that previous Prime Ministers had on occasion taken policy decisions in small groups of ministers (Inner Cabinets) before Margaret Thatcher. Her novelty lay in developing a style of leadership that took to the limits what a Prime Minister could do without the Cabinet (*Madgwick 1994*). This was itself a contributory factor in the Cabinet rebellion that removed her from office in 1990.

Paradoxically after the 1997 and 2001 General Elections Tony Blair felt strong enough to further reduce the power of the Cabinet. Meetings were fewer and shorter in almost a replication of the Thatcher practice.

Other weaknesses in this perspective are:

- A tendency to ignore the constraining influences pressing on a Prime Minister within the executive, Parliament and party.

- Less attention is given to the mix of personality and style of governing of various Prime Ministers.

The cabinet government view (traditional)

Margaret Thatcher's removal as Prime Minister in 1990 reinforced the premise that in British politics it is difficult to govern without the support of the Cabinet. The traditional Cabinet government view of prime ministerial power was of a chief executive governing through a collegiate of ministers who were consulted and involved in policy-making at the highest level.

The principle arguments of this theory are:

- It is virtually impossible for a Prime Minister as one person to dominate a Cabinet of 20 other ministers.

- Policy decisions can go to small bilateral groups of ministers including the Prime Minister but final authority remains with the full Cabinet.

Prime Minister and Cabinet decide policy together (collegiate power) which is implemented through

Party   Parliament   Civil service

The Cabinet government view

Secondary themes are:

- Prime Ministerial patronage power over ministerial appointments is checked by the practicality of having a balanced Cabinet representative of the party spectrum.

- The power to dissolve Parliament for a general election confers little political advantage on a Prime Minister.

Checks and balances on Prime Ministers

Claiming that the restraints operating on a Prime Minister's power were as significant as the strengths (*Jones 1980*, *1990* and *King 1985*), makes a convincing case against Prime Ministerial government; it is impossible for a Prime Minister to govern without the support of the Cabinet, the party, public opinion and Parliament. There are many examples: Harold Macmillan's removal of a third of his Conservative Cabinet in July 1962 lost him popularity from which he never recovered. In the eighties Margaret Thatcher was persuaded to accept the Rhodesian/Zimbabwe settlement and the necessity to enter the European Exchange Rate Mechanism against her will (*Thatcher 1993*). John Major faced difficulties in divided Cabinets over a European referendum, the privatisation of the Post Office, VAT on fuel and the Maastricht Treaty. After 1997 Tony Blair faced party criticism over the Dome Project, fuel costs and old age pensions increases, which caused Cabinet unease.

John Major and the restoration of Cabinet government

John Major's period of office as Prime Minister from 1990 to 1997 signalled a return to traditional Cabinet government style partly because he was a compromiser seeking to lead by consensus. Whether this weakness in Cabinet eventually led to his 1997 election defeat by Tony Blair's New Labour Party is debatable. For a variety of reasons, including smaller Commons majorities, different personality, consensus approach to running the government, John Major appeared a less dominant **Cabinet chairman** to Margaret Thatcher's **chief executive**. He restored Cabinet discussion to its central place in policy-making and endeavoured to hold together a balanced Cabinet of left, centre and right deeply divided over Europe. Margaret Thatcher's Premiership was characterised by certainty and conviction, John Major's by comparison was continually dogged by fears for his own survival (*Young 1994*).

Tony Blair as Prime Minister

Tony Blair came to office in 1997 with a very large majority of 179 which gave him the authority as a reforming Prime Minister to carry through much of his legislative programme according to timetable, in his first year. By 1998 the Labour government had embarked on a long list of reforms including the signing of the Social Charter of the Treaty of Maastricht, the banning of handguns, more money into education and health, implementation of the minimum wage and constitutional changes embracing devolution and reform of the House of Lords. Tony Blair personally played an active role in negotiations over Europe and the settlement of the Northern Irish question and the Millennium project. In all this he operated as a focused chief executive, silencing critics within his own party but at the same time realising his dependence on powerful cabinet colleagues – Gordon Brown, Chancellor of the Exchequer, John Prescott, Deputy Prime Minister and Robin Cook, Foreign Secretary.

With his second election win in 2001, Tony Blair demonstrated that he was prepared to stamp his authority on the New Labour cabinet even if in the last resort he had to sack ministers to achieve this aim. The removal of Robin Cook as Foreign Secretary in the post election reshuffle and his replacement by Jack Straw demonstrated his impatience with those who did not share the New Labour project. The survival of Gordon Brown as Chancellor of the Exchequer once again showed the reluctance of a Prime Minister to remove a powerful Cabinet colleague. The resignations of Stephen Byers at Transport (2002) and Estelle Morris at Education and Skills (2002) demonstrate the importance of retaining the Prime Minister's confidence if a minister is to keep his or her job.

Questions

1 Why are Prime Ministers more powerful today than in the past?

2 What is the central point of the prime ministerial government debate?

3 What is the principle advantage of the Cabinet government debate?

CHECKLIST

✓ The survival of John Major as Prime Minister from 1990 to 1997 was due as much to circumstances as to any particular strengths he demonstrated.

✓ By the 1997 general election John Major presided over a hopelessly divided Conservative Party that was returned to Parliament with 165 seats down from the 336 of 1992. Although he did not face a Cabinet revolt like that which removed Margaret Thatcher from office in 1990, John Major's Cabinet divisions between those who wanted closer European political and economic integration (Europhiles) and those against (Europhobes) proved insurmountable.

✓ The governments of both Margaret Thatcher and John Major in their own ways demonstrate the importance of Cabinet support for any Prime Minister.

✓ Although Tony Blair after 1997 and again from 2001 successfully controlled his Cabinets, one cannot discount the fact that at some future time he could face difficulties if the New Labour project is blown off course. Therefore the view that the survival of a Prime Minister is inextricably bound up with relationships to the Cabinet, still stands. There seems little point therefore in attempting to analyse the Prime Minister's position away from this construct.

Core executive theories (modern)

Current theories of prime ministerial power are complex and all-embracing. They focus on the relationships surrounding the Prime Minister as chief executive and recognise that the **power of other elites** and the **fragmentation of policy-making** between them affect the Prime Minister's authority within the core executive.

As a **chief executive** the Prime Minister presides over and manages a core executive of institutions,

networks and practices which include the Cabinet and its committees, ministerial groups, meetings and negotiations (*Dunleavy and Rhodes 1990*). In this role the Prime Minister's formal powers cover the armed services (Commander in Chief), the legislature (policy leader and head of the largest single party in both Houses of Parliament), the administration (head of the civil service as First Lord of the Treasury) and foreign affairs (chief spokesperson for the nation).

There are two basic core executive views:

1 **The segmented decision making model**

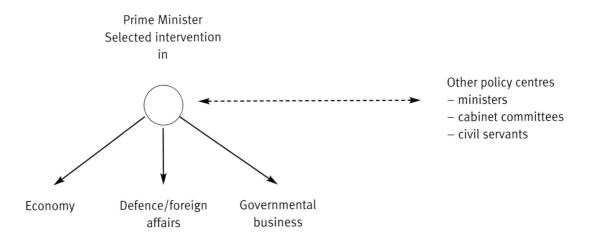

This view claims that power is now so fragmented in the British core executive that the Prime Minister only selectively intervenes in major policy areas, for example the economy, foreign affairs, state security/defence and governmental business

(*Rose 1984, Dunleavy and Husbands 1985*). This narrow prime ministerial focus leaves other policy centres with ministers, Cabinet committees and civil servants.

2 The bureaucratic coordination model

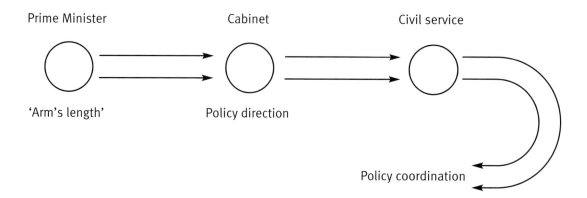

According to this view the civil service has an independent power in policy-making forcing the core executive of Prime Minister and Cabinet into the background (*Heclo and Wildavsky 1981*). Policy-making diffuses through a vast bureaucratic elite who have a vested interest in encouraging a presidential arm's length style of leadership. This inevitably reduces the role of the Prime Minister to one of **tie-breaking** or **power-broking** interdepartmental and Cabinet disputes.

CHECKLIST

✓ **Both core executive theories are administrative in the sense of focusing on policy networks of ministers and officials around the Prime Minister and elitist in trying to show how they exist within the core executive competing elite and centres of power.**

✓ **In each position we can detect precedents in the arguments about the location of power in the core executive and the 'who governs' debate in the civil service.**

✓ **Although conspiratorial in nature, for example in the claim that no core executive can adequately control the modern state, core executive theories have moved forward the debates on prime ministerial power and authority.**

Managing the core executive

In managing the core executive a Prime Minister will be preoccupied with:

- Deciding and implementing public policy at the highest level, primarily the aim and objectives of the political party (**policy initiation**).

- Governing the country at the head of an administration, mainly through the Cabinet and civil service (**policy implementation**).

At any time performance in these roles will depend on a mix of factors: personality, style of leadership, environment and party political considerations. How they come together will affect the judgement made of a Prime Minister's handling of the **government machine**.

Style and personalities

Kavanagh (*1991*) identifies two styles of Prime Minister: **Mobilisers** and **Reconcilers**. Mobilisers are impatient for change, keen to press on with ideas and motivate others. Reconcilers try to maintain the consensus and cohesion of the Cabinet and will compromise if necessary to reach this position.

Norton (*1988*) uses a fourfold categorisation of the personalities of Prime Ministers: **Innovators**, **Reformers**, **Egoists** or **Balancers**.

INNOVATORS	REFORMERS
Set the agenda; expect to lead others	Seek to implement the party programme
EGOISTS	BALANCERS
Enjoy the power of premiership for own sake	Seek a compromise or middle ground between functions

Prime ministerial personalities, based on Norton (1988)

Margaret Thatcher showed the traits of belonging to the Innovator category whilst John Major was clearly a Balancer. His apparent indecision and perceived weaknesses in governing were partially explained by his inability to control all the factions in the Conservative Party. Tony Blair, certainly after his second election victory in 2001, appeared in both the

Innovator and Reformer categories in seeking personally to oversee the New Labour reforms in public service delivery.

Evaluation of Kavanagh and Norton

There are obvious similarities between the style and personality categories of *Kavanagh* and *Norton* (Mobilisers and Innovators, and Reconcilers and Balancers). Although Margaret Thatcher appeared to adopt a Mobiliser style of leadership – she had larger parliamentary majorities than John Major giving her more authority over the party (*Thatcher 1993*) – there were occasions when she had to operate as a Reconciler.

Autocratic and collegiate

An **autocratic** dominant prime ministerial style can lead to loss of support and respect of colleagues when the party is unpopular; Sir Geoffrey Howe's resignation speech from Margaret Thatcher's Cabinet demonstrated this. A **collegiate** style of management with more equality between ministers is less likely to antagonise but can lead to charges of weakness as with John Major. Tony Blair after four years in office gives the impression of being both autocratic and collegiate. His conduct of Cabinet proceedings are less formal than either Thatcher's or Major's and he is prepared to delegate in areas of major policy for example education and foreign policy. Yet he insisted on absolute unity from his Ministers through the strict maintenance of **collective responsibility**.

The Cabinet and Prime Minister's Office

The authority of the Prime Minister is based on the electorate, the party, Parliament and the Cabinet. As the supreme policy-making body the Cabinet must be carried **politically and administratively**. The removal of Margaret Thatcher in 1990 and the split Cabinets of John Major demonstrate that relationships are difficult to maintain. The Prime Minister has responsibility for the following formal powers over the Cabinet:

* appointments, dismissals and reshuffles of ministers;
* structures and memberships of Cabinet committees;
* control of Cabinet agendas;
* management of Cabinet meetings;
* policy initiation and direction.

These formidable powers are supported by a Number Ten staff (or Prime Minister's Office) a Policy Unit and various ad hoc arrangements of ministers, partial

Cabinets (ministers from departments whose policy is under discussion) and Kitchen Cabinets (mixed groups of advisers of various kinds). Tony Blair's Prime Minister's Office in 1998/1999 comprised a Chief of Staff, Jonathan Powell, a Number Ten Policy Unit with David Miliband as Director of Policy, and a Political Unit under Sally Morgan Political Secretary. The Number Ten Press Office was headed by Alastair Campbell as Chief Press Secretary. His was an increasingly controversial and politicised post working closely with the Prime Minister. In addition to this group of advisers of approximately 40 persons Blair frequently consulted his former 'spin doctor' Peter Mandelson, until 1998 Minister without Portfolio with various responsibilities to drive policy forward.

Tony Blair increases his power after 2001

After the 2001 General Election victory Tony Blair reorganised both the support staff and his personal office to achieve a greater degree of control and focus on the delivery of government services. A new tripartite system of organisation was set up inside Downing Street reporting directly to the Prime Minister, headed by Jonathan Powell, Chief of Staff, Alastair Campbell, Director of Communications and Strategy and Anji Hunter as Head of Government Relations. It is too early to comment on this arrangement except to record the criticism that it has led to confusion over roles and responsibilities in Number Ten and the civil service.

The civil service

A Prime Minister is assisted in the management of government and the core executive by the centralised civil service structure – in this Richard Crossman was correct. Power flows from the Prime Minister as First Lord of the Treasury down through Permanent Secretary responsible for the Civil Service. Control of this **bureaucracy** theoretically guarantees the **implementation** of the Prime Minister's programme even though **neutrality** is one of the characteristic features of the officials. This bureaucracy will respond to whichever party is in power.

The charge of **politicisation** of the civil service made against Margaret Thatcher because she took a personal interest in the replacement of her permanent secretaries has not been substantiated. She may have advanced her favourites (*Hennessy 1989*) but the authoritative Royal Institute of Public Administration report of 1985 found no real evidence to substantiate charges of political interference. Clearly the fact that Margaret Thatcher was Prime Minister from 1979 to 1990 gave her the opportunity to replace a majority of her senior civil servants, but she had no direct control over the Senior Appointments Selection Committee even though she asked for greater freedom of choice (*Armstrong 1985*). Martin Sixsmith made similar claims of politicisation under the Tony Blair government in 2002 after his resignation as Director of Communications.

USA comparison

It is instructive to compare the political powers of an American President over the civil service with those of the Prime Minister. Since there is no politically neutral system of appointments to the American senior ranks, the service depends on political partisanship and patronage in a way that is not found in the British system – another reason why talk of the development of a presidential Prime Minister is misleading.

Questions

1 Define what is meant by core executive theories.

2 Give one difference between John Major's and Tony Blair's style of leadership. Is it important?

The Prime Minister's environment

The Prime Minister's environment is increasingly complex. *Norton* (*1988*) suggests **three variables** within which he operates:

1 **The global economy.** Furthest away from the Prime Minister and subject to least prime ministerial influence. Yet as national leader the Prime Minister protects British interests in, for example, negotiations over European Monetary Union (EMU) and the Single Currency (EURO). After being elected Labour Prime Minister in 1997 Tony Blair announced that Britain would not join EMU at the first round in 1999 and reserved judgement to enter at a later stage.

2 **The climate of expectation.** Every government is faced with new demands as public expectations of the quality of life continue to rise. The Prime Minister reflects public opinion but must be cautious not to promise too much. Tony Blair's 1997 general election manifesto entitled 'New Labour Because Britain Deserves Better' set out 10 promises to be fulfilled over the first five years of a Labour government.

Recognising electorate fears of previous high spending Labour governments Blair promised in a 'contract with the people' not to raise the basic or top rate of income tax during this period. By continuing with restraint in public expenditure and by passing the power over interest rates to the Bank of England the Prime Minister was showing awareness of electorate perceptions that New Labour should be given an opportunity to demonstrate caution in economic management.

3 **The proximate political situation.** The immediate political environment around the Prime Minister over which he/she has most control includes the Cabinet, civil service and machinery of government. This vast structure is managed through the Prime Minister's Office including a system of advisory staffs. Under Tony Blair there has been a substantial increase in the numbers of advisers working for the Prime Minister leading to criticisms of 'cronyism' or jobs for the boys from William Hague in 1998.

FACTFILE

- The formal Number Ten Office and the informal groups of advisers act as a civil service department serving the Prime Minister but it is an untidy arrangement.

- Because of the complexity of coordinating the government machine, it is frequently suggested that a more formalised bureaucratic organisation be established as recognised Prime Minister's Department.

- All Prime Ministers to date have rejected these proposals preferring the informality of a system of secretaries and advisers. The former Cabinet Secretary Sir Robin Butler felt that the present arrangements whereby ministers would help in the coordination of government was sufficient and worked well (*Price 1998*).

- John Major set up a Number Twelve Committee in 1995 to improve coordination of government.

- In 1998 Tony Blair had approximately 20 political advisers working in his Private Office excluding MPs and civil servants. After the government reshuffle of July 1998, he established a new post of Minister for the Cabinet Office with Jack Cunningham expected to act as a coordinator and enforcer of government policy, working closely with Sir Richard Wilson, the Cabinet Secretary. After 2001 this function was given to John Prescott, Deputy Prime Minister.

Authority of the Prime Minister

Around the nucleus of the Prime Minister's environment are three fields of authority within which he must successfully operate: Parliament, party and public opinion.

Parliament

The Prime Ministerial government thesis made much of a Prime Minister's control over Parliament – essentially the House of Commons. In the British system of parliamentary government the party that controls the House of Commons becomes the executive; the future of the two is bound together. Prime Ministers must of necessity secure a good working majority to ensure control and the passage of their legislation through the House. Margaret Thatcher was fortunate in achieving the high figure of 100 plus majorities from 1979 to 1990 over her opponents and we have seen how this impacted on her style of leadership. What is less well known is the **correlation** of **dissent** or **backbench rebellions** to those administrations with **good majorities**. *Norton (1994)* showed how Conservative backbench MPs were more rebellious during the eighties precisely because there was little fear of bringing down their government.

Within the House of Commons, Prime Ministers will be judged on their performance at the Dispatch Box and in debates when speaking on the floor of the House. Their most opportune moments to impress are provided by **Prime Minister's Question Time** when they face the opposition and other critics. Traditionally held as a **device for maintaining executive accountability** to the legislature, most commentators now agree the institution has lost its focus (*Madgwick 1994*). Considerations of time, party advantage, publicity and (marginally) the televising of Parliament have served to reduce Question Time to a spectacle. Partly for this reason, Tony Blair reformed question time after the 1997 general election.

Prime Ministers have the right to call for a **dissolution of Parliament** by making a formal recommendation to the monarch for a general election. As with all powers of the Prime Minister, there are opportunities and constraints working for and against them. Prime Ministers will obviously seek the opportune time when the party's popularity is at its highest to call the election and within the statutory five year limit (Representation of the Peoples Act 1949) will have a degree of manoeuvrability.

Occasionally the threat to call a dissolution is made by Prime Ministers to **silence backbench critics** in their own party (the doomsday scenario). Both Harold Wilson and James Callaghan threatened back benchers, and in a desperate attempt to secure **ratification of the Maastricht Treaty** in 1993, John Major let it be known that if he lost the vote he would regard it as a loss of confidence in his government and call a dissolution. Although he was successful on this occasion, the criticisms of his leadership continued until the 1997 General Election defeat.

Opponents of the present dissolution power (specifically Tony Benn) wish to move to a **fixed term** system (as in Europe and America) when the date of the election is known. This would

- remove Prime Ministers' discretion in timing a general election and
- curtail their freedom to use the device as a control mechanism over backbenchers.

This argument lacks conviction; realistically the result of a general election can go either way. In 1970 Harold Wilson's decision to call a general election produced a Conservative government with a 31 seat majority. The **doomsday scenario** would be little more successful to a desperate Prime Minister. Any dissolution called to silence backbench critics would split a political party and lead to electoral oblivion at the polls.

Party

Party unity is essential to the survival of any Prime Minister. John Major showed during his struggle with the **Euro-sceptics** that he was prepared to discipline those who refused to support his leadership. In 1994 a number of Euro-rebels were expelled from the Conservative Party by the device of **withdrawal of the whip**. This was either a sign of strength from John Major who finally decided to act to prevent further party schisms, or a desperate move from a beleaguered Prime Minister anxious to restore unity to a divided party. The event showed the dangers facing a Prime Minister experiencing **policy differences** with a sizeable section of his party.

The introduction of a more **democratic mechanism** for selecting the leader in 1965 changed the **relationship between Conservative Prime Ministers** and their **backbenchers**. Now they are dependent on the maintenance of good relations and up until the **rule change** in July 1995, could be challenged annually if there was enough backbench support for a leadership election contest. Both Edward Heath (1976) and Margaret Thatcher (1990) lost the leadership of the Conservative Party partly because they ceased to enjoy majority support and their aloof behaviour alienated their own backbenchers. As if conscious of their failures, John Major made strenuous efforts to contact personally a majority of backbench MPs in the Conservative leadership election of June 1995 with good results.

Part of the success of Tony Blair as Prime Minister after 1997 was his ability to build on changes to the Labour Party structures introduced by his predecessor Neil Kinnock. After 2001 the policy-making power of the party was further diluted as Tony Blair centralised power under his authority through the Millbank party headquarters.

Public opinion and the media

The **formation of public opinion** is helped by the media and presentation of politics in newspapers and on television. Prime Ministers since the eighties have been more aware of the importance of presentational skills in the attempt to win votes and influence the electorate. In the sixties and seventies politicians were less skilled in public relations and appeared unaware of its importance in elections. Now party management of general election campaigns is highly professional – nothing is left to chance. In the 1997 and 2001 General Elections Tony Blair and leading Labour politicians were carefully packaged for the media and public. So called '**spin doctors**' like Peter Mandelson and Alastair Campbell ensured that events were given the right 'spin' creating favourable impressions for New Labour in the electorate mind. Now dress, appearance and public speaking skills are all carefully orchestrated by outside '**consultants**' to create positive public images rather like selling commercial products. It follows in this public relations war between the parties that it is advantageous to a party to have young photogenic politicians as opposed to the old or unfashionable. This was graphically demonstrated in 1997 when the young modernised Tony Blair opposed the older 'grey' boring image of John Major. In 2001 he himself was faced by the younger looking William Hague as the new Conservative leader, but this did not play well with the electorate.

Prime Ministers have most opportunity for media exposure as chief executive and party leader. This focus can strengthen their role, authority, power and prestige or conversely can undermine them by constant reference to their government's short-comings, unpopularity or policy mistakes. As if to recognise this focus particularly in and after the 2001 General Election, Tony Blair appeared to take on the role of Chief Communicator for New Labour by carefully managed TV and press conferences assisted by Alistair Campbell, his press secretary and head of the new Communications and Strategy Unit.

A Weakened Prime Minister

In his second term Tony Blair has faced mounting criticisms over his style of government, which in turn has deprived him of much popular support. The war in Iraq and its aftermath have done most to weaken his authority both within the Labour Party and in the country. These and controversial issues like immigration and university top-up fees, coupled with the pressures of the office, may have contributed to his health scare in 2004. His development of a presidential style of leadership, which has reduced the Cabinet to an advisory body, is also blamed for shortcomings within his government.

Summary

1. **Studies of the power, authority and role of Prime Ministers have become more sophisticated over the years.**

2. **Early or traditional theories were mainly descriptive in their analysis (the prime ministerial versus Cabinet government debate).**

3. **Recent theories focus on wider parameters – style, personality, environments and competing centre of power – and you should be aware of these (core executive theories).**

4. **Questions on the Prime Minister are often related to the Cabinet since as a chief executive the Prime Minister cannot really be divorced from it.**

Sample question and answer

AS Level question

1   How does the Prime Minister relate to Parliament?

The Prime Minister's relationship to Parliament requires a discussion of the following points:

- Necessity for a working majority in the House of Commons.
- Control of Commons timetable and procedure to reach legislative objective.
- Dissolution power to call a general election, and how real a threat to backbench critics.
- Patronage posts of approximately 100 government MPs (payroll vote) ensuring government majority in any divisions (votes on debates or legislation).
- Backbench dissent as a threat to the Prime Minister's government.
- Performance at Dispatch Box (Prime Minister's Question Time).
- Management of the party through the Whips' Office and public perceptions of the Prime Minister's ability (assisted by the media).

PREVIEW

In this chapter you will revise the following:

- **The importance of the convention of Cabinet collective responsibility.**
- **The problems of Cabinet efficiency in policy-making and coordination.**
- **Relationships with the Prime Minister and their effects on the structures of Cabinet.**
- **Constitutional and practical interpretations of the operation of Cabinet government.**

Origins and structures

Development of the Cabinet

The origins of the modern Cabinet system (some think the concept originates from the Cabal named after the initials of Charles II's ministers – Clifford, Arlington, Buckingham, Ashley and Lauderdale) can be traced to the eighteenth century when the Hanoverian monarchs (George I, II and III) refused to attend its meetings. Gradually the Cabinet acquired the function of presenting policy advice to the monarch through a leading minister – eventually the Prime Minister. In the changed political climate of the nineteenth century *Bagehot* (*1867*) described the Cabinet and its ministers as 'the hyphen' or 'buckle' which joined 'the legislative part of the State to the executive part of the State'. By the close of that century traditional Cabinet government had emerged with a collegiate of ministers including a Prime Minister deciding policy at the highest level.

FACTFILE

- **The Cabinet (with the Prime Minister) is at the apex of the machinery of government as the central controlling body of the executive.**
- **Traditionally, the study of Cabinet government was approached through the perspective of public administration largely because the emphasis was on structure and their efficiency. However, the Cabinet has a dual purpose – it is both an administrative and a political unit bringing together policy formulation and policy implementation at the highest level. For this reason political considerations are bound up in any analysis.**

Conventional parameters

The working of Cabinet government is based on **conventional practice** or rules which have evolved over time. Apart from the 1937 Ministers of the Crown Act (ensuring the payment of salaries), Cabinet Ministers and Prime Minister managed to operate within constitutional parameters which do not have the backing of law; they are followed because it is politically expedient to do so. The major conventions or characteristics governing Cabinet operations are:

1 **Collective responsibility** Collective responsibility for policy decisions supported by all Cabinet members. In practice this now includes the whole executive – ministers of Cabinet and non-Cabinet rank.

2 **One party dominance** Selection of the executive from one political party. Cabinet members are chosen by the Prime Minister from the majority party in the House of Commons. Exceptions to this rule can occur if a coalition government is produced by the House of Commons or if crises (wars, economic slumps) necessitate the formation of a national government representing all the shades of opinion.

3 **Accountability** Answerability or accountability of the Cabinet to the House of Commons and ultimately the electorate. There are two aspects to this:

a) Sovereignty of Parliament has in the modern sense passed to the majority party in the Commons which implies the Cabinet and Prime Minister. Within Parliament, therefore, the Cabinet is responsible to a legislature dominated by itself.

b) Although the executive dominates the House of Commons, there is provision for the removal of the Cabinet in the convention. If a government is defeated on a motion of no confidence, it must resign because it no longer commands the support of the House. Although first established in 1841, this **sanction** only removed three administrations in the twentieth century, the last being the 1979 Callaghan Labour government.

Party discipline prevents the government losing its majority in the House of Commons. In 1979 special circumstances deprived James Callaghan of his majority and ability to defeat the motion of no confidence.

Knowing that they rarely face defeat at the hands of the House, successive Prime Ministers have used the threat of a vote of no confidence to instil party loyalty into rebellious Commons backbenchers. *Bagehot*

(*1867*) first observed that the Cabinet 'could dissolve the assembly which had appointed it' and, although appointed by one Parliament, it could appeal to the next. John Major's threat to turn the ratification of the Maastricht Treaty into a vote of confidence issue in 1993 successfully demonstrated that a desperate Prime Minister can constitutionally risk a general election to achieve his objective.

CHECKLIST

✓ **The Cabinet is the supreme executive committee of the government. It exists primarily to:**

- **Initiate and implement government policy.**
- **Coordinate the work of the administration.**
- **Settle disputes from lower down the ministerial hierarchy.**
- **Provide party political leadership to the Commons and the nation.**

✓ **In a narrow sense it is a committee comprised of between 20 and 24 senior ministers who meet on a regular basis under the authority of the Prime Minister.**

✓ **In a broad sense it is at the heart of what *Madgwick* (*1991*) calls the central executive territory which includes the Prime Minister and his office, the Cabinet Office, Cabinet and ministerial committees and senior officials and advisers.**

Membership of the Cabinet

Membership is conventionally restricted to the most senior politicians in the government. Within the Cabinet there are approximately 20 Secretaries of State responsible for the main departments. They are assisted (beyond the Cabinet) by Ministers of State and the more junior Parliamentary Under Secretaries. The ministerial support for Secretaries of State depends on the size of their respective departments – those combining a number of service or functional responsibilities (Defence and Environment are good examples) will have a greater establishment than smaller departments like Northern Ireland.

Size and balance of the Cabinet

The size of the Cabinet is governed by political and administrative considerations. Politically the heads of the main spending departments will be included as they contribute to and implement government policy as it affects their own area. Theoretically a Prime Minister will also **balance** the Cabinet to ensure all

shades of party opinion have an outlet at the highest level. In practice both Margaret Thatcher after 1983 and John Major from 1995 tended to balance their Cabinets to the right and centre respectively. Tony Blair's first New Labour Cabinet of 1997 included a balance of new and old left but after his second election victory in 2001 he gave the impression that he was less concerned with political balance than with driving forward government policy with a Cabinet of loyal Blairites. However, although he removed Robin Cook from the prestigious post of Foreign Secretary, he kept him in the Cabinet as Leader of the House of Commons. Three other 'old' Labour stalwarts also remained: Gordon Brown at the Treasury, John Prescott as Deputy Prime Minister and Clare Short at International Development. This may have been a reflection of his 'Big Tent' strategy or it demonstrated again how difficult it is for a Prime Minister to remove powerful colleagues from a Cabinet.

1	Downing Street and Prime Minister	Tony Blair
2	Cabinet Office and Deputy Prime Minister	John Prescott
3	Treasury and Chancellor of the Exchequer	Gordon Brown
4	Foreign and Commonwealth Office	Jack Straw
5	Education and Skills	Charles Clarke
6	Health	Alan Milburn
7	Home Office	David Blunkett
8	Work and Pensions	Andrew Smith
9	Culture, Media and Sport	Tessa Jowell
10	Lord Chancellor's Department	Lord Irvine of Lairg
11	Environment, Food and Rural Affairs	Margaret Beckett
12	Transport, Local Government and Regions	Alastair Darling
13	Defence	Geoff Hoon
14	Trade and Industry	Patricia Hewitt

* Tony Blair's Cabinet includes nine other posts not shown in this list, making a total of 23 Ministers.

The 14 main departments in the Labour Cabinet after the reshuffles of 2001/02.

FACTFILE

- **Despite continuing upward pressure to expand the Cabinet in keeping with the growth of government responsibilities, Prime Ministers have managed to keep to an optimum of more efficient workable size. This has been achieved by a process of merger and amalgamation of smaller ministries into larger departments ensuring that all areas of government activity are still represented in the Cabinet.**

- **Smaller Cabinets have the obvious advantage that they make it easier to reach decisions. *Gordon Walker* (*1970*) claimed that a Cabinet larger than 17 or 18 ceased to be a council that could easily reach a collective view. Recent Prime Ministers have found it impossible to accommodate political and administrative pressures within that number. Margaret Thatcher (1979–90) and John Major (1990–97) had 22 and 23 Cabinet Ministers respectively. Tony Blair had 22 Ministers in his original Cabinet of 1997 and 23 after the 2001 election.**

Central features

The whole operation of Cabinet government is underpinned by conventional practice. The most important convention is collective responsibility – without it the Cabinet as we know it could not function. Although the convention has faced considerable pressure for change, to which it has adapted, it still remains the underlying central principle of Cabinet government.

Collective ministerial responsibility

The classic description of collective ministerial responsibility was first given by *Lord Salisbury* (*1878*) in a statement much repeated but still operative: 'for all that passes in Cabinet, each member of it who does not resign is absolutely and irretrievably responsible, and has no right afterwards to say that he agreed in one case to a compromise, while in another he was persuaded by his colleagues'. In practice this has come to mean that public acceptance of government policies is a prerequisite for Cabinet membership. Within a Cabinet of 20-plus ministers there cannot (does not need to) be unanimity for all decisions, but publicly the appearance of unity or solidarity must be given. In its modern form, therefore, collective ministerial responsibility implies:

- Public agreement by all Cabinet members to all government policy decisions.

- Wherever possible the open avoidance of public criticism of government policy by serving Cabinet Ministers.

- A willingness to resign from the Cabinet if a member cannot reconcile private doubts over the direction of government policy with public pronouncements.

Operation of these principles (now part of the guidelines issued to all new ministers) occasionally leads to political controversy. This is likely to happen when a policy split divides a Cabinet resulting in:

- resignations;

- media leaks or unattributable briefings;

- special arrangements.

Resignations

There are many factors working for or against a ministerial resignation for collective policy disputes in a Cabinet. Considerations of political ambition will for the most part keep ministers in a Cabinet. During the Wilson Cabinets of 1974–76 both Tony Benn and Michael Foot were critical of government foreign policy but did not resign. Acceptance of collective responsibility is so strong that resignations from Cabinets on these grounds are relatively rare.

Only five ministers resigned from Margaret Thatcher's governments during the period 1979 to 1990.

John Major's Cabinets since 1992 were less troubled by resignations for collective responsibility reasons. This did not mean that the Cabinets were without policy conflict but rather that the constraints keeping ministers in his Cabinets were greater than the impact of the policy disputes. This was evident during reported policy clashes over the possibility of adoption of the European Social Chapter during 1993 when a number of ministers were said to be on the point of resignation. In late 1994 Cabinet splits were reported over attitudes towards a proposed referendum on Europe. By 1995 divisions in the Cabinet and Conservative Party over Europe (Euro-enthusiasts versus Euro-sceptics) had been so publicly obvious (and therefore damaging of collective responsibility) as to force John Major to settle the issue by a Conservative leadership election contest in June/July 1995.

In opposition before 1997 and as Prime Minister since, Tony Blair had rigorously applied collective responsibility to his Cabinets. Stressing the importance of working together he always emphasised that a Cabinet divided against itself would not succeed. Possibly fear of losing the 2001 General Election also kept ministers in line with the result that there appeared publicly to be fewer splits in the New Labour Cabinets when compared to the last government of John Major.

Only after the events of the Iraq war did Tony Blair lose two Ministers from his Cabinet in 2003 for collective responsibility reasons. Foreign Secretary Robin Cook and International Development Secretary Claire Short both resigned because of opposition to the British involvement in the war in Iraq – a policy neither felt they could support.

Questions

1 What factors determine the size of the Cabinet?

2 Describe collective responsibility in your own words.

3 Why are there fewer ministerial resignations under collective responsibility rules today?

4 How is the Cabinet held accountable?

Media leaks or unattributable briefings

The conduct of the business of the Cabinet depends on **secrecy** – collective responsibility would break down without it. Ministers would not speak their minds in the privacy of the Cabinet room if they knew their respective positions on policy issues could be publicly identified. However, it is clearly impossible for a Cabinet of 20 plus ministers and all the attendant servicing documents to remain totally private. According to *Madgwick* (*1994*) approximately 200 people see Cabinet papers – except those relating to the most sensitive pieces of government information.

Cabinet secrecy (and collective responsibility) is breached by periodic deliberate approved 'leaking' of information to press and lobby correspondents. All governments suffer from unattributable leaking by ministers or Prime Ministers who use the media to publicise policy positions of respective parties 'off the record'. *Gordon Walker* (*1970*) first claimed that leaking was part of Cabinet conventional behaviour – that it functioned to reconcile the public fiction of unanimity in Cabinet with the reality of dispute in private. The former Conservative minister, *Alan Clark* (*1995*), appeared to support this view when he claimed that selective leaking had become part of the machinery of government, because it proved so useful to ministers. In a detailed analysis of leaks in the Major government, *Castle* (*1995*) claimed there were more than 25 government leaks during 1994/95

without any culprits (civil servants, ministerial aids and others) being publicly identified. The most notable were:

	Leak	Date	Suspect
1	DTI cash	August 1994	Civil servant
2	ID cards	January 1995	Unknown
3	Joint Framework Document	February 1995	Pro-Unionist elements
4	Scott Inquiry	June 1995	Government
5	Education spending	September 1995	Department for Education and Employment
6	Lottery cash	October 1995	Department of National Heritage

Government leaks 1994/95

The damaging impact of leaks on the conduct of government is probably overrated. The Cabinet Office, which is responsible for tracing culprits, appears complacent and as *Clark* (*1995*) points out, leaks do contribute to more open government allowing greater public debate of policy issues.

Leaks under Blair

The Blair governments to 2001/02 appeared superficially to have suffered fewer leaks than either the Major or Thatcher governments partly because party discipline was so rigorously enforced. Occasionally 'whispering' campaigns against ministers surfaced in the media and leading Labour figures like Robin Cook, Clare Short, John Prescott and Peter Mandelson were attacked. During and after the 2001 election campaign the media highlighted leaks on the so-called rift between the Tony Blair and Gordon Brown partnership. Apparently Brown was to be offered the leadership after Blair stood down but this rumour was vigorously denied by Downing Street and by the Prime Minister himself. Further 'leaks' can be expected in the Blair government including difficulties on joining the EURO and attitudes to greater European integration.

FACTFILE

- **Cabinet secrecy is also breached by the publication of memoirs or diaries of former politicians when recollections of events in the Cabinet are placed in the public domain or prove embarrassing to government. The original *Crossman Diaries* published in 1977 proved embarrassing to the Wilson Labour government, more for revelations about the minister/civil service relationship than for any specific reference to Cabinet policy.**

- **The Radcliffe Committee of 1976, set up specifically by Harold Wilson to review the publication of ministerial memoirs and their effects on collective responsibility, revised the rules governing future publications and heavily criticised Crossman for breaching confidentiality. Ministers were restricted to a 15 year ban on the use of Cabinet papers (for the public this remains a 30 year ban) and had now to submit their manuscripts to the Cabinet Secretary for clearance against tests of acceptability protecting state security and government confidence.**

- **It is now fairly standard practice for ex-ministers to write about their public life and this causes little concern in government. After each general election a spate of memoirs usually appears from defeated government ministers – now they are taken less notice of.**

Special arrangements

A final attempt to overcome an unresolved Cabinet policy dispute where resignations are to be avoided is the practice of **agreements to differ**. Theoretically impossible within the convention of collective responsibility which implies unanimity between colleagues, there have been occasions when Prime Ministers have suspended collective responsibility in order to reconcile differing factions within their Cabinets.

- Harold Wilson allowed those Labour ministers opposed to European Community membership to publicly campaign against his government's position in 1975.

The Prime Minister in the above situation was anxious to avoid a split Cabinet and relaxed collective responsibility to allow for this. For similar reasons James Callaghan, Labour Prime Minister in 1977, allowed Cabinet Ministers to dissent from the vote on the European Assembly Elections Bill.

The work of the Cabinet

As the senior committee of the executive, the Cabinet brings together departmental heads (Secretaries of State) and the Prime Minister to decide governmental policies and how they will be implemented. There are three broad areas of work at this level of government.

1 **Parliamentary and legislative matters**   The legislative programme discussed in Cabinet will be closely related to proposals contained in the party's manifesto but will need constant adaptation and change. The longer a government remains in office the more difficult it is to present a new programme to the electorate. New legislative proposals are either

   (a) **completely new policies** produced in consultation with advisers, ministers, pressure groups and other interests, closing a legislative gap or perceived weakness in existing laws or

   (b) **adaptation or adjustments** to existing policies often brought to Cabinet level (with the agreement of the Prime Minister) by a minister supported by civil servants.

   The Cabinet will prioritise these legislative proposals and arrange for their introduction into the parliamentary timetable. Sometimes these discussions will involve the Prime Minister and relevant departmental ministers in a **partial Cabinet** as opposed to a full Cabinet.

2 **Foreign Affairs**   The full Cabinet (or Cabinet Council (*Madgwick 1994*)) regularly discusses foreign policy. Important decisions have to be taken over the correct stance towards further European integration and relations with the European Union, both of which split the Conservative Party under John Major. Relations with the rest of the world and current issues also need Cabinet attention. In the first year of Tony Blair's New Labour administration (1997–98) affairs brought to Cabinet could have included the Queen's state visit to India, the British handover of the Hong Kong colony to China, the signing of the final Northern Irish Peace Agreement of April 1998, and Britain's presidency (under Tony Blair) of the European Union for the first half of 1998.

3 **Coordination of government**   A major part of the work of the Cabinet involves oversight and coordination of government policy. All policy affects departments differently but some coherence is needed at the highest level if government is to reach its objectives. Any interdepartmental disputes over the allocation of resources will be referred to the Cabinet and Prime

Minister for mediation and settlement, but neither can interfere in the internal working of a department. The relationship between the Prime Minister and Cabinet Ministers discussing coordination is one-sided. A Prime Minister can see matters in the round; ministers tend to be 'blinkered' by departmentalism – a tendency to view policy matters through the eyes of their departments (*Crossman 1979*).

Cabinet meetings

Traditionally the Cabinet meets on a Thursday for two or three hours of discussion and deliberation. Meetings follow a set pattern and are chaired by the Prime Minister assisted by the Cabinet Secretary. The agenda is circulated beforehand and the minutes are under the control of the Prime Minister and Cabinet Secretary respectively. The recording of Cabinet deliberation has given rise to claims of 'cosmetising' or interference with the record. Michael Heseltine in his dispute with Margaret Thatcher over the Westland Affair claimed that the minutes of one particular Cabinet meeting did not accurately reflect his views. The minutes of the Cabinet are important because the record of the Prime Minister's conclusions form the basis of the policy to be adopted in the administration and copies are forwarded to the respective ministers in their departments for implementation. Clearly any cosmetising of the minutes could have repercussions lower down the government hierarchy.

The conduct of proceedings in Cabinet varies according to the style and personality of the Prime Minister. Margaret Thatcher led from the front preferring decisiveness and direction in discussion to deliberation and debate. Her preference for discussions with inner Cabinets of trusted ministers, **bilateral meetings** with ministers and officials, use of Cabinet committees to bypass Cabinet and personal involvement in pushing policies were all cited as evidence for the prime ministerial government thesis. The replacement of Margaret Thatcher by John Major in 1990 marked a return to a more collegiate open style of running the Cabinet, but Tony Blair after 1997 and 2001 appeared to play down its importance preferring, like Thatcher, to discuss matters in 'bilaterals'. In reducing meetings to under one hour and further limiting their frequency, Tony Blair could be accused of adding to the long term decline of the Cabinet as a deliberative body. Clearly meetings of less than one hour offer little opportunity for any lengthy examination of the issues.

In December 2001 the former Cabinet Minister Mo Mowlam publicly criticised Tony Blair for being too presidential in the way he handled his Cabinet. She claimed that Cabinet government was dead because ministers no longer decided policy collegiately. Both Blair and his deputy, John Prescott, refuted her claim.

CHECKLIST

✓ **The support system of Cabinet government is provided by the Cabinet Secretariat and a system of committees working in the Cabinet Office – the engine room of Cabinet (*Hennessy 1986*).**

✓ **The Secretariat is under the control of the Cabinet Secretary who acts as the Prime Minister's unofficial Chief Secretary. It was founded in 1916 by Lloyd George with the primary purpose of bringing order to the work of the Cabinet, which had managed with informal arrangements to that time. The Secretariat services the full Cabinet and committees, is responsible for the circulation of the minutes and generally manages Cabinet business ensuring that its decisions are implemented.**

✓ **Currently there are five small secretariats, focusing on the following specific areas of government work:**

 1 **economic policy;**

 2 **overseas and defence information;**

 3 **European business;**

 4 **home affairs;**

 5 **security and intelligence matters.**

Cabinet committees

The Cabinet Office oversees the operation of the Cabinet committee system which does much of the preparatory work of the full Cabinet. Until 1992 and John Major's open government initiative, the numbers and structures of the committees were covered by collective responsibility and Cabinet secrecy. However, it was generally known that there were two types of main committee and this has now been confirmed:

1 **Standing committees** cover the areas of main departmental work, for example overseas policy and defence, economic and domestic policy, legislation, public expenditure. In 1992 John Major had 27 of these committees including a number of sub-committees. Margaret Thatcher by contrast had 35 standing committees during her 11 years in office and her predecessor James Callaghan had 25 (*Hennessy 1978*).

2 **Ad hoc committees** are formed for current specific purposes. Typical issues covered in the

government of Margaret Thatcher included replacement of Polaris Missiles with Tridents, planning for teachers' and miners' strikes, and changes in local government structures. John Major made less use of these committees than Margaret Thatcher, preferring instead to use the full Cabinet. Tony Blair after 1997 made a radical departure from the convention that opposition members do not appear on these committees by appointing the Liberal Democrat Leader Paddy Ashdown to the Joint Cabinet Committee on Constitutional Reform.

A large number of these committees are chaired by the Prime Minister or the Deputy Prime Minister. From 1995 until 1997 Michael Heseltine as Deputy Prime Minister chaired nine Cabinet committees and worked closely with John Major in an 'overlord' capacity coordinating policy through the Cabinet. John Major retained control of the memberships, chairmanships and terms of reference for the committee system as is usual practice for the Prime Minister. Tony Blair reformed the committee system by scrapping four of John Major's committees (nuclear defence, competitiveness, coordination and presentation of policy and sub-committee on terrorism). Two surprises in Blair's appointments to committees were Deputy Prime Minister John Prescott given a coordinating role (rather like Heseltine) on four central committees and Peter Mandelson, Minister without Portfolio, placed on 11 of the 20 Cabinet committees. The main Cabinet committees under Tony Blair (1997) were:

- Defence and Overseas Policy
- Economic Affairs
- Home and Social Affairs
- Public Expenditure
- Environment
- Local Government
- Intelligence Services
- Northern Ireland
- Constitutional Reform Policy
- Devolution to Scotland/Wales. England Regions
- Queen's Speeches/Legislation (Future)
- Legislation

Cabinet committees research subjects before full Cabinet discussions or consider policy passed down to relieve an otherwise 'overloaded' executive. They have delegated authority from full Cabinet; their decisions are binding on the government and do not have to be referred back unless they cannot reach agreement or compromise. The **main advantage** of this system is that it allows the full Cabinet to function. A lesser advantage is better coordination across departments. By including a wide range of ministers and officials in standing, ad hoc and other committees (ministerial) the system associates larger numbers than Cabinet in policy-making at the centre of government. The main problem in the committee system is that it can reinforce the Prime Minister's hold over Cabinet and be used – as in the case of Margaret Thatcher – to take policy-making power away from full collegiate decision making. The terrorist attacks on the New York World Trade Center in September 2001 demonstrated how committees can be used in emergency situations. Tony Blair convened the COBRA, the Civil Contingencies Committee, to increase security at Britain's airports and control flights over London, in response to the mass destruction and hijacking of planes in the United States. In October, after the joint USA/UK Declaration of War against terrorism and the action against Afghanistan, the Labour War Cabinet met for the first of a series of meetings.

The COBRA committee met again in November 2002 to co-ordinate the Government response to the first firefighters' strike for 25 years.

Reform of the Cabinet

Departmental view

As the Cabinet is both an administrative and political institution, so the problems associated with it reflect political and organisational constraints. Politically there may be a lack of direction at the top of British government partly because Cabinet members do not have the time or lack the inclination to focus on the longer term (*Wass 1984*). This criticism appears to support the ideas of departmentalism noticed by *Headey* (*1974*) and confirmed by *Crossman* (*1979*) and *Barnett* (*1982*) that ministers were too preoccupied with their department's problems to worry about those collectively aired in Cabinet. If ministers were always preoccupied with their departments' concerns, then the traditional idea of Cabinet government as a body of 20 plus centralised ministers deciding policy was flawed. Even before the advent of Margaret Thatcher, the Cabinet was losing power to the Prime Minister. Policy decisions were increasingly being taken outside in the Cabinet committee system, in advisory groups and in bilateral meetings between the Prime Minister and other ministers.

Policy Cabinets

As early as the 1940s commentators first noticed weaknesses in both the composition and the coordinating abilities of the Cabinet. *Amery (1947)* argued that the Cabinet was ideally suited to management of the short term daily problems of government but departmental problems prevented ministers looking strategically forward. He suggested the establishment of a **small Policy Cabinet** made up of six 'super ministers' without departmental responsibilities. They would coordinate and direct policy without the problems normally associated with traditional Cabinet Secretaries. *Winston Churchill (1951)* experimented with a system of coordinating ministers or **'overlords'** in an attempt to bring strategic thinking into his Cabinet but for a number of reasons, including confusion in ministerial responsibility, it failed.

Large versus smaller Cabinets

Churchill's 'overlords' experiment was an attempt to reduce the size of Cabinet to more manageable proportions. Large Cabinets are not effective in wartime and smaller Cabinets are not efficient at other times. Even the 1918 Haldane Committee on the Machinery of Government recognised this difficulty. Despite this, modern Prime Ministers have improved Cabinet coordination by:

- Using 'inner' or 'partial' Cabinets and bilateral meetings (Margaret Thatcher).

- Changing the structure of administration by merging/enlarging departments. Most modern departments – Defence, Education and Employment, Environment and Transport and Regions are merged from older ministries, and the balance frequently changes (Harold Wilson, Margaret Thatcher, John Major, Tony Blair).

- Giving coordinating responsibility to a Deputy Prime Minister. A practice started by John Major with Michael Heseltine and continued by Tony Blair with John Prescott.

- In a new departure after the government reshuffle of July 1998 Tony Blair appointed Jack Cunningham as a new Minister for the Cabinet Office specifically tasked with improving coordination between the Cabinet and Prime Minister's Office. Working closely with the Cabinet Secretary Sir Richard Wilson he had access to the Prime Minister and introduced improvements to the Cabinet committee system. After the 2001 election this function was given to John Prescott as Deputy Prime Minister. Jack Cunningham had by that time left the Cabinet.

Cabinet personnel after 2003

By 2004 all Tony Blair's original Cabinet of 1997 had been reshuffled with the exception of the 'big three'. Only Tony Blair as Prime Minister, John Prescott as Deputy Prime Minister and Gordon Brown as Chancellor of the Exchequer remained in post. Other Ministers like David Blunkett, Jack Straw and Margaret Beckett remained in the Cabinet but had different portfolios. The Lord Chancellor, Lord Irvine, was replaced in 2003 by Lord Falconer in a new departure as transitional Lord Chancellor and Secretary of State for Constitutional Affairs, pending the abolition of the Lord Chancellorship after the next general election.

Theorising about the Cabinet

Today there is little doubt that the role of the Cabinet as the supreme policy-making centre in British government has become less important than in the past. Under Tony Blair, meetings are of shorter duration and the Cabinet has a reduced advisory role sanctioning policy developed elsewhere. By consulting Ministers and officials in bi-lateral meetings, Tony Blair continues with practices developed by Margaret Thatcher, the last strong Conservative Prime Minister. Paradoxically this reduction in the powers of the Cabinet and treatment of her colleagues was a contributory factor in her eventual removal by those unhappy with her leadership. This is unlikely to happen to Tony Blair because Labour leaders in office cannot be deposed in this way but it does not contribute to his authority and standing in the party.

Summary

1 We have seen some of the problems relating to the efficiency of the Cabinet and attempts to overcome them by Thatcher, Major and Blair. If in the traditional sense the Cabinet has joined what *Burch (1988)* calls the honorific part of the constitution, then this is an inevitable consequence of the growth in the powers of the Prime Minister.

2 Policy shortcomings are not easily overcome either. The short-lived Central Policy Review Staff (CPRS, 1971 to 1983) gave sometimes unpleasant advice to Prime Ministers but in the end was abolished by Margaret Thatcher because of duplication of work already done in the Cabinet Office or for political reasons. It is possible that Tony Blair or his successors could in the future re-establish some form of policy review machinery, either in the Cabinet Office or in the Prime Minister's Office at Downing Street.

3 The idea of a traditional Cabinet making policy decisions on a collegiate basis is no longer an accurate description of events at the centre. But the Cabinet still fulfils useful functions under the convention of collective responsibility, including associating ministers with policy, coordinating the Cabinet committee system and as the leading political committee of the governing party.

Sample questions and answers

AS Level questions

1 Explain collective responsibility.
2 How is it operated in government?

1
- *Explain the importance of conventions in Cabinet government   give flexibility etc.*
- *Define collective responsibility (Lord Salisbury's definition) – classically Cabinet ministers are all held responsible.*
- *Explain why doctrine is still followed – unity in government, need to face criticism in House of Commons.*
- *Discuss the changing convention – ministers rarely resign today because of different way policy is decided.*

2
- *Give examples of the working of the convention.*
- *Show how the classic principle has been relaxed – agreements to differ.*
- *Discuss why Prime Ministers allow relaxation of principle.*
- *Look at resignation of Howe, Heseltine and Lawson. Discuss their implications for the convention.*
- *Examine practice of leaks – how it affects convention, desirable/undesirable.*
- *Make some evaluation of the changed convention – is there any point keeping it? What purpose is it serving? Secrecy in government. How important to policy-making?*

PREVIEW

In this chapter you will look at the following:

- The effectiveness of Parliament in controlling the executive.

- The role of the House of Commons in legislation, scrutiny and debate.

- Members of Parliament as representatives.

- The House of Lords as a second chamber.

- Parliamentary reform of the Commons and Lords.

FACTFILE

- **Bicameral legislature** – a two House legislature comprising the House of Lords and the House of Commons. Theoretically the House of Lords is superior as the Upper House. Politically the House of Commons has superiority because of its electoral accountability.

- **Golden Age of Parliament** – a reference to the mid nineteenth-century situation when the House of Commons had more independence from the executive because the party system had yet to fully develop.

- **Government by committee** – the passing of legislative initiative to committees of the House of Commons thereby weakening the government's control over the House.

Perspectives on Parliament

Theoretical views of Parliament focus essentially on the House of Commons as it plays a more important role in legislation than the House of Lords. There are three basic models based around the historical, reformist and legal aspects of Parliament.

Legal institutional model

For a brief period in the nineteenth century (the so-called Golden Age 1832–68) parliamentary strength over the executive was at its maximum. Sovereignty resided in a House of Commons that was able to change governments, force the removal of ministers and decide legislation on its merits. The House of Commons was able to do this because the party system and affiliations of MPs had yet to crystallise around a government/opposition axis. By the twentieth century the stranglehold over Parliament by the party machine meant in effect that MPs lost their independent status and became subject to party political control.

This model accepts the constitutional position of a legal system subordinated to Parliament. The judiciary apply or interpret the law; they do not get drawn into arguments about the efficacy or otherwise of legislation. Parliament has a limited impact on policy-making, largely because the party system guarantees the government a working majority which in turn implies executive control over legislation. It is accepted, therefore, that the role of Parliament has changed in the modern period – the legislature is weak, the government strong. Parliamentary strength will only return with a coalition government in the Commons (achieved through electoral reform or under the existing system); this would make the executive more dependent again on the legislature.

Westminster model

From this perspective it is recognised that Parliament has never played a major policy-making role. According to *Adonis* (*1990*) the House of Commons has never sought to usurp the functions of government but plays a marginal role. **Positively** this embraces:

- Being a debating forum for government and opposition.

- Keeping the party battle in focus for the media and the public.

Negatively the Commons is weak because:

- Government controls debate and the legislative timetable.

- Scrutiny of legislation by standing committee is largely ineffective.

- Investigative work of government by specialist committees is not productive.

- Political partisanship dominates procedure in the House of Commons reducing checks on the executive to party controversy.

This rather negative view of the House of Commons is now regarded as **orthodox** simply because a government with a good majority will always prefer executive power over the parliamentary.

Transformative model

According to some writers, Parliament since the eighties has redefined its powers and reasserted its role as a check on the executive (*Norton 1981*). Parliament does, therefore, impact on executive policy-making even if in small ways. Changes in the operation of the House of Commons include:

- There is now more **backbench dissent** resulting in oppositional behaviour from government MPs willing to defy their leadership. This was particularly evident during the governments of Margaret Thatcher and John Major.

- The new **departmental select committees** (since 1979) have extended scrutiny over the executive raising public awareness of policy weaknesses which have in some cases been corrected.

- Votes on **conscience issues** have had increased significance as MPs are given **free votes** away from party dictates. The list of issues is long, ranging from capital punishment, abortion laws, divorce, house conveyancing, to Sunday shopping and televising of Parliament.

CHECKLIST

✓ **The House of Commons has assumed primacy in the British parliamentary system as the sole elected national assembly representing the wishes of the people – a criterion regarded as essential for democratic government.**

✓ **Although technically the Lower House in a bicameral legislature, the Commons is more important than the House of Lords in current parliamentary practice.**

The House of Commons

Personnel and procedures

There are now 659 Members of Parliament (including the Speaker) representing constituencies in England, Wales, Scotland and Northern Ireland. Each constituency returns one MP elected on the simple majority system under a party label. Now it is virtually impossible to get into Parliament without the support of a political party; the days of the independent Member have long gone. Once in the House, party strictures are strong. Except for the creation of the Social Democratic Party in 1981 when 27 Labour and one Conservative MP left their respective parties to join the SDP, only four MPs have '**crossed the floor**' of the Commons to join other parties in recent years. In 1976 Reginald Prentice, a former Labour Cabinet Minister, joined the Conservative Party after rejection by his local party. In 1995 Alan Howarth, Conservative, defected to Labour because of policy differences with his government. That same year, Emma Nicholson, Conservative, defected to the

Liberal Democrats for policy reasons followed by Peter Thurnham in 1996 who continued to sit as an Independent Conservative. In 1998 the Conservative MP Peter Temple Morris announced that he was joining the Labour Party and would sit on that side until the next general election (according to media reports he was promised a Life Peerage by Tony Blair).

The Speaker

The Speaker is the chairperson of the House of Commons with a long list of responsibilities including:

- chairing debates;
- controlling procedure;
- managing the business of the House;
- representing the House on official and informal occasions.

Speakers do not vote in divisions except to break a deadlock when they cast a tie-breaker vote usually (by tradition) supportive of the government of the day. Selected for a new Parliament (or after death or retirement of their predecessor), the convention of the House is for the majority party to nominate a successor after discussion with the other parties. When Betty Boothroyd (Labour) replaced Bernard Weatherill (Conservative) in 1992 she had the distinction of being the first female House of Commons Speaker after securing a majority of 372 votes in an open election. After her retirement in 2000 she was replaced by Michael Martin, another former Labour MP and Deputy Speaker.

Whips and party discipline

Party discipline is essential to the life of the Commons – without it the House could not satisfactorily conduct its business. To this end the major parties choose a number of MPs as Party Whips whose function is to maintain discipline amongst their MPs. *Silk* (*1995*) likens their role more to that of **personnel managers** rather than draconian figures disciplining their backbenchers. Each party selects a Chief Whip (on the government side he arranges the business of the House) who cooperate with each other to ensure the smooth running of legislation through the 'usual channels'.

Party Whips also act as the 'eyes and ears' of the party leaders carrying back information on the opinions and morale of the backbenchers. In order to control attendance in divisions (when the House votes on a proposal – legislative or debate) government and opposition Party Whips issue **the whip** which is an instruction to attend for a division. If the government has a small majority it is likely that it will do its utmost to win divisions. However, since the collapse of the Labour government of James Callaghan in 1979 after losing a vote of no confidence, governments tend to **ignore defeats** in the Commons unless they affect a crucial part of their programme, as in the case of the passage of the Maastricht ratification process 1992–93.

Dissident MPs

The whip is divided according to importance of the instruction to attend: the **one line whip** requests attendance; **two line whips** insist on attendance unless the MP is paired (cancelled out) with a member on the opposite side; the most serious is the **three line whip** where attendance is mandatory. The ratification of the Maastricht Treaty highlighted divisions within the Conservative Party where rebellious (dissident) MPs ignored any type of whip and voted against their government on a number of occasions. This in turn lead John Major to:

- use the threat of a dissolution of Parliament (and hence a general election) in the form of making a final defeat on the Maastricht Bill into a motion of no confidence in the government in July 1993;

- expel eight Conservative Euro-rebel MPs from the Parliamentary Party in November 1994 by withdrawing the whip in punishment for refusal to support the government over the vote on increases to the European Union budget.

Paradoxically, dissent by government backbenchers originally highlighted by *Norton* (*1980*), during the long Conservative administration of Margaret Thatcher and continued under John Major, had ramifications on the role of Parliament. Because of large Conservative majorities the official Labour opposition was less effective than opponents on the government side. And independent behaviour by MPs is generally regarded as returning power back to the floor of the House of Commons. However, as *Madgwick* (*1994*) notes, the object of protests against legislation by government backbenchers is to secure influence over it, not to bring about eventual defeat in a general election. The large Labour majorities in the 1997 and 2001 general elections reversed these parliamentary roles.

Now the Conservative Party facing their second Parliament in opposition under their new leader Iain Duncan Smith from 2001 are a reduced force. Unless there is dissent within the ranks of Labour MPs there is little prospect of the government being seriously challenged in the House of Commons. Indeed so ineffective were the Conservatives under William Hague that by late 2001 there was talk of the Liberal Democrats replacing the Conservatives as the Official Opposition.

Questions

1 Briefly explain the following perspectives on Parliament.

a) Legal – Institutional

b) Westminster

c) Transformative

2 Why is the Speaker expected to be impartial?

3 Why do MPs not 'cross the floor' of the House of Commons (defect from one party to another) more often?

Functions of the House of Commons

CHECKLIST

It is generally accepted that the House of Commons has five or six functions depending on the emphasis between the formal and real powers of Parliament (*Norton 1981*).

✓ **The function of legitimation is the overarching agreement given to the executive to govern by the House of Commons from which it draws its legitimacy to rule. The Commons also gives legitimisation to the laws passed by the government – without this approval there can be no legislation. Clearly a government that loses control over the House (a lost majority) cannot claim any legitimacy from the Commons and must tender its resignation.**

✓ **British government is representative and responsible (*Birch 1964*), which implies a representative tie to the electorate through the Commons. MPs indirectly represent all the constituents in their area whether they supported the MPs or not. Since government ministers are recruited from MPs by the Prime Minister, a career in the House of Commons is usually a prerequisite for high office. Ministers are therefore trained in parliamentary procedure and carry their representativeness into government.**

✓ **As a forum of national debate the House of Commons is fulfilling an informative and educative role. There are many opportunities for the House to debate government policy including:**

- **Queen's speech;**

- **opposition days;**

- **emergency debates;**
- **finance bill;**
- **confidence debate;**
- **debates on bills.**

As governments usually win the vote after debates (divisions), and much of what is said is party political point scoring, critics tend to focus on their negative impact. Whilst it is true that the Commons is a 'talking shop', *Norton* (*1981*) makes the point that Parliaments are exactly that. The value of debate is in exposing weaknesses in the performance of government ministers, which the electorate will evaluate in general elections.

Legislation and scrutiny

The main functions of the House of Commons – **legislation** and **scrutiny** – are possibly the most important and demand more extensive analysis.

Legislation

The legislative activity of the House of Commons involves the whole House overseeing the passage of bills, giving sanction to the government's programme. Except in the case of private members' bills, MPs do not in the strict sense have **legislative initiative**, rather they concentrate within their respective parties on influencing the content of legislation. Because most legislation originates with the government, which has a majority on standing committees dealing with it, the broad direction of policy is unlikely to be affected greatly by any amendments proposed by opposition MPs.

Types of legislation

The bills which come before the House of Commons are either **private** or **public**. The former relate to a specific interest; the latter affect the community at large.

Government bills

Most public bills are sponsored by the executive. **Government bills** have the greatest chance of reaching the legislative statute book because they are prioritised by government control of the Commons timetable. Some of the government's legislative intentions will be spelt out in the Queen's Speech, which is delivered to parliament each November at the opening of a new session. Other legislative proposals will be laid before the electorate in the governing party's manifesto, which forms a loose **mandate** for office once in power. Governments also acquire public legislative powers through statutory instruments (SIs) which follow a different route from ordinary bills.

Private members' bills

A small percentage of parliamentary time is allocated to private members' bills which do not usually reach the statute book for lack of government support. As public bills they will often tackle social or moral issues which governments prefer to leave for fear of electoral ramifications. Occasionally they will highlight an area of growing public concern where the government will act after the failure of the private member's bill. MPs successful in the ballot to introduce a bill (other ways include the 10 minute rule after the day's proceedings, or Standing Order 58, by giving notice to the Speaker) are often approached by outside interests anxious to promote legislation of their own. In early 1995 the Labour MP

PUBLIC BILLS – Affect public as a whole

1)	GOVERNMENT BILLS	Most legislation affecting public
2)	PRIVATE MEMBERS' BILLS	Mainly controversial topics (capital punishment, abortion, law etc.)

1) Introduced by government
2) Introduced by backbench MPs

Types of legislation

PRIVATE BILLS – Affect private interests

For example, LOCAL GOVERNMENT by-laws giving special powers to a local authority

John McFall was persuaded by the League Against Cruel Sports to introduce his Wild Mammals (Protection) Bill which was in effect written by the League. The subsequent revision of this Bill introduced by the Labour MP Alan Meale, enabled it to pass both Houses of Parliament by February 1996 as The Wild Mammals (Protection) Act.

Private bills

Private bills form a small part of the legislative output of Parliament. Governments are generally not in favour of granting special powers to public bodies like local authorities because this impinges on the concept of parliamentary sovereignty and makes it harder to control legislation. For this reason private bills go through an elaborate and expensive process of being 'proved' by special committees of both Houses of Parliament, before embarking on their different stages. Typical powers granted to local authorities under this type of bill include regulatory laws to control the activities of local markets, small business and other activities. *Silk* (*1995*) gives numerous examples including the Birmingham City Council Act 1985 which allowed motor racing on public roads in the city.

Legislative stages

To become law, bills must pass through legislative stages in both the House of Commons and the House of Lords. Bills that begin in the Lords (less politically contentious) end in the Commons and those starting in the Commons end in the Lords. The final stage, the royal assent, is a formality; the monarch does not personally sign bills (the Clerk to the Parliaments affixes the royal assent in Norman French).

Of these respective stages, the committee stage is possibly the most important from the point of view of the opposition who can table amendments to bills more effectively at this stage. Bills go before **standing committees** (committees of debate organised along party lines) where they are examined clause by clause.

Amendments will be considered and sometimes accepted by the government if they improve the effectiveness of the bill, but not if they alter policy considered important or attempt to wreck it. Wrecking amendments, together with effective management of the timetable, are a major reason why government managers bring in the time motions of the **guillotine** or **kangaroo**. Both restrict the amount of time spent in debate and in consideration of a bill and are frequently criticised by opposition parties as being undemocratic.

Executive control of the legislative timetable for bills also ensures that the vast majority of accepted amendments made to general legislation in standing committees are government sponsored with opposition and backbench amendments hardly succeeding.

STAGE	WHERE TAKEN	COMMENTS
First reading	Floor of House	Formal introduction; no debate
Second reading	Floor of House	Debate on principle of Bill
Committee	Standing committee in Commons	Clause examined; amendments can be made
Report	Floor of House	Bill reported back to House; amendment possible
Third reading	Floor of House	Final approval; no amendments in Commons
Lords or Commons Amendments	Floor of House	Consideration of amendments by other House
Royal assent		Bill becomes Act of Parliament

Stages of parliamentary legislation

Comment on the legislative process

The effectiveness of the House of Commons is related to any policy influence that can be brought to bear over government controlled legislation. Because the functions of the modern Commons are subsumed under party control – in effect majority government – the legislative role is weak. This is particularly evident from the following criticisms.

Scrutiny

Scrutiny of the work of the executive is possibly the most effective area of the House of Commons business in the sense that it focuses on the politically sensitive aspect of **policy implementation** rather than **policy initiation**.

Scrutiny of government takes two forms:

1 Spontaneous contemporary examination through questions to ministers.

2 Procedural investigation of administrative activity through departmental select committees. Select committees are the more effective check on policy, or have most influence because they traditionally operate on non-partisan (non-party political) grounds from a parliamentary perspective.

FACTFILE

- **The legislative stage is too lengthy, complex and time consuming (*Norton 1995*). As MPs insist on their rights to debate principles and details of controversial bills – both in standing committee and on the floor of the House – attempts to reform procedure have yet to succeed.**

- **Parliament has little input in the pre-legislative stage. Bills coming into the commons are at an advanced stage of formulation thus reducing MPs' influence. Suggestions for improvement include the placing of committee stage at the beginning of the legislative process where the wider implications of a bill can be examined (*Norton 1995*).**

- **Structurally standing committees are not able to offer a convincing check on executive legislative powers. As presently arranged, they are formed to consider bills under heads A, B, C, D etc., then disbanded after their work. This ad hoc nature and dispersal prevents the accumulation of member expertise which would assist public policy scrutiny.**

- **Only a fraction of statutory instruments (SIs) made under Acts of Parliament are examined by the Commons Select Committee on Statutory Instruments. Now approximately 3000 to 4000 SIs are produced each year giving additional powers to the executive. The vast majority are formally 'laid before Parliament' and are signed into law – 'nodded through' – with little or no debate (*Booker 1995*).**

Questions to ministers

Question Time was traditionally held up as the parliamentary institution which enshrined ministerial accountability to the House of Commons. Tony Blair, after becoming Prime Minister in 1997, was determined to remove the adversarial nature from Prime Minister's question time. By moving it to a one hour session each Wednesday instead of the previous practice of two separate fifteen-minute sessions (Tue/Thur) he hoped to make it less confrontational and more informative to Parliament. Critics have noticed this reduces the Prime Minister's appearances in the Commons and it still leaves other ministerial questions in their former arrangement.

Sleaze and corruption of MPs

The Committee on Standards in Public Life (Wicks Committee)

The activities of some Conservative MPs in accepting payments from outside interests (generally known as 'sleaze', cash for questions or cash for influence) in particular David Tredinnick, Graham Riddick, Timothy Smith and Neil Hamilton – for placing questions to ministers lead to the establishment in 1994 of the committee on Standards in Public Life under its first Chairman Lord Nolan. Prior to the activities of these MPs there had been questions raised over members and their financial links to outside lobbies or other organisations. Although covered by a voluntary **Register of Members' Interests** since 1975, there were unrecorded cases of MPs receiving hospitality, gifts, payments or commissions for raising matters inside Parliament on behalf of special interests. The Select Committee on Members' Interests (in 1995 replaced by Select Committee on Standards and Privileges) recommended strengthening safeguards against corruption of MPs by tightening the rules on disclosure of financial relationships. The first report of the **Nolan Committee** (1995) **on Standards in Public Life** set out seven principles by which Members of

STRENGTHS	WEAKNESSES
1 Directly confrontational (government v. opposition)	1 Time not adequate for many questions
2 Attracts media attention	2 Ministers can avoid straight answers
3 Easy to follow	3 Prime Ministerial Question Time can degenerate into party political battle
4 Can reveal gaps in government knowledge	4 MPs who want more detail prefer written questions which get written answers
5 Supplementary questions can surprise ministers	

Strengths and weaknesses of Question Time

Parliament and others would be judged – selflessness, integrity, objectivity, accountability, openness, honesty and leadership. The committee's main recommendations were accepted by the Major government and have resulted in the establishment of a Parliamentary Commissioner for Standards (Elizabeth Filkin) responsible for maintaining a more informative Register of Members' interests and a New Code of Conduct for MPs. Other changes implemented were full disclosure of outside earnings relating to parliamentary work and restrictions on employment for lobbying organisations.

Departmental select committees

The most effective form of scrutiny of the work of the executive has always come from the **investigative** or **select committees** of the House of Commons. These were first established in the nineteenth century and have become a regular feature of parliamentary life since that time. Various piecemeal reforms were carried out to committees (in the 1950s and 1960s) until 1979 when the then Leader of the House of Commons, Norman St. John Stevas, implemented the decision by the House to extend the system to cover government departments. The new departmental select committees (DSCs) were the first attempt to regularise the scrutiny system with committees that could examine 'the expenditure, administration and policy' of the main government departments.

Other committees include the Public Accounts Committee, Environmental Audit, Public Administration and European Scrutiny. Committees have substantial powers given to them by Parliament and can call for **'persons, papers and records'**. They publish unanimous reports of their deliberations (which the government replies to) and, unlike standing committees, operate in a non-partisan parliamentary way.

Committees have attracted their share of **criticism**. They cannot compel MPs, ministers and other witnesses to attend.

Civil servants only attend with express permission of their permanent or deputy secretaries and then they are governed by the **'Osmotherly Rules'** regulating their conduct. Access to information is restricted: committees have no express powers to examine departmental records, nor to compel witnesses to answer their questions. This was graphically demonstrated by the stonewalling actions of the Maxwell brothers in refusing to answer questions before the Social Services Committee in 1992. A final difficulty is the fact that the government is not obliged to act on a committee's recommendations – although it makes a response. Such behaviour limits any **policy influence** committees may have over the executive. Norton talks of the marginal influence of DSCs on government policy although generally he believes this has had positive results.

There is little doubt that select committees have improved the scrutiny function of the House of Commons over the executive. According to *Norton (2000)* the following improvements are a direct result of the work of the committee system.

* The House of Commons is better informed about government work through MPs' specialised critical activity in select committees.

COMMITTEE	AREA OF WORK
Agriculture Culture, Media and Sport Defence Education and Employment Environment, Transport and Regions Foreign Affairs Health Home Affairs Science and Technology Northern Ireland Scottish Affairs Social Security Trade and Industry International Development Treasury/Civil Service Welsh Affairs	All matters relevant and relating to expenditure, administration and policy of each respective department

Departmental select committees of the House of Commons from 1998

- Committees have had a deterrent effect on the behaviour of government in the knowledge that their affairs are publicly scrutinised.

- There is now more openness in government as a direct result of committees examining ministers in public and placing more information into the public domain than previously.

- Groups and outside interests are given more access to policy makers by being called before or submitting evidence to committees.

- Although difficult to quantify, the reports of select committees may have greater policy influence than is obvious. Many recommendations are later adopted by the government and proposals may find their way into improvements in policy.

Occasionally proposals are made to increase the effectiveness of select committees still further – increased budgets, longer sitting days, greater links with the floor of the House of Commons.

C H E C K L I S T

✓ **Executives in parliamentary systems are generally reluctant to see increased powers given to scrutiny committees for fear of losing policy initiatives to what in effect becomes government by committee.**

✓ **Reformers sometimes compare the weakness of the British select committee system to the strengths of American congressional committees. This is not particularly useful for constitutional reasons – the US federal system and separation of power allow the existence of powerful legislative and investigative committees as a check on an otherwise overpowerful President.**

✓ **The British Prime Minister and executive operate within a parliamentary system answerable to a House of Commons.**

Commons reform

The reformist New Labour governments of 1997 and 2001 adopted a less traditional attitude to changes in the House of Commons whilst preserving its orthodox role. Previous approaches to Commons reform had been based on two opposing views.

1 **The weak view** Generally identified in the writings of *Crick* (*1970*) who claimed that Parliament's role was educational and supportive of constituents. The policy-making function rests with the executive and the House of Commons should concentrate on scrutiny and criticism.

2 **The strong view** Associated with the work of *Walkland* (*1979*), who argued for an ending of the adversary party political battle which denigrates Parliament. Two-party dominance of the House of Commons will only end with electoral reform.

Evaluation

The choice facing reformers revolves around a weak Parliament and strong executive (the present situation), or a reformed stronger Parliament and weak executive. A possible middle way was that adopted by Tony Blair after 1997. The Labour government were examining the merits of electoral reform (the Jenkins Commission) which if adopted will have far-reaching consequences in Parliament. Internally Tony Blair has altered Prime Minister's Question Time, and made other procedural changes through a new **Select Committee on Modernisation of the House of Commons**. This committee, under the chairmanship of Robin Cook, Leader of the House, proposed that the Commons finished work by 7pm. This was accepted by the House in late 2002 and implemented by January 2003. Friday sittings were also scrapped with the House completing its business on the first four days of the week.

Questions

1 What do you consider the most important legislative stage of a bill and why?

2 Briefly what is the value of the Commons department select committee system?

3 Why is the House of Commons ineffective in controlling the government?

Members of Parliament

The public image of the House of Commons is closely bound up with the behaviour of Members of Parliament. Before the televising of the House of Commons in 1989, people's perception of the House owed much to sound broadcasts (started in 1975) and newspaper coverage. The general impression given was of a disorderly place absorbed in a party political battle with MPs of radically different ideologies arguing about legislation and government policy. Televising of the House has produced a change in parliamentary behaviour – MPs appear **less confrontational** in debate, as they seek to create favourable impressions with the electorate (*Adonis 1990*). Structurally (because of the government–opposition seating arrangements) the classic impression given of the House of Commons was of a place where representatives of the working class (Labour) faced representatives of the middle and upper classes (Conservative and Liberals (Democrats)) in an adversarial contest. Such a picture is now less relevant and no longer an accurate description of events.

Theories of representation

There are two basic theories of representation used to account for Members of Parliament.

1 **Representative or Burkean theory**   According to this view MPs are representatives of their constituents and owe their constituents their better judgement in any decisions relating to their behaviour in the Commons. They **do not slavishly follow** their constituents' dictates but consider opinions in an overall evaluation before casting their vote. These ideas have their origins in the writings of the Whig philosopher and eighteenth century MP *Edmund Burke (1729–97)*. Burke was no democrat – he preferred aristocratic rule (because aristocrats were trustful) and was opposed to the extension of the franchise to women and the labouring classes.

   Burke's ideas have become influential because of his emphasis on the freedom of MPs from restraining ties of their electorate. Yet in the modern House of Commons MPs are tied to party machines (except in 'free votes') so it could be argued that Burke's philosophic notion of pure representation has never been achieved.

2 **Delegate theory**   The delegate theory of MPs has more recent origins and can be traced to early this century with the extension of the franchise and the creation of the Labour Party. Essentially this view recognises a stronger electoral tie between MPs and their constituents. Since their constituents elect them to Parliament, they should (like a delegate) **subordinate** their **personal views** and vote according to their constituents' dictates, or the party constitution. Left wing Labour MPs put more emphasis on this perspective largely because of the tradition of mandated (instructed) delegates to the Labour Party Annual Conference and associated trade union conferences. There is also a philosophic left wing connection to the idea that the Labour MPs should endeavour to keep to the socialist principles established in their constitution. The attempt by the Labour left to ensure the permanent mandatory reselection of MPs can be seen against this background.

Social background of MPs

MPs are predominantly male, middle aged and middle class. Apart from the under-representation of the working class in their ranks, women and members from the ethnic minorities also have less chance of becoming MPs. Two reasons are advanced for this situation.

1 Parties tend to select so-called 'safe' candidates for parliamentary elections. There is a generally held

FACTFILE

- **Clearly British MPs lean more to the Burkean or representative view of representation. Labour, Conservative and Liberal Democrats are not mandated in the true sense of the word as delegates for their constituents. Indeed, there are those on the right who regard the delegate theory as positively harmful to the orthodox idea of a 'free' representation.**

- **This contrasts with the philosophic position of members of the US Congress who are part delegate and part representative because of the federal nature of US representation at local, state and national level.**

belief supported by research that black candidates, women and members of the working class are seen as liabilities by the electorate and are therefore not selected by the mainstream parties.

2 Working class representatives, women and ethic minority group members tend not to present themselves as candidate for fear of selection failure and this reinforces the low numbers succeeding.

Comment on social background

Parliament has never socially mirrored the nation or 'selectorate' that it represents. This does not imply a conspiracy to under-represent the majority for indirect representatives have in that sense always been elitist. However, there is now a general feeling that women and ethnic minority communities should have more MPs and the major political parties are moving in this direction. The Labour Party introduced rule changes that allowed all-women shortlists in safe Labour seats (EMILY's List) from 1993 until 1996 when the practice was dropped. However enough women were adopted to remain in place for the 1997 general election when Labour gained 101 women MPs or 35 per cent of that party's total. The Conservative Party secured the election of 18 women MPs in 1997 only 12 per cent of its total. The position for representatives from the ethnic minorities was less favourable with 9 MPs elected in 1997 in all political parties representing approximately one per cent of the make-up of the Commons. In the 2001 general election these figures hardly changed. Only 118 women were elected to the House of Commons or 18 per cent of the total of 659 MPs. Ethnic minority representation rose to a total of 10 Asian or black MPs, all on the Labour side of the House.

Class background of MPs

The House of Commons is a middle class institution – most MPs are drawn from professions, with university education an important criterion. Examination of the occupational background of successful parliamentary candidates in the 1997 general election showed business and private sector professionals dominating the Conservative Party whilst public sector teachers and lecturers dominated the Labour Party. This pattern was repeated in the 2001 election. This development, which has been tracked since the 1945 Parliament, has two implications.

1 The class background of all MPs has **converged** towards the middle class. The Conservative Party is no longer dominated by the upper class and the Parliamentary Labour Party has few MPs of working class origin.

2 The **social gap** between the electorate and MPs was always greater for the traditional Labour Party and its working class base than the Conservative Party and its middle class base. In the 1997 general election New Labour made specific successful appeals to the middle classes and so closed the gap. In the 2001 election Labour managed to attract 36 per cent of the middle class vote compared to the Conservative 38 per cent middle class vote. For the first time Labour is beginning to look increasingly like the middle class party in terms of electoral support. No longer can it be described simply as a party of the working class.

Functions of MPs

According to *Adonis* (*1990*) MPs' functions can be subsumed under the following headings:

1 **Party loyalist/activist** The majority of MPs are loyal to the party that puts them into Parliament.

2 **Constituency representative** Constituency work takes vast amounts of MPs' time. Surgeries, local public relations and correspondence from constituents have increased pressure on MPs.

3 **Member of the Commons** The main work of MPs includes debates, committee work, divisions and general legislative activity, embracing private members' bills. In carrying out their role (which each MP interprets independently) they face pressures from their party, constituents and parliamentary work, all of which lead to questions of their effectiveness and how it could be improved.

The effectiveness of MPs

The effectiveness of MPs is often judged against their performance in the House of Commons, which in turn relates to pay and conditions of service. Conditions of work in the Commons were frequently criticised as inadequate in terms of office space, secretarial support and working environment. MPs worked long hours and needed more support services if they were to carry out their roles effectively.

The occupation of a new award-winning Portcullis House Parliament building by 2001 gave all MPs European and American style office space and facilities, ending the disadvantage of inadequate accommodation. MPs have yet to receive the remuneration and professional support of their counterparts in the US Congress but they are fast approaching parity with European parliamentarians, and can no longer claim inadequate reward for the job.

Other changes to the House of Commons

The Commons Modernisation Committee continued to experiment with changes to procedure after 2001. Apart from shorter sitting times, there has also been a reduction in the period of the summer recess. Unfinished bills, previously lost at the end of each session, can now be carried over to the next sitting with obvious advantages. These and other changes continue to attract criticism from traditional MPs whilst being favourably received by the new intake of women members as being more family friendly.

CHECKLIST

✓ The first report of the Nolan Committee on Standards in Public Life did not favour the severing of outside links by MPs – the acceptance of its recommendations brought back into focus the question of the full or part time status of the House of Commons. Many MPs were resentful of the disclosure rules because they highlight the consultancies and contacts that bring substantial financial reward. These MPs support the idea that outside employment/occupations beyond Parliament enrich their experiences and add to their role as representative of varied interests. They do not wish to become closeted full time parliamentary professionals.

✓ The counter view that MPs should concentrate on their parliamentary work is propagated mainly by those with fewer outside contacts. They claim that Parliament should be the sole occupation of MPs and that those without outside employment are able to discharge their duties properly. *Norton* (*1994*) identified a growing trend among the newer MPs to regard Parliament as a main professional career. The difficulty for such MPs is the counter argument that if they lose their seats at a general election they will have no occupation to return to. Many lawyers and other professionals maintain their alternative occupations for just such an eventuality.

The House of Lords

There have been many attempts to reform the House of Lords, all of which have failed. From this it can be concluded that there is a broad nature of agreement between all the main parties that the Lords should continue in existence playing its major role as a second chamber criticising the executive (*Brazier 1991*). Even though the composition of the House is now questioned, there appears little controversy over its role and functions. As presently organised the Lords does not threaten executive dominance of the legislature and no present or future government wants to see the House rival its power over the commons. Those who want reform generally feel the Lords should be more effective in its legislative role and more democratically accountable in its representative function.

The powers of the House of Lords

The powers of the House of Lords are subject to the operation of the Parliament Acts 1911 and 1949. The first Act removed powers over financial bills. The second Act restricted delaying power to one year (effectively one parliamentary session). It is important to clarify this position.

In practice the House has worked out its relationship to the executive in the Commons through an arrangement referred to as the **Salisbury Convention**. The fear facing the newly elected Labour government of 1945 was that the Conservative dominated Lords would frustrate the wishes of the electorate by delaying legislation for two years under the 1911 Parliament Act. Accommodation was reached with the Conservative Leader of the Lords in 1945 that the House would not seek to prevent the passage of legislation contained in a party's election manifesto. In effect, therefore, bills in a government's manifesto have the authority of an electoral mandate and are not opposed outright by the Lords. The House

does retain the right to propose amendments to bills, however, but these are rarely pressed if the government insists on its legislative detail unaltered.

Clearly this power to amend and delay bills from the Lower House can be beneficial in forcing ministers to reconsider legislation. Sometimes the Lords will claim the support of public opinion for their actions as in the case of the 1998 rejection of the Crime and Disorder Bill because of an amendment to lower the age of consent from 18 to 16. This made Home Secretary Jack Straw remove the offending amendment after discussions with the gay and homosexual lobby.

In operating their legislative powers peers tend to behave with circumspection as if direct challenges to the executive can lead to reform proposals of the House on the grounds of preventing popular legislation. The power to delay bills under the 1949 Parliament Act (passed by a Labour government anxious to further restrict the Lords) is rarely used because the Commons can subsequently pass bills to royal assent without the Lords if the latter attempt rejection. In recent times the only bill delayed was the 1991 War Crimes Act which became operative in 1993.

Constitutional safeguard

The powers and functions of the House of Lords are inseparable in that how it behaves or functions is governed by its power. It has a major role as a **constitutional safeguard** against arbitrary conduct by a government in the Commons. It can prevent absolutely any bills to extend the life of Parliament beyond the statutory five year term. This last **absolute veto** provides the greatest single argument for retaining the Lords, for if it was abolished this function would have either to pass to the Commons or to the courts which do not have power over the executive.

Deliberation and scrutiny

The first televising of the House of Lords in 1985 brought publicity to the debating qualities of members of the upper House. Although of high standard debates rarely affect anything of major significance (*Adonis 1990*). Paradoxically, debates illustrate the representative composition of the House for a large number of life peers have wide interests and experience of life even though many are past retirement age. Again, the much criticised hereditary peers also had younger members in their ranks – some of the newer life peers are also younger.

The scrutiny function of the Lords follows much the same process as the Commons and as all bills have to

Study and Revise AS and A2 Level Government and Politics

pass both Houses before the royal assent, any amendments made by the House will need:

1 agreement by the Commons,

2 rejection by the Commons or

3 substitution of a Lords amendment by a Commons amendment.

Usually the House backs down in the face of concerted Commons (government) pressure and accepts the agreed version of a Bill which then goes for royal assent.

The Lords has established scrutiny select committees in Europe, Science and Technology and Delegated Powers which operate on a similar pattern to those found in the House of Commons in addition to its standing legislative committees. The scrutiny function is completed by Question Time which has less significance than its Commons counterpart. Peers can ask oral or starred questions of the government spokespersons and also receive written answers. One measure of the **revival** of the House since the early eighties is the increase in the number of questions now being asked (*Adonis 1990*).

Composition and political affiliation

There are four categories of membership and political affiliation in the House of Lords:

Membership	
• Bishops (includes 2 Archbishops)	25
• Hereditary Elected	92
• Life Peers	537
• Law Lords	27
Total at November 2003	681*
*Includes peers who are not currently attending.	

Party Strengths	
• Conservatives	210
• Labour	185
• Liberal Democrats	64
• Cross Bench (Independent)	179
• Bishops	25
• Other	7*

Figures at November 2003.
From *The Work of the House of Lords* House of Lords Information Office 2004.

Since the admission of **life peers** in 1958 (Life Peerage Act), breaking the hereditary stranglehold over the House, the political imbalance between the Conservative leaning **hereditary peers** and the rest has been moderated. Although those who take the Conservative whip outnumber the other parties, three factors condition this prospect:

1 A considerable number of peers (173) do not take a party whip and prefer to sit as **crossbenchers**.

2 The majority of Conservative hereditary peers (backwoodsmen) were inactive. However, they gave the Conservative Party an in-built majority and attended to protect their interests. The controversial Poll Tax (Community Charge) 1989–90 was introduced by the Thatcher government with their support in the Lords. This was a major factor in the Blair governments move against the House after 1999.

3 Attendance figures to the Lords have increased to a daily average of 300 (*Norton 1993*), making it more likely that the Labour and Liberal Democratic parties can rely on their memberships in divisions. Life peers (many Labour and Liberal Democratic, but also Conservative; since 1983 few hereditary peers have been created of any party) tend to be more active and see their legislative role in the House as their major occupation.

New Labour and reform of the Lords

Before the 1999 Blair government the last serious attempt to reform the House of Lords came with the Parliament (No.2) Bill of 1968/69. The main provision in this bill was to remove the voting rights of hereditary peers and thus created a fairer political balance between the political parties. This bill failed because Conservative opponents could not support the extinction of the hereditary element in the constitution and Labour wanted more radical change. Both attitudes are relevant in the current political climate. Tony Blair in the 1997 Labour manifesto promised that his government would end the right of hereditary peers to sit in the Lords and ensure that no political party had a majority. This marked an **evolutionary** move for Labour who in previous elections had pledged to abolish the House altogether. New Labour are apparently satisfied with the legislative role of the House – disputing only the unfairness of the present composition. The fact that by late 1998 the Blair government had been defeated a **total of 31 times** by the upper House lent support to Labour arguments that the Lords was overdue for reform. Tony Blair's comfortable majority in the Commons gave him the necessary authority and power to complete this process.

Stage one reforms

After the 1997 general election Tony Blair established a committee of both Houses of Parliament to undertake a review of reform proposals and recommend how those changes would be implemented. These proposals were initiated through a **Cabinet Subcommittee on Lords Reform** under the chairmanship of the Lord Chancellor Lord Irvine. The interim proposal was that the hereditary peers be phased out in a new reform bill in late 1998 with approx. 600 Life Peers (200 Labour, 200 Conservative, 130 Crossbench, 70 Liberal Democrats) constituting the new Lords. A Royal Commission was established under Lord Wakeham to examine the prospects of long term reform based on a part elected, part nominated chamber. The Labour government accepted Wakeham's proposals and passed the **1999 House of Lords Act** effectively removing the hereditary peers (with the exception of 92) in the first stage of a two stage full reform of the whole House.

Stage two reforms

Stage two reforms were fudged as the Labour government appeared uncertain of the way forward. The difficulty with removing hereditary peers (some were created Life Peers) whilst maintaining the legislative functions of the House was twofold. First there was the danger of increasing prime ministerial patronage power through Life Peer creations making the Lords into a kind of super quango (non-governmental organisation). Second a reformed House of Lords with a guaranteed existence could become more of a rival to the democratically elected House of Commons.

Tony Blair was aware of the problems but brought forward proposals in the Queen's Speech in 2001 to remove the remaining 92 hereditary peers and move towards a part elected part appointed House, through an Appointments Commission, as advocated in the Wakeham Report.

The House of Commons could not reach agreement on any of the Stage Two Reforms and in late 2003 the government published plans for a new House of Lords Bill that will remove the remaining hereditary peers and create a Statutory Appointments Commission. Gordon Brown in his Budget Speech of March 2004 said the government was looking to an all-appointed House after the next general election.

Summary

1 The British Parliament (the Queen, the House of Commons and the House of Lords) has long been subject to academic debate about its effectiveness in terms of both legislation and control over the executive.

2 Although reforms have been introduced – the 1999 House of Lords Act and the departmental select committee since 1979 – the parliamentary legislative system is effectively still dominated by the executive.

3 This raises questions about the role of Parliament – should it be an adjunct to government policy-making or should it have an existence of its own evaluating proposals on their merits?

4 The corresponding role of Members of Parliament is also subsumed under these considerations, as is the importance of the House of Lords as a reviewing chamber.

Sample question and answer

A2 Level question

1 Discuss critically the role of the House of Commons.

This question demands a thorough understanding of the role of the House of Commons against the background of executive dominance. It is important to show the positive attributes of the House although current debate focuses on the shortcomings. An examination of the different perspectives on Parliament would be useful followed by careful discussion of the legislative, deliberative and scrutiny function of the Commons. The legislative role of Members of Parliament needs evaluation including their performance in departmental select committees. Finally, there should be an analysis of reform proposals of the Commons set against the orthodox role of the modern House.

PREVIEW

In this chapter you will revise the following:

- **The reforms of Conservative and Labour governments and changes to the nature and structure of the service.**

- **The prevailing relationships between higher civil servants and ministers and how this has changed.**

- **The role and power of senior civil servants in relation to the administration of government policy.**

Theories of civil service power

Theoretical debates about the civil service continue to concentrate on the proper role and function of civil servants and the structure of departments. In this tradition writers argue from the particularly narrow focus of the special relationship prevailing between ministers and their departmental permanent secretaries, to the all-embracing general perspective of powers within the whole civil service. There are **five main** theoretical constructs or models of power relationships within the civil service which contribute to our understanding.

FACTFILE

- **Civil servant – administrative officials in the employment of central government departments distinguished from the uniformed military services.**

- **Bureaucracy – a hierarchical arrangement of officials working in central government departments. The most senior reside at the apex of the structure and orders flow from the top downwards.**

- **Mandarins – the most senior officials running government departments reporting directly to ministers. The ranks of permanent secretary to assistant secretary are generally included in this category.**

- **Whitehall – the generic name given to the main central government departments which had their origin in the street of that name. Some departments are still located there; others have been dispersed around London.**

Liberal democratic

This traditional perspective of civil service power is sometimes referred to as the public administration model, with the implication that civil servants are divorced from the political aspects of governing. According to the constitution, British civil servants implement the policies of their government ministers – they are not influenced by party considerations, and do not make policy decisions. This **orthodox** view of the service appeared to come under attack during the governments of Margaret Thatcher 1979–90 ironically because officials were perceived as too traditionalist to implement a radical programme of reform. The overall effect of these reforms (which are still continuing) is to move the bulk of the service axis back to pure administration and away from policy-making, with the emphasis on the managerial and administrative skills of civil servants. There is some evidence that the structural changes in departments introduced by Tony Blair after 2001 was also a reflection of perceived weaknesses of traditionalism still surviving in the service.

Constitutional bureaucracy

This view draws attention to the power of civil servants operating in a democratic state, running the government machine on behalf of democratically elected politicians. The sociologist *Max Weber (1864–1920)* first drew attention to the power of government officials in his analysis of the bureaucratic form of administration. Although bureaucracy was a necessary form of administration because it was the most efficient and rational organisation, there was always a danger of powerful officials beyond the control of democratically elected politicians. The democratic state had to guard against **bureaucratic absolutism** or rule by officials because the amateur status of politicians (who are continually elected or rotated in posts) compared unfavourably with the professional strength of permanent officials.

Although Weber's prescript is an ideal type that has not developed in the British constitution (procedural and structural safeguards prevent its emergence), the dangers are there. *Rose (1991)* has drawn attention to the constant reshuffles that occur in the ministerial hierarchy reducing the time a single politician spends running a department. This inevitably places the onus on professional impartial conduct by senior officials advising ministers. After 2001 Tony Blair carried out many changes to the departmental/ministerial structure, further proof again that constant reforms can weaken continuity.

Power bloc

According to this perspective senior civil servants have the power to obstruct radical policies of governments which they find unacceptable. As a group the higher civil service is drawn from a fairly narrow social class base, which in turn leads to charges of **elitism** and **unrepresentativeness** at the top. Previous Labour ministers (Richard Crossman and Tony Benn) have testified to the difficulties they experienced from civil servants opposed to their policies which made their relationships adversarial rather than professional, although others have testified that the service is responsive to the needs of its ministers. According to John Garret the mandarins have been able to resist the more radical reforms of the Thatcher, Major and Blair governments in the sense that the same type of people are still at the top of the services.

Bureaucratic over-supply

A frequent criticism of the civil services from the early eighties focused on administrative expansionism or oversupply. Because the service was immune from the pressures of the free market (funded by tax payers and government) it was able to develop a relatively privileged position in terms of personnel, pay and conditions. At a time when the economy was experiencing a downward turn due to recession, the civil service appeared resistant to reductions in its level of operations. Although more concerned with efficiency, the reforms implemented by the Labour governments after the **Fulton Committee Report (1968)** had not seriously affected personnel or budgets. In a seminal study of the civil service *Lord Crowther-Hunt and Kellner (1980)* concluded that the vested interests of the higher civil service had prevented the implementation of many of the Fulton recommendations. Overstaffing and expansionism in the civil service continued until the Thatcher government reforms began to take effect after 1980.

Whitehall community

Some descriptions of the upper reaches of the civil service focus on the collegiate nature of the service at this level. Stemming from the work of *Heclo and Wildavsky (1974)* the emphasis is placed on the village-like atmosphere of Whitehall where most of the permanent secretaries personally know each other. The relationships in this 'cosy world' contribute to the smooth running of the administration through formal and informal contacts between ministers and civil servants. Much of the preparatory groundwork for policy implementation is carried out through cross-department and interdepartmental committees where

useful networks assisting ministers are built up. Although this model is valuable for understanding the interlocking relationships at the top of the service, its main weakness lies in its narrow focus on the London elite of administrative officials *(Theakston 1992)*.

CHECKLIST

✓ **The current civil service structure is generally thought to date from the mid-nineteenth century.**

✓ **The influential Northcote–Trevelyan Report of 1854, regularised what in effect was an inefficient, corrupt and unaccountable service into a coherent system of officials managing government departments. The work of service was classified for the first time into intellectual and mechanical categories and a system of examinations and qualifications for entry introduced.**

✓ **The removal of nepotism on entry was an important reform but the introduction of mechanical and intellectual classes was a divisive feature in the service until the reforms of the 1960s.**

✓ **Apart from some procedural changes in the 1930s (the Tomlin Commission of 1931 described civil servants as servants of the crown, other than holders of political or judicial office, employed in a civil capacity) the service remained basically within its nineteenth-century ethos until the advent of the Fulton Report in 1968.**

The nature of the service

Reformism

The establishment of the Fulton Commission in 1966 by the Labour government of Harold Wilson can be seen against a background of two general concerns:

- **Managerialism** In keeping with Harold Wilson's ideas of technological change, civil servants were regarded as inefficient administrators, primarily because of their generalist (non-specialist) backgrounds. More attention would be paid to management of resources and personnel in the future.

- **Classlessness** The Labour government were keen to promote equality of opportunity and saw restrictions on mobility in the existing system of civil service classes. There were also concerns expressed over the narrow social class backgrounds of many senior administrators. It was hoped that opening up the service to wider recruitment would rectify this aspect.

In his report Lord Fulton made the following criticisms of the civil service.

- The service was dominated by the **philosophy of the amateur** administrator. Potential senior civil servants were chosen because of intellectual generalist skills, not specialised or relevant qualifications.

- There were **too many grades** of civil servant making the service appear restrictive of talent. The grades of classes were a barrier to advancement.

- Management skills were given a low priority in the service. The professional administrative grades tended to regard themselves as **policy advisers** to ministers rather than **managers** of subordinates delivering services to the public.

- The service was too insular or inward looking; the closed career structure did not encourage the adoption of 'best practice' management techniques and personnel from private industry. Part of the difficulty here related to the traditional lifelong career pattern of professional civil servants. They expected to reach the highest grades without facing external competition. To employ 'irregulars' on secondment from industry would encroach on this idea.

- Training and coordination of work across departments were also singled out as areas which could be improved. Fulton contrasted the English practice of **'on the job' training** once in the service with the French elitist practice of graduate civil service preparation through the Ecole National d'Administration (National School of Administration).

- There was too much secrecy surrounding the whole structure of the civil service.

Impact of the Fulton reforms

Fulton reported in 1968 under the Labour government of Harold Wilson which had set up the inquiry. As the party lost office for the four years 1970–74, the Conservative government of Edward Heath was charged with the initial implementation of the reforms. A returning Labour government from 1974, first under Harold Wilson, then James Callaghan, continued some implementation of these reforms against early civil service resistance. An early critic of the implementation of the reforms, *Lord Crowther-Hunt (1980),* claimed the **slowness** of the reform resulted from obstruction from higher civil servants opposed to changes which would damage their authority. Despite this criticism it is possible to see

the Fulton reforms as the precursor of the sweeping changes that would be introduced into the service by the government of Margaret Thatcher and continued into the nineties under John Major. The Blair government from 1997 did not move radically away from the following changes:

- The service introduced a single unified grading structure. The former clerical, executive and administrative classes were placed in a unified **Administrative Group** in 1972 with the upper grades subject to open competition. From 1995 the White Paper 'The Civil Service: Taking Forward Continuity and Change' created new senior civil service grades 1–5 (also open to outside competition) based on earlier 1986 reforms.

- Training of civil servants was improved with the establishment of a **Civil Service College** in 1970 designed to offer in-service management courses for middle and senior civil servants. Initially there was some criticism of the quality of training courses. After July 1989 more attention was given to creative management thinking and the adoption of business-like training methods. The Centre for Management and Policy Studies has now absorbed the college.

- Better coordination of the personnel function of the service resulted from the creation of a separate **Civil Service Department** in 1968. Although this department appeared to improve the management of recruitment practices, it was abolished by the Conservative government in 1981 and its powers passed back to the Treasury and separate departments. Now some of these functions are carried out in the Civil Service Employer Group of the Office of Public Service.

- Although Fulton felt there was too much secrecy surrounding the work of the civil service, he did not make specific recommendations on the closed relationship between permanent secretaries and their ministers. The question of 'openness' in government received a set-back with the prosecution of two civil servants (Sarah Tisdall 1984 and Clive Ponting 1985) under the 1911 Official Secrets Act for passing government information to outside contacts. The revised 1989 Official Secrets Act ended the defence of disclosure of information in the public interest and did not focus specifically on 'openness' in public life. John Major's Citizens' Charter initiative of 1991 could be seen as an attempt to provide the public with more information on service entitlement from civil servants. It did not improve the quality of public debate over policies in the civil service, which was an aim of Fulton.

• Some attempts were made to break the insularity of the civil service with the greater use of **'outsiders'** from the private sector on secondment under short term contracts. Civil service unions did not welcome the employment of managers from outside the service for the reasons mentioned above, although successive governments continued to develop this feature. Following the 1994 Oughton Report and government White Paper 'The Civil Service: Continuity and Change', attempts were made to modify the closed career ethos of the service by the introduction of the following reforms:

  1 External advertising of senior posts, although most will in fact be held by insiders.

  2 The introduction of new contractual practices for senior staff including fixed term contracts, performance related pay and appraisal systems.

• Fulton's criticisms of the service's 'generalist' or amateur administrative philosophy was bound up with recruitment practices which appeared to favour non-specialist graduates capable of reaching the highest ranks. Those with 'Oxbridge' generalist degrees tended to be most successful, both in terms of entry and eventual management of the service.

A service based on an 'elite' of generalists recruited mainly from Britain's two premier universities was said to be out of step with current thinking on democracy and equality irrespective of educational background. Fulton's recommendation for more emphasis on 'relevant degrees' in recruitment was not implemented, possibly because the service preferred generalists who would not be over-committed to one policy at the expense of others. Ten years after Fulton, *Lord Crowther-Hunt (1980)* could still claim that the service was dominated by generalists because its recruitment practices favoured a narrow 'Oxbridge' elite. Specialists were there but they failed to reach the elite – they were 'on tap but not on top'. A major problem for the service is accommodating to this criticism which is still current.

Questions

1 What was the significant feature of the Northcote–Trevelyan Report of 1854?

2 What was the thinking behind the Fulton Report of 1968?

3 Why did Fulton criticise the civil service?

4 Why did the Fulton reforms take so long to be implemented?

Structures and responsibilities

The civil service, like most large private organisations, is organised along bureaucratic lines with power flowing hierarchically from the most senior to junior posts. For purposes of analysis the most important categories of civil servant are those in the Administrative Group organised from 1995 with five upper grades from First Permanent Secretary (1) to Assistant Secretary (5).

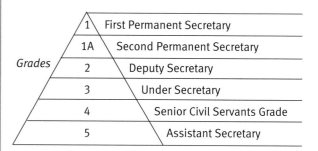

Grades		
	1	First Permanent Secretary
	1A	Second Permanent Secretary
	2	Deputy Secretary
	3	Under Secretary
	4	Senior Civil Servants Grade
	5	Assistant Secretary

The top open structure groups in the civil service (from 1995)

This group is formally responsible for:

• policy advice to ministers;

• general management; and

• administration.

These categories of civil servant (traditionally the old administrative class), retain their elitist generalist character despite changes in recruitment practices. The top four grades (the Mandarins) tend to concentrate on policy advice to ministers with the remainder responsible for general senior management of their departments.

Recruitment

Entry into the upper civil service is highly competitive, with graduate general candidates facing elimination tests for ability and aptitude, together with interviews run by the **Civil Service Selection Board**, through the Civil Service Employer Group in the Office of Public Service. Shortlisted candidates face a final selection process (Final Selection Board) designed to test their suitability as future senior civil servants whose work will include policy advice to ministers. Those successful are recruited into the Fast Stream Development Programme regarded as potential high fliers destined to reach the highest ranks of the civil service in a long career spanning many decades.

'Oxbridge bias' and the Fast Stream

Since the Fulton Report criticisms the Civil Service Commissioners have made conscious efforts to try to redress the 'Oxbridge' bias in recruitment to the Fast

Stream, which is still evident from the statistics of those successful to this grade.

The 1997/98 Report of the Fast Stream Recruitment showed that of those successful to the Fast Stream Development Programme 277 were recruited out of 10,000 applicants; 43.5 per cent of these were graduates of Oxford or Cambridge universities. These figures are little different to the 1991–92 Report of the Civil Service Commissioner which first officially recognised the problem. To their credit the Commissioners have tried to attract non-Oxbridge candidates and 56.5 per cent in 97–98 came from other universities, but breaking the dominance of Arts graduates from Oxbridge is proving resistant to change. It is difficult to find a reason for this 'bias' except that there is a long tradition of students from Britain's oldest universities applying to the Civil Service which is reflected in the statistics and success rates.

A possibly more serious charge against recruitment practices to the higher civil service, against the background of equality of opportunity, is in the area of gender and ethnicity. According to *Theakston and Fry (1989),* women are under-represented at the highest ranks of the civil service and those with an ethnic minority background rarely succeed at the Final Selection Board stage of recruitment (Civil Service Commissioners Report, 1991–92).

Ministerial relationships

FACTFILE

- **In their official relationships with ministers, civil service behaviour is governed by a number of key traditional features designed to keep separate their administrative function from the political or policy-making role of politicians.**

- **In addition to these four features (permanence, expertise, anonymity and impartiality) civil service behaviour was first regularised by the 1985 code of conduct issued by the Cabinet Secretary as 'Notes of Guidance on the Duties and Responsibilities of Civil Servants in Relation to Ministers'.**

- **This eventually became the statutory code of ethics issued by the Major government as 'The Civil Service Code' in January 1996, and clearly emphasises that civil servants are crown servants with a duty to support the policy decisions taken by the ministers of the day, whatever the political complexion of the government.**

Characteristics of the higher civil service

Permanence

Permanence is one of the distinguishing features of the British civil service originating in the Northcote-Trevelyan reforms of 1854. Then the intention was to remove the service from **political patronage** and influence. Now this feature provides for a continuity of administration against the fairly short span of ministerial appointments *(Rose 1987)*. Compared to the American system of 'spoils' or patronage administrative positions which change with each new Presidency, the British system has much to commend it. The downside with permanency is that it can lead to complacency – a general criticism of bureaucracy. Civil servants are often preoccupied with their own career aspirations to the exclusion of other considerations. This became more evident as Margaret Thatcher's reforms of the civil service began to take effect *(Parkinson 1992)*.

Expertise

Public administration is an art, not a science. British civil servants are experts in administration. Although generalists by nature, they build up **valuable expertise** (by training, Fast Stream civil servants move across departments gaining valuable skills), which they place at the service of their ministers. Ministers for their part are not chosen for relevant political expertise in departmental responsibilities either and will come to rely on the integrity of the officials both in the quality of policy advice given and in its implementation in the department.

Anonymity

Constitutionally anonymity of civil servants implies that officials are not publicly identified with the policy successes or failures of the government and this principle is generally adhered to. However, there have been instances where ministers have tended to publicly **blame civil servants** for administrative failures which have given the appearance of policy shortcomings. This tendency to blame civil servants occurred with the dismissal of Derek Lewis, Director General of the Prison Service Agency, in October 1995. The Home Secretary Michael Howard publicly blamed Lewis (though not strictly a civil servant in the traditional sense) for the shortcomings in the prison service revealed by the 1995 Learmont Report into the Parkhurst Prison breakout in early 1995. In 1998 Robin Cook, Foreign Secretary, appeared to blame junior civil servants in the Sierra Leone arms controversy (Arms to Africa Affair).

Impartiality

Civil servants are politically neutral, impartial and most have little difficulty with this aspect of their work. Essentially this implies that they do not hinder government objectives (even if they cannot accept the policy) by actively promoting the counter interests of the opposition parties but loyally serve their ministers, whatever political complexion. Because they are **carefully screened** on selection it is doubtful if civil servants do form strong attachments to any partisan policies. *Ponting (1986)* (dismissed from the service after his acquittal in 1985) claimed the ideal civil servant was positively neutral and could work for any purpose with few strong beliefs.

Constitutionally such a view of the civil servant accords well with the traditional Liberal Democratic or Public Administration perspective of loyal servants anxious to do their minister's bidding. In reality the politically cautious nature of civil servants (*Sir John Hoskyns* called them 'passionless' *(1983)*) could lead to problems or misunderstandings with a radical or reformist government. Although the former permanent secretary *Sir Anthony Part (1980)* claimed the civil service hoped to influence ministers towards the common ground – the ground on which the majority of people could be persuaded to move – it appears more likely that civil service behaviour is increasingly pressured by political events.

Civil service impartiality became more problematic under the long period of Conservative administrations. Some blurring of the political and administrative functions may have occurred as civil servants come to play a more active role in defending government policies. On a number of occasions Sir Robin Butler, the Cabinet Secretary (an impartial civil servant), gave public explanations for ministers accused of wrong-doing (receiving free gifts, money or holidays) and has admitted that civil servants actively intervened in the legislative process (presumably on the instructions of their minister) to draft amendments to bills. **The Scott Inquiry** of 1994 (published 1996) into the **Arms to Iraq Affair** also revealed collusion between civil servants and ministers over information given to Parliament. These and other incidents have increased the pressure on civil service traditional impartiality, and prompted John Major to establish the statutory code of ethics setting out more clearly the political and administrative divisions of the civil servant/minister relationship.

Power in the civil service

CHECKLIST

✓ **Power relationships in the civil service depend on a variety of factors, the most important of which are:**

- **personalities and competence;**
- **length of service of the administration;**
- **ministerial turnover;**
- **political events.**

✓ **Constitutionally political power resides in the minister; administrative power in the permanent secretary and other civil servants. This area of focus – the minister/civil servant relationship – is difficult to analyse because of the lack of publicity surrounding it.**

✓ **Clearly whichever theoretical model is used (Liberal Democratic, Constitutional Bureaucracy, Power Bloc, Bureaucratic Over-Supply, Whitehall Community), the day-to-day working relationship between ministers and their advisers is conditioned by practicalities. Discounting conspiracy theories, the dictum 'the minister commands, the civil servants obey' is probably nearer the truth (*Barberis 1996*).**

Personalities

Civil servants appear to prefer strong competent ministers who know which policies they prefer to implement. If they give the lead the civil service will follow. Former strong ministers would include Michael Heseltine (Conservative), Dennis Healey (Labour) and Peter Walker (Conservative). Occasional criticisms of civil service power from former Labour ministers Richard Crossman and Tony Benn can be partially explained by personality clashes between the minister and his permanent secretary. On one occasion Richard Crossman asked Prime Minister Harold Wilson to intervene in a dispute with his permanent secretary Dame Evelyn Sharp. Tony Benn claimed that the civil service would 'contain' a minister they disliked or distrusted. The permanent secretaries' network within Whitehall could be used to undermine prime ministerial confidence in a minister.

Length of service of the administration

The impression is sometimes given

- either that civil servants are 'captured' by their ministers after long periods of office, thereby compromising impartiality,

- or that the ability of civil servants to reverse previously established policies implies a lack of integrity and the promotion of good government (*Johnson 1982*).

Whatever view is accepted, the longer a government stays in office the greater the risk of the neutral civil service being identified with the political persuasion of it. Both Conservative and Labour governments have criticised the civil service on entering government after periods of opposition. After 13 years in opposition from 1951 to 1964, ministers in Harold Wilson's Labour government complained of civil service hostility. Margaret Thatcher's Conservative ministers produced similar claims after taking power from James Callaghan's Labour government *(Ridley 1991)*. The Blair government by contrast faced a civil service with an 18-year record of serving conservatism but this had caused few problems by 1998. The Conservative government in the first half of the nineties faced charges of '**politicisation**' of the civil service, mainly because Margaret Thatcher took a personal interest in the selection of her permanent secretaries. Careful examination of the facts has not substantiated the politicisation charge. Margaret Thatcher refused to follow the orthodox practice of previous Prime Ministers who accepted the decisions of the Senior Appointments Selection Committee, but instead demanded involvement in vetting suitable candidates. In November 1995 Sir Robin Butler denied the service has been 'politicised' even though he had rejected ministers' requests to act politically.

Ministerial turnover

Ministerial turnover – the short length of time ministers stay in office – obviously had a bearing on their civil service relationships. The average length of stay in a department appears to be around two years, and this is not a long time to become familiar with its work (*Madgwick 1994*). In the Cabinet changes of July 2001 there was a considerable shakeup of ministerial functions. Seven departments were radically affected and four new departments were created: Environment, Food and Rural Affairs; Transport, Local Government and the Regions; Education and Skills; and Work and Pensions. Inevitably these changes always put the onus on permanent secretarial support to ministers (political advisers also assist ministers). As administrative amateurs with very little prior knowledge of their department's work, they are reliant on the professional competence, efficiency and honesty of their officials. Clearly there are unethical ways that permanent secretaries can influence ministers in this relationship – **controlling the flow of information, presentation of policy options, coordinating other officials to achieve an**

outcome, procrastination and delay are all examples. Yet in the last resort ministers are answerable to Parliament for their department and it must be supposed that whatever shortcomings there are, career civil servants have an interest in a good working relationship with their minister.

Political events

Ministers and officials must respond to day-to-day political events and to the longer term strategic direction of the government. The structural changes imposed by the Harold Wilson Labour governments following the Fulton Report proposals may have met some resistance from a service concerned to preserve its privileges or departments (departmentalism). Similarly, the reforms introduced by Margaret Thatcher initially met objections from those opposed to rapid change – Sir Ian Bancroft, Head of the Civil Service, was prematurely retired in 1981. John Major continued with this policy of confronting the civil service with change. in a speech to the Future Management in Government Conference (November 1995) Sir Robin Butler warned of a lowering of civil service morale caused by the changes sweeping Whitehall. Although this had increased feelings of insecurity in civil servants, Sir Robin was not against the Next Steps agencies that were eventually introduced.

> ## Questions
>
> 1 Explain the origin and concept of the philosophy of the amateur administrator.
>
> 2 How and why is 'Oxbridge' bias in recruitment to the higher civil service defended?
>
> 3 Which of the four features of the higher civil service (permanence, expertise, anonymity and impartiality) do you consider the most important and why?

Individual ministerial responsibility

The doctrine of individual ministerial responsibility is central to the operation of the civil service for **ministers are personally accountable** to Parliament for the work of their department. This convention is now so closely linked to collective responsibility that it is hard to separate the two doctrines. Some argue that individual responsibility is subsumed under collective responsibility *(Watkins 1995)*. If the Prime Minister wishes to keep a minister he will protect that minister under the Cabinet collective. This may have been the case with Michael Howard in October 1995 resisting demands for resignation after the removal of

Derek Lewis as Director General of the Prison Service. *Pyper (1994)* claims that sometimes the doctrine of individual responsibility is used to shield the whole Cabinet, like an 'air raid' shelter thrown over the government. He gives the examples of the resignation in April 1982 of Lord Carrington, Humphrey Atkins and Richard Luce protecting Margaret Thatcher from criticism following the Argentine invasion of the Falklands, and Leon Brittan's resignation in 1986 during the Westland Affair crisis.

Despite these political complications, there are fairly straightforward implications in individual responsibility. Ministers are answerable to Parliament for the operation of their departments. This may be disadvantageous to them because:

- it is physically impossible for them to know all that occurs in their departments and
- they may have only been in the post a short time.

In the strong form of the convention they must defend their department in Parliament against criticism of any policy and administrative mistakes and be prepared to resign for any shortcomings so exposed. The weak form of the convention, as now operated, appears to separate policy error for administrative malpractice. Increasingly ministers are refusing to accept culpability for maladministration in operations matters, particularly in the case of **Next Steps** de-regulated agencies.

Resignations

Increasingly ministers are failing to resign for administrative as opposed to policy errors. *Pyper (1994)* has distinguished two types of responsibility within individual responsibilities – **'role responsibility'** and **'personal responsibility'**. The former relates to official responsibility as a minister of the crown discharging constitutional functions. The latter relates to personal behaviour of ministers in their private life. Although it is difficult to draw conclusions, it is apparent that the largest number of individual responsibility resignations from both Margaret Thatcher's and John Major's Cabinets to late 1995 fell into the category of private misconduct or personal responsibility. Cecil Parkinson, David Mellor, Michael Mates and Tim Yeo were all sacrificed by the Prime Minister because their positions became untenable with the party, the public and the Cabinet. From a civil service point of view, personal resignations have little impact except the loss of an able minister who may have advanced the department.

Role responsibility resignations are more serious because they illustrate

- shortcomings in a department's administration practices,

- defects in the advice given to ministers by their civil servants or
- policy failures by governments.

The classic example of resignation for role responsibility is the **Critchell Down Case** of 1954. The Minister for Agriculture, Sir Thomas Dugdale, resigned for the action of his civil servants, even though he was not kept fully informed of events leading up to the crisis. By the second Blair administration to 2004, four Ministers had resigned their posts from the Cabinet for individual responsibility reasons in addition to the resignations of Robin Cook and Claire Short (collective responsibility).

1 **Peter Mandelson** 2001, Hinduja Northern Ireland – passport scandal.
2 **Stephen Byers** 2002, Transport – Railtrack problems.
3 **Estelle Morris** 2002, Education – administrative failures.
4 **Alan Milburn** 2003, Health – personal reasons.

All the above fall into the category of role responsibility even though Alan Milburn resigned for family reasons.

Non-resignations

If role responsibility resignations have declined, it could be argued that the convention of individual responsibility has lost one of its important supportive sanctions. Many examples of maladministration have occurred in the operation of government without the sanction of resignation. Ministers have successfully defended their actions, or placed the blame lower down the administrative hierarchy. The division between policy responsibility and administrative action is now being used to protect ministers, possibly at the expense of civil servants. Yet this appears to breach the informal Maxwell-Fyfe Guidelines (1954) suggesting that ministers defend civil servants who acted under their orders (*Pyper 1994*).

In the Vehicle and General Car Insurance Case of 1972, the minister, John Davies, avoided resignation as his own officials were publicly blamed. James Prior, Secretary of State for Northern Ireland, survived the scandal surrounding the escapes of republican prisoners in 1984. Home Secretary Michael Howard survived the controversy surrounding the publication of the Learmont Report of October 1995 into the Parkhurst Prison breakout. In removing Derek Lewis as Head of the Prison Service Agency Michael Howard successfully demonstrated to Parliament that he was only accountable to Parliament for 'policy' and not 'operational' failures. In his open support for the Home Secretary, John Major demonstrated that he was not prepared to lose his minister. But the case had implications for the whole accountability function of Next Steps agencies.

Change and Reform

The Efficiency Unit

Using the Cabinet Office structure, Margaret Thatcher established an Efficiency Unit under Sir Derek Rayner. Rayner's task was to reduce waste in government and implement greater efficiency in service delivery. Implementation of the recommendations from the 'Scrutinies' of the unit produced considerable cost savings in civil service operations, and the next head of the Efficiency Unit, Sir Robin Ibbs, produced the Next Steps Reports from 1987 which were to have far-reaching effects.

The Next Steps Reports

The general philosophy behind the various Next Steps Reports on **'Improving Management in Government'** was to sever the connection between administration and policy in the existing civil service, in order to remove political obstacles to efficiency. It was argued that since the majority of civil servants (some 95 per cent) were involved in service delivery, they could profitably be divorced from policy-making without any adverse effects. In his final report (1988) Ibbs recommended the separation of the higher civil service (the policy advisers) from the administrators. The former would remain in the service; the latter would be hived off or devolved into semi-autonomous management groups or agencies as part of the drive towards deregulation. In summary, this policy (which fitted well with market forces ideology prevailing in the Conservative Cabinet at that time) satisfied the following criteria:

- Private industry would be given a chance to tender for public service contracts now held in the civil service.

- The bulk of the civil service would be made less political.

- Further personnel reduction in the mainstream civil service would be possible.

- Greater drives to management and cost efficiency would be possible.

The process of implementing Ibbs' proposals began with Margaret Thatcher's government and was taken on by John Major after he became Prime Minister in 1990.

John Major and Next Steps

The priorities were addressed in the 1988 Next Steps Report: work (**service delivery**), management (**skills**) and value for money (**costs**). Civil service departments were expected to examine these features before deciding if functions could be placed into agencies. Under John Major's premiership the creation of agencies continued. By 1992, 75 were in existence employing over half of all civil servants. The initial intention was to achieve agency status for up to 75 per cent of civil servants by the end of a 10 year period ending in 1998. By April 1997, 170 Next Steps agencies were in existence with nearly 80 per cent of civil servants working along these lines. Other developments from 1991 through to 1993 included the adoption of compulsory competitive tendering to allow the introduction of market forces into departments after market testing exercises.

Evaluation of Next Steps programmes

1 **Management theories** Discounting political motivations, there are clear precedents for the Next Step programme in management theory. Breaking up a state bureaucracy theoretically overcomes problems of inefficiency. The introduction of the **Citizens Charter** by John Major in 1988 to try to achieve excellence in public service can be seen against this background. A new ethos – or new public management which might save public taxes – or reduce civil service inefficiency/expenditure was also wanted. The

writers *Burns and Stalker (1966)* in their classic book *The Management of Innovation* first showed how efficiency could be improved in large organisations by breaking bureaucratic (mechanistic) structures into smaller more responsive (organic) units or groups. Next Steps agencies fit this model. More recent influences on the Major government were the academics *Osborne and Gaeblar* (1992) who argued for the introduction of entrepreneurial skills, competition, pursuit of markets and profits in a new reinvented government. Such objectives towards the creation of a different civil service culture appear to have continued under Tony Blair's New Labour government from 1997, with a management style that was forward thinking, reformist and not introspective.

2 **Political and administrative concerns** Politically Next Steps agencies raise a number of issues. According to *Butcher (1995)* two pressing concerns are parliamentary accountability and the break up of the national civil service. The accountability issue is not new for previous QUANGOS (Quasi-Autonomous Non-Governmental Organisations) have also operated at an 'arm's length' approach from ministers. Indeed, many of the old nationalised industries also worked within similar parameters. The case of Michael Howard and Derek Lewis, however, does illustrate the problem of defining power and responsibility in the new agencies and raises the whole issue of the relationship of chief executives to Parliament and the consequent questions of the blurring of ministerial responsibility.

The break up of the national civil service structure has in a sense already begun with the Next Steps agencies, privatisation plans for some of these and the introduction of compulsory competitive tendering. This may have repercussions for sponsoring departments, and could lead to the erosion of the British public service ethic which is held in high regard throughout the world.

Tony Blair and the civil service reforms

The reforms of the eighties and nineties were largely accepted by Tony Blair and New Labour after 1997 and continued into their second term from 2001. The following reforms all represent adaptations or innovations of previous civil service management techniques adopted by New Labour but having their origins in the Conservative governments of Margaret Thatcher or John Major.

1 **Service First Programme** replaced the Conservatives' Citizens' Charter. Citizen satisfaction is gauged through a People's Panel of 5000 respondents.

2 **Public–Private Partnerships** replaced the Conservatives' Private Finance Initiative. Private organisations can tender for government work subject to efficiency criteria.

3 **Next Step Agencies** By 2000, 105 Executive Agencies had been established, employing approximately three-quarters of the total of 500,000 civil servants.

4 **Personnel and Staffing** The Gershon Efficiency Report of 2004 recommended a reduction in the size of the civil service and a redeployment of staff from London. This policy change was announced in the Budget Speech of March 2004.

Summary

1 **Traditionally the study of the civil service revolved around the structures and parameters of administration.**

2 **As a central concern of public administration the service was thought to be beyond politics, and political power.**

3 **For purposes of analysis it is instructive to include both, to divide the political from the administrative aspects of the service; both in their own ways have been subject to considerable change over the last decade.**

4 **Critical attention now focuses on the role of civil servants; their relationship to ministers and the overall structure of the administration in the light of constant reform changes, under both Conservative and Labour governments.**

Sample question and answer

A2 Level question

1 The minister commands, the civil servants obey. Critically discuss this statement.

In their relationships to ministers civil servants will exhibit personal qualities within the professional parameters of their work. They will also be powerful, pliable or as weak as their ministers allow assuming a Liberal Democratic or Public Administration view of the service. One quality of senior civil servants is the ability to be flexible – to give different advice to ministers regarding the policies of separate governments. This may lead to a lack of integrity and promotion of good government (Neville Johnson) but it essentially protects the impartiality and anonymity of the civil service – two important traditional features. Civil servants become valuable and trusted advisers to ministers (Michael Heseltine) because they build up expertise in administrative matters which they place in the service of the government of the day.

The claim that civil servants are too powerful is usually taken to mean they over-step the mark in their relationship to ministers. Sometimes this may happen (the service prefers strong ministers to lead from the front) if there is a personality clash or if civil servants are unprofessional. At the top of the civil service hierarchy a minority of officials (permanent secretaries mainly) deal with policy advice to ministers; the vast majority do not do this work. With the introduction of the Next Steps agencies, less than five per cent of the existing service will have policy dealings with ministers.

For the elite advising ministers there are theoretical approaches that emphasise possible manipulation: Power Bloc, Bureaucratic Over-Supply and the Whitehall Community models all describe techniques of administrative control of politicians (selection or filtering of policy options, re-routing documents, procrastination, delay, control of information, informal and formal contacts).

Civil servants as permanent officials therefore have considerable power to affect the course of events. Although Max Weber warned of the dangers of bureaucratic absolutism (the manipulation of amateur politicians by professional administrators) as a general comment this does not appear to happen in the modern British civil service. The dictum that the minister commands and the civil servants obey is probably as relevant today as it has always been. The sweeping reform changes introduced into the civil service by Margaret Thatcher and John Major have pushed the opportunities for a manipulative civil service further into the background.

Criticisms of civil service power prior to the Next Step reforms have come from both sides of the political spectrum. Richard Crossman and Tony Benn for the Labour Party complained of civil service hostility to nationalisation plans and Nicholas Ridley, when a member of Margaret Thatcher's Conservative government, also drew attention to the procrastination of officials implementing the privatisation policies. Since politicians in both major parties have criticised the impartiality of the civil service, it might be fair to conclude there is no conspiracy on the part of officials to manipulate governments. Even though politicians may see only approximately one per cent of the work of their department, they are accountable to Parliament for it. Their advisers (the civil servants) are accountable to the minister both publicly and privately. Since the Ponting Affair (1985) civil servants have a duty to their minister and the crown and cannot escape the charge of responsibility by claiming a public duty to release information.

Civil servants are flexible – they know they have to implement one government's policies and be prepared for a change of policy following a general election. The ethics of the service dictate that they impartially administer policies without hindering those they dislike. But they could form attachments to those policies which support their departments (departmentalism) and defend the status quo against change – this may be the middle or common ground talked of by Sir Anthony Part. There could therefore be a temptation not to give total commitment to a particular policy – this can be construed as civil service power. There was some evidence that Margaret Thatcher initially felt unhappy with the lack of perceived commitment to her policies from senior civil servants in the early eighties. Her gradual appointments to the permanent secretary posts (on leaving office in 1990 she had taken an interest in the appointment of 24 out of 27 permanent secretaries) may have altered the balance of persuasion in her favour.

The charge of political bias (not politicisation, which Margaret Thatcher did not implement) in the civil service centres on the idea that officials frustrate the wishes of a minister. It could simply be that the service protects itself against getting too closely attached to any one policy for fear of losing impartiality. The Major government's (1995) statutory code of ethics has helped to clarify the respective policy/administrative responsibilities of ministers and officials.

Finally, whether we consider civil servants too powerful or too pliable depends on theoretical views of politics. From a consensus viewpoint a neutral civil service searches for the centre ground, an important non-political position. From a conviction viewpoint, success in politics depends on strong policies with pliable civil servants. This appears to be the position at the present time. British civil servants are not too powerful; on the contrary they may be weak.

Parties in democracies

Political parties are an essential ingredient in democratic society. They can be described as voluntary organisations designed to aggregate people of like-minded interests concerned to produce policies which they hope will be implemented once they achieve government power. Their most important functions are:

Representation In placing themselves before the electorate, parties hope to secure enough votes to form governments. Since the state does not organise parties in a democracy, this function would not be carried out otherwise. By organising the vote, parties are helping the representative process – they will represent the views of electors who support them either in government or in opposition. In terms of structure, a major problem in representative parties has been the creation of bureaucracies at the top since the majority cannot actively organise the party. The classic writer *Michells (1949)* first drew attention to what he called **'the Iron Law of Oligarchy'**, whereby representative power inevitably falls into the hands of a party elite. The three main political parties in Britain – Conservatives, Labour and Liberal Democratic – are to some extent led by a parliamentary elite, although all have developed more democratic structures since *Michells* wrote.

Participation Parties are important vehicles for political participation bringing people into politics. Political activity for the majority appears limited to casting a vote for a party in local or national elections. The minority are politically active, attending meetings, helping to get out the vote or participating as politicians. Although **political apathy** is low in Britain measured by turnout in general elections (between 70 per cent to 80 per cent average (*Butler and Kavanagh 1992*)), **political involvement** in terms of party membership, attendance at political meetings and helping to run political parties is also low. *Parry, Moyser and Day (1992)* estimate that

seven per cent of the electorate, only 2.3 million people, are members of political parties.

There are three generally accepted reasons put forward as explanations of apolitical behaviour:

1 **Apathy** – political participation is regarded as a futile process bearing no relationship to the disinterested.

2 **Cynicism** – cynical views of the political process relate to the feeling that politicians and the political process are corrupt.

3 **Alienation** – political alienation is a situation where individuals see no connection between their lives and the government. In their classic study of the civil culture *Almond and Verba (1963)* found greater degrees of political alienation in Britain, Germany and Italy than the United States.

Party types

Political parties can be classified sociologically into two broad general types: **mass** parties with a broad base or **elitist** with a narrow support base. The former are found in Western democratic countries, the latter were typical of the parties in the former Soviet Union and Eastern Bloc countries.

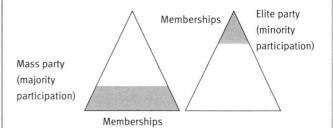

Memberships — Elite party (minority participation)

Mass party (majority participation)

Memberships

Mass parties and elite parties

The essential point about these diagrams is that there is said to be a healthier relationship between the leaders and the citizens in a mass party with larger memberships, and more chance of achieving **bottom up** policies when that party comes to power. Elite parties represent an active minority governing electorate on behalf of themselves or supposedly in the interests of the mass (the old style Communist Party of the Soviet Union). Such an arrangement would produce **top down** policies, with little citizen involvement.

Party systems

Democratic political systems depend on the existence of a number of parties competing for power. It is hard to characterise the British political system as either **one party**, **two party** or **multi-party**; party competition has passed through periods of adversarial politics into consensus and back again. A common feature of all democratic systems is a struggle for political

FACTFILE

According to *Duverger (1966)* political parties can be subdivided according to membership into three categories:

- **Caucus party – membership based on a limited elite or caucus (small grouping) who holds the strings of political power. The nineteenth-century Conservative and Liberal parties were of this category.**

- **Cell or militia party – based on a cell or militia structure, highly centralised and disciplined. Usually found in parties engaged in revolutionary activity. The Irish Republican Army were organised along cell lines before the Northern Irish ceasefire and peace process of 1994 to 1996.**

- **Mass membership party – based on large fee paying memberships either directly or indirectly related through affiliated organisations. The Labour Party's affiliated membership arises from trade unions affiliated to the party and individual members paying the political levy. The Conservative Party has no affiliated members.**

power along one, two or any number of dimensions. Consensus and cleavage are an integral part of this competition (*Lipset 1963*).

A one party system

Britain does not have a one party system in the orthodox sense of a single party holding all the political power in a state. The long period of Conservative government in the mid-nineties raised the spectre of **one party dominance** in a dominant party system which constantly returned a single party to office even though there were other large competing parties in existence. On closer examination it is obvious that two factors contributed to this situation:

1   The weakness of the opposition parties. Because the Labour and Liberal Democratic Parties opposed each other as well as the Conservative Party, their parliamentary strength was dissipated, allowing the Conservatives to remain in office.

2   The simple majority electoral system used in the United Kingdom favours larger parties at the expense of the smaller. The opposition vote was greater at 58 per cent in the 1992 general election, yet the Conservatives formed their fourth consecutive administration on a 41.9 per cent share of the vote.

The Situation with the Blair Governments

The above features were returned with the election of the Blair government. After his second win in 2001, Labour became the dominant governing party and the Conservatives the weak, divided opposition. As Conservative and Labour roles were reversed, it was again possible to conclude that Britain had entered a new period of one-party dominance.

A two-party system

The traditional description of the British party system has always emphasised the importance of two parties competing for the power of government. Historically, party competition has for the most part been between two factions: first the Whigs and Tories (eighteenth and nineteenth centuries), then the Liberals and Conservatives (early twentieth century) and finally Conservatives and Labour (late twentieth century). But because this party system is never static we cannot predict with certainty that this pattern will remain in the future. It is possible that **political cleavage** always finds an outlet in two dimensions; certainly *Ingle (1993)* found this pattern occurring over 300 years of British history. It is also sometimes claimed that the British people prefer an either/or choice between two parties alone leaving little room for centre parties. A system of two-party dominance does prevent the emergence to power of extremist parties because the majority of the electorate, or the **median voters** (those with equal numbers to the left and right in a political continuum), are at the centre ground.

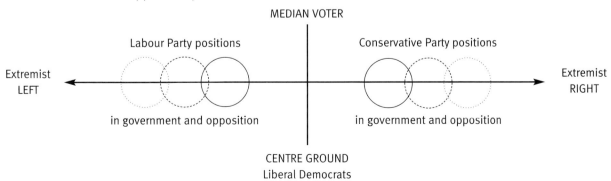

The two party political continuum and median voter

Centre parties are squeezed by the two main parties. This occurs electorally as the Conservative and Labour Parties take votes from the Liberal Democrats, and ideologically as Conservatives and Socialists adopt centre policies they feel they can make their own. Environmental issues are a good case in point. For long they were championed by the Liberal Democrats, only to be picked up by the Conservatives in government and Labour in opposition. After the 1997 general election the situation was reversed with a New Labour government emphasising green issues.

Advantages of two-party competition

The two main advantages of a two-party system are:

1 **Strong responsible government**. The system virtually guarantees the winning party a good majority in the House of Commons. This in turn ensures the majority party is responsible to the wishes of the electorate.

2 **Alternation in government**. A two-party system with an official opposition waiting to take power is a better guarantee of democracy because it enables alternative policies to be placed before the electorate. Although the Conservatives had remained in continuous office since 1979, there was the electoral probability that the Labour Party or a combination of Labour/Liberal Democrats would replace them in the future. Under the **pendulum theory** of party competition (popularised by *McKenzie 1963*) the regular alternation in power of an 'in' and 'out' party is a sign of a healthy democracy. The problem with the long run of Conservative dominance in the eighties and nineties was the danger of the Labour Party being associated in the minds of the electorate with the image of a natural party of opposition against the Conservative Party image of a natural party of government (*Crewe 1992*).

Disadvantages of two-party competition

Two disadvantages of two-party competition relate to:

- **An economic model**   A major tendency with modern governments is to exploit the political market place for their own ends. The governing party can manipulate the economy so as to produce policies which the electorate find attractive. If a government is able to continually satisfy median voters (the 'feelgood' factor), it increases its chances of remaining in office. This partially explains the success of Margaret Thatcher's three consecutive general election victories of 1979, 1983 and 1987, and was a factor in the previous long run of Conservative victories from 1951 to 1964.

- **An adversarial model**   The two-party system favours the outlooks of adversary politics. Under this model political debate is channelled through two aggressively competing avenues – a **left spectrum** versus a **right spectrum**. The first serious analysis of these effects was carried out by *Finer (1975)*. He showed how the system of government/opposition made the parties more polar than they otherwise would be. Party leaders are encouraged to make ideological commitments to the extremist wings of their respective parties giving the impression of radical policies to the electorate. Once in power, governing parties tend to reverse many of the policies of their predecessors irrespective of their merits. Political debate between major parties concentrates on differences between them, on destructive rather than constructive criticism (*Ball 1987*). Part of the appeal of the Liberal Democrats has always been that they seek to capture the essence of consensus – that the majority of the electorate do not cluster at the extremist need of the political spectrum.

Questions

1 What was Michell's 'Iron Law of Oligarchy'?

2 What is the difference between a mass party and an elite party?

3 Who are median voters and how do they relate to the party system?

4 What is the pendulum theory of party competition?

A multi-party system

From an electoral (but not parliamentary) point of view, Britain has a multi-party system. There are always three or more parties competing for electoral support, which in turn gives greater choice to the voter: Conservatives, Labour, Liberal Democrats, Scottish Nationalists, Welsh Nationalists and Northern Irish parties. However, this choice appears to have little impact on who governs, largely because of the simple majority electoral system. It could therefore be argued that since minor parties have little chance of gaining power (even the Liberal Democrats' 2001 18.3 per cent share of the vote only gained them 52 MPs), those who support these parties are effectively disenfranchised unless party labels on MPs are disregarded from a total representative point of view. *Dearlove and Saunders (1991)* emphasise the importance of the electoral system in translating voter choice into party systems. Because the electoral system favours the main parties, they distinguish between the **two-party** system in Parliament, the **dominant party** system of the executive and the **multi-party** system of election.

The British multi-party system does not in normal circumstances translate into House of Commons arithmetic. In the European model, weak governments are dependent on alliances in strong Parliaments. Except for a brief period in the late seventies, when the Labour minority government of James Callaghan were dependent on the then Liberal party for office (the Lib-Lab Pact), the British electoral system prevents this happening.

Despite the sweeping changes introduced by New Labour after 1997, they resolutely refused to alter the simple majority system for electing MPs to the Westminster Parliament. Until such a system is changed it is highly unlikely that Britain will move to a multi-party parliamentary model.

Conservatism and the Conservative Party

Political commentators used to describe the modern Conservative Party as the most successful party to have operated in the British political system. If the main indicator of political success is the ability to win elections and form governments, taking the period 1900 to 1996 the Conservatives alone or with allies were in power over two thirds of that time. After the Labour successes of 1997 and 2001 commentators were less likely to refer to the Conservative Party in this way.

Conservative ideology

The philosophical basis of Conservatism lies in the idea of individualism – that individuals are responsible for their own existence and standard of life. The task of government is therefore limited to protecting the citizens in the state, not the correction of any inequalities that exist in society. As individuals are created with different abilities, so there will always be those who acquire more wealth and property than the rest. Government should protect the acquisition of this private property since it forms the basis of a free society.

Conservatives are therefore suspicious of political philosophies that aim to level people down or restrict the freedom of individuals to create wealth. **Human nature** is inevitably flawed – people do not necessarily improve their condition over time and there is no blueprint for a perfect or future society. Applied to the institutions of the state, this philosophical creed teaches caution and revolutionary change. Intellectually the ideas of *Edmund Burke* (*1729–97*) did much to establish the

---

CHECKLIST

These features find their way into modern Conservative ideology.

✓ **Pragmatism** – The Conservative Party has always prided itself on being pragmatic – of adjusting policies to suit political circumstances. For this reason the party is often portrayed as being less ideological than the Labour Party and Liberal Democratic Parties.

✓ **Flexibility** – Although the nineteenth-century Conservative (Tory) Party was fiercely upper class or aristocratic, it always allowed members of the middle class into its ranks. This flexibility gave the party an edge when it came to accommodating to new social groupings in the twentieth century. The social background of modern Conservative MPs is therefore little different to that of their opponents. Indeed, it could be said that John Major's background was more 'ordinary' than Tony Blair's.

✓ **Adjustment** – The Conservatives were quick to adjust to the electoral changes brought about by the expansion of the franchise in the late nineteenth and early twentieth centuries. As a result, they have successfully combatted the electoral challenge of Socialism and held on to a sizeable share of the working class vote.

---

notion that revolutionary change threatened the status quo and was to be resisted. Burkianism has influenced modern Conservative thinking.

Modern Conservatism takes much from the leader of the party because the leader characterises its policies which in turn underpin the philosophy. There are two current strands in Conservative thought that can be identified:

1 **One Nation Conservatism**   One Nation Conservatism has its origins in the work of Benjamin Disraeli, Conservative Prime Minister and leader of the party from the mid 1800s. Disraeli created Conservative Central Office in 1870 with the express purpose of bringing together the separate elements in the party which would now focus on securing the vote into a national party in the nineteenth century by successfully confronting the Liberal challenge for the working class vote; Disraeli wanted Conservatism to move away from narrow aristocratic sectional interests.

These ideas were again emphasised throughout the first 80 years of the twentieth century as Conservative Prime Ministers came to embrace progressive policies which assisted the working classes (*Whiteley et al. 1994*). Prime Ministers Winston Churchill (1951–55), Anthony Eden (1955–57), Harold Macmillan (1957–63), Alec Douglas-Home (1963–64) and Edward Heath (1970–74) all in their own ways advocated a mixed economy and welfare state ideas in economic management, education, housing and social welfare. When Margaret Thatcher replaced Edward Heath as Conservative leader in 1976 (she did not become Prime Minister until 1979), the ideas of One Nation Conservatism were held responsible for the policy failures of the seventies and a new strand in Conservative thinking was identified.

2 **New Right or Neo-Liberal Conservatism** Part of the attraction of One Nation Conservatism had always been the lack of philosophical dogma in comparison with the creed of Socialism. For Conservatives there was no blueprint for a future society or a written party constitution restricting activity. But this freedom had allowed **Conservative leaders to interpret their philosophy**. Now the policies of failure (Edward Heath's government) forced the new leader Margaret Thatcher to turn to the ideas of Liberal Conservatism. In doing this Margaret Thatcher was not introducing ideology into Conservative Party politics as some have claimed; ideology had always existed in the party. As circumstances changed, so the leadership would emphasise one strand of thinking against others. By the 1980s Conservatives were trying to recapture a radicalism that would distance them from the **consensus policies** of One Nation Conservatives (or 'Wets' as they so disparagingly came to be called) and the ideas of Socialism.

New Right Conservative thinking (or Thatcherism) embraced a number of radical policies. To some it was an attack on the social democratic ideas embraced by both One Nation Conservatives and the Labour Party. To others it was a general set of political principles embracing council house sales, privatisation, trade union legislation and monetarism (*Kellner 1988*). Margaret Thatcher was influenced in these New Right policies by a variety of thinkers opposed to collectivism and the power of the state including *Alfred Sherman*, *Milton Friedman*, *Sir Keith Joseph* and *Freidrich Hayek*. Part of the objective was to reduce state interference in the affairs of the individual, cut government spending, reduce taxation, target welfare spending on the poor and encourage the development of 'popular capitalism'; the property enfranchisement of working class people living in council owned property.

Despite Margaret Thatcher's success in pursuing these policies (she won three consecutive general elections), the Conservative Party removed her from office in 1990 for a variety of reasons (electoral unpopularity, Poll Tax problems, rising unemployment, opposition from within the Cabinet, problems with European relationships, and backbench dissent in the House of Commons). Her successor John Major made little impact on mainstream Conservative ideology and to many he was more of an administrator than a thinker, bringing together the disparate factions of the party.

Conservative Party organisation

The Conservative Party organisation can be described as unitary or autocratic in that power flows from the top down, with authority concentrated in the leader's hands. In terms of structure there are four components in the party but little internal democracy. The four parts are:

1 The Parliamentary Party comprising MPs and parliamentary committees.

2 Conservative Central Office, including the professional staff of full time officials.

3 Constituency Associations.

4 The Annual Conference.

Structures

Conservative Party structures were reformed by William Hague in 1998 after his 'Fresh Future' proposals were accepted by the membership. A major proposal was the acceptance of OMOV (one member, one vote) which democratised the process for electing Conservative leaders. This was first used in the selection of Iain Duncan Smith in 2001 after the resignation of William Hague. Other structural reforms included the abolition of the National Union of Conservative Associations (1867–1998) and its replacement by a Management Board, the creation of constituency policy forums headed by a Policy Forum General Council and a new national party convention. This organisation still has its origins in the advisory structures established in the nineteenth century organised to provide the leadership with support. Despite the surface democracy of the new structures, critics within the party, particularly the Charter Movement, claim that the constituency policy forums are more a form of window dressing in that they do not really involve the rank and file in actual policy-making (*Kelly 2001*). Central Office and the membership are still very much subordinated to the parliamentary leadership and the leader.

The place of the leader

> **F A C T F I L E**
>
> - **The standard work on the distribution of power in the Conservative and Labour Parties was McKenzie's British Political Parties, first published in 1955. Writing of the Conservative leader, he said that the leader leads and the party follows – as long as the leader is successful at winning elections.**
>
> - **Although, therefore, leaders are in an unrivalled position of superiority in the party (deciding policy, choosing Cabinet colleagues and Party Chairman) they are vulnerable to electoral failures. Their security of office is problematical and they can now be challenged in office.**

From 1965 the leader was elected by ballot of the Conservative Parliamentary Party. Edward Heath (1965), Margaret Thatcher (1975), John Major (1990) and William Hague (1997) were all chosen by this method. After the Hague Reforms of 1998 the party moved to a more democratic selection method (OMOV) but retained the power of MPs over the procedure. First MPs vote in a secret ballot, then party members are offered up a postal ballot of two contenders. Consequently after William Hague's resignation following the second Conservative election defeat in 2001, the Parliamentary Party were able to reject Michael Portillo (seen by some as the favourite to replace Hague) in favour of Kenneth Clarke and Iain Duncan Smith. In the final ballot of party members Iain Duncan Smith won a 61 per cent share of the vote to Kenneth Clarke's 39 per cent of an 80 per cent turn out and so became Conservative Leader.

Challenges to Conservative leaders

The change to an electoral system reduced the authority of the Conservative leader who was now dependent on the opinions of backbench MPs in an open contest. Both Edward Heath and Margaret Thatcher were elevated to the Prime Ministership by the backbenchers and subsequently removed by them. In July 1995 John Major faced the most serious challenge to this leadership from the Cabinet member John Redwood. Major survived this threat largely because of the reluctance of Michael Portillo, the right-leaning defence Secretary, to stand against him and because of the decision of the heavyweight Michael Heseltine not to enter the contest, leaving his supporters the opportunity of backing the Prime Minister.

After William Hague changed the rules for challenging a Conservative leader, which now included the involvement of the wider party, he felt it necessary to seek the early support of the membership in a 'back me or sack me' ballot in which he was successful.

William Hague

John Major's immediate resignation on losing the general election of May 1997 was a new departure. Previous leaders had hesitated before being challenged. Major's departure was a recognition that the party wanted a rapid change this time. William Hague at 36 was the youngest of the other challengers: Kenneth Clarke, John Redwood, Peter Lilley and Michael Howard.

In an analysis of why Hague won, *Norton* (*1998*) claimed that he was the least objectionable, with the bulk of party loyalist Eurosceptic support.

The small number of Conservative MPs that selected William Hague (the others had lost their seats in the election) raised again the criticisms from the wider party that the leadership electoral system should be replaced by some form of elections college involving all the party faithful. William Hague appeared to accept this idea when he announced party reforms to restructure the organisation and increase the membership which had fallen to approximately 100,000 (*Hetherington 1997*).

Iain Duncan Smith

When William Hague lost the 2001 election with 166 Conservative MPs elected he immediately followed John Major's example and resigned, bringing into operation the new electoral machinery involving all party members after a parliamentary ballot of Conservative MPs. The serious contenders for the leadership were Iain Duncan Smith, Kenneth Clarke and Michael Portillo.

After the ballot of the membership Iain Duncan Smith emerged as the favourite, but headed a very divided party. Divisions over Europe and the left/right scism faced the new leader who was said to be 'on trial' as they were waiting in the wings to challenge him if the parties fortunes did not pick up.

Iain Duncan Smith may have won the election against Kenneth Clarke for similar reasons surrounding his 1997 defeat. Clarke was seen by many in the party as too old, at 61 to face the younger Tony Blair. Also Iain Duncan Smith had the advantage of being relatively new and unknown and therefore could distance himself from the failures of William Hague's leadership. The candidature of Michel Portillo – regarded by many as the person to lead the Conservative Party back to power – was lost because MPs refused to take the risk of going with a more adventurous leader.

Michael Howard

Iain Duncan Smith did not last long as Conservative leader and was forced out in 2003 after losing a vote of no confidence. The party circumvented the Hague rules (which demanded an election by MPs and a final choice by party members) and Michael Howard was chosen as the new leader. Behind-the-scenes lobbying had ensured he was the strongest candidate and the party decided this time there was little point in holding a leadership election contest. Iain Duncan Smith was chosen that way and he was a disappointment so there would be no repetition of that mistake. The choice of Michael Howard was hailed as a success in the short term. A more aggressive parliamentary opposition style and improvement in the opinion polls gave the Labour Party some cause for alarm at this change in fortunes for the Conservatives. And the removal of Iain Duncan Smith again showed how ruthless the party hierarchy could be in displacing failed leaders.

The Annual Conference

The power of the Conservative Party Annual Conference has traditionally received less attention than the power of the Labour Party Annual Conference because of its lack of formal power over policy-making and the party leadership. The emphasis has always been on publicising loyalty to the Conservative leadership in a party where power flows from the top down. Research by *Kelly* (*1994*) has shown that the importance of the Conservative Annual Conference has to be seen against a background of regional and sectional conferences where policy criticisms are raised. Certainly since 1965 the party leader has attended the whole conference giving an appearance of policy input from the rank and file who draw leadership attention to issues of current concern to ordinary members. In addition the establishment of constituency party forums representing a new way of making policy in the Conservative Party may have the effect of reducing dissent at conferences as they seek to square policy differences before the annual meeting. Conservative conferences have had the policy-making power of Labour Conferences, but the existence of policy forums means that rank and file members are given some inputs to Conservative leaders before important decisions are taken. They do not of course have to be taken notice of.

Groups within the Conservative Party

There are a bewildering number of groups within the modern Conservative Party, each representing a faction or ideological position. The most obvious splits occur across the European dimension – in his analysis of the new Conservative Parliamentary Party of 1997 *Norton* (*1998*) found three main groups – Eurosceptic right, party faithful and pro-European Left. William Hague on his election as leader appealed for unity across these factions but they still remain. One group agitating for internal democracy is the Charter Movement founded in 1981. The Conservative 2000 Foundation formed by John Redwood, the twice defeated candidate for the leadership, occupies the Eurosceptical right together with the No Turning Back Group, the Bruges Group, Conservative Way Forward and others. Factions on the left include the Bow Group, the One Nation Group and the Tory Reform Group.

Questions

1 Give and explain one central feature of Conservatism.

2 What is the difference between One Nation Conservatism and New Right or Liberal Conservatism?

3 What is the difference between the electoral base of Iain Duncan Smith and that of William Hague?

Socialism and the Labour Party

Although the Labour Party had fewer electoral successes than the Conservative Party until 1997 and 2001 it did succeed in eclipsing the Liberal Party in the early part of the last century as the second force in British politics. Because of its origins as an extra-parliamentary party, the Labour Party has

- paid more attention to internal democracy in its organisational structure;

- divided policy formulation between the Annual Party Conference and the leadership;

- appeared more divided than the Conservative Party because of its commitment to a political creed (socialism) which has produced a variety of interpretations.

For these and other reasons the task of governing what is a federal party structure has always been more difficult for a Labour leader. This partially explains why Tony Blair introduced structural reforms after becoming leader in 1994 to reduce the power of the trade unions and other groups in the party.

Labour ideology

CHECKLIST

✓ **Philosophically the Labour Party has its roots in socialism. The problem for those deciphering socialism and its significance for the modern Labour Party is to interpret the different strands that made it up. When the Labour Party was founded in 1900, four constituent elements were instrumental in its make-up, but only one (the Social Democratic Federation) had a strong ideology. The four elements were: the trade unions, the Social Democratic Federation, the Fabians and the Independent Labour Party.**

✓ **These disparate groups produced a version of moderate evolutionary socialism with ideas of a fairer and more just society, to be achieved through parliamentary adjustment of capitalism. Human nature, they claimed, was collectivist rather than individualist and could reach perfection. To reach this society, the state would have to intervene and run industry for the collective good.**

✓ **In 1918 the Labour Party committed itself to a written constitution which future socialist governments would implement. The most important feature of this constitution was Clause IV which committed the Labour Party to nationalisation or common ownership of the means of production, distribution and exchange. This clause and the first 1918 constitution would survive unchanged until 1995 when they were replaced by a more moderate second constitution, with a modified Clause IV without the commitment to nationalisation.**

Ideological debates

Throughout the history of the Labour Party there has been debate over the nationalisation issue as a token of the commitment to socialism. The general division between the left and right of the party has always existed as each tried to eclipse the other. We can regard the left as having a stronger commitment to **fundamentalist** socialism (hence **fundamentalists**) mirrored in their blueprint for a future socialist society: anti-capitalist, decentralised, state ownership and equality between the classes. Those opposed to what they regarded as extremist socialism – an electoral liability in their eyes – sought to modify the commitment to socialism by **revising** (hence

revisionists) Clause IV. During the post war years the fundamentalists were lead by Aneurin Bevan, later Tony Benn and Ken Livingstone; the revisionists by Hugh Gaitskell, Anthony Crosland and Prime Ministers Harold Wilson and James Callaghan. Later Neil Kinnock, John Smith and Tony Blair lead the Labour Party from the revisionist right. Neil Kinnock successfully defeated the left (expelling the Trotskyist Militant Tendency in the early eighties) and Tony Blair finally completed the modernisation (or revision) of the party constitution by late 1995. His introduction of communitarianism is discussed below.

Why the modernisers triumphed

There has always been tension between the fundamentalist and revisionist wings of the Labour Party (by 1995 the two wings were renamed traditionalists and modernisers) (*Kelly 1995*). The modernisers have generally centred on the Parliamentary Labour Party whilst the traditionalists have their strength in the extra-parliamentary elements – constituencies and affiliated organisations. As the parliamentary wing of the party has always sought to present itself as the alternative party of government, it has closely followed the wishes of the electorate in adapting policies to it. One reason why modernisers fought so hard to remove the old Clause IV was that they correctly perceived that from the 1960s nationalisation as an issue became an electoral liability for Labour (*Jones 1994*).

Traditionalists by contrast had emphasised the protest side of Labour politics. In their view the Labour Party would not lose sight of its roots in the urban working class and trade unions. Nationalisation and public ownership (rather than moderniser public control) were crucial ways to redress the class balance between rich and poor. During the years in opposition to Margaret Thatcher's centralisation policies over local government, **New Urban Socialists** like Ken Livingstone argued that the Labour Party should rebuild socialism from the localist position to convince voters that Labour policies could work (*Gyford 1985*). The activities of Left Labour controlled councils would prove as much of an embarrassment to the Labour leadership of Neil Kinnock as to the government of Margaret Thatcher.

Labour Party organisation

The organisation of the Labour Party is **federalist** in the sense that political power and policy-making are divided between the leader, the Annual Conference, constituencies and trade unions. The origins of the party outside Parliament are reflected in this structure. A central point of debate in Labour Party politics has always been the degree to which the extra-parliamentary organisation controls the parliamentary wing. As a reformist party anxious to implement policies which would change the status quo, the Labour Party had radical inputs from its memberships, plus a written constitution partially beyond the control of its parliamentary leadership. This did not matter when Labour was in opposition, but once it started to form governments it was inevitable that the parliamentary leadership would want a free hand to govern.

McKenzie (1963) first addressed this problem. In his examination of the power and policy relationships in the Labour Party, he reached the controversial conclusion that because of the convention of governing (Cabinet responsibility) final authority rested with the Labour leadership, not with the Annual Conference. Certainly Labour leaders since the sixties behaved as though this was a correct interpretation. Hugh Gaitskell (party leader 1955–63) battled with the Annual Conference over Clause IV; Harold Wilson and James Callaghan both ignored the more extreme Conference resolutions (on, for example, the abolition of the House of Lords). McKenzie's thesis was therefore helpful to the right wing parliamentary leaders of the Labour Party, particularly the assertion that once in office the restraints on a Labour Prime Minister from the Annual Conference and National Executive Committee (NEC) fell away. In effect, therefore, a Labour Prime Minister was as strong constitutionally as a Conservative Prime Minister. Although this theory was challenged by *Minkin* (1980) who reasserted the traditional authority of the Annual Conference, it would have a profound effect on the party's internal structural reforms.

Structural changes

The ideological disputes mentioned above also had their counterparts in the internal organisation of the party. Accepting McKenzie's ideas, the Labour left (led by Tony Benn) campaigned for greater internal democracy in the party (the Campaign for Labour Party Democracy) on the grounds that stronger controls were needed over the leadership to ensure the implementation of socialist policies through a Labour government. Responding to these changes through a **Special Conference in 1981** the party decided on the following reforms:

- Election of the leader and deputy leader to be democratised to the whole party rather than Members of Parliament.

- MPs to face mandatory reselection on an annual basis (changed in 1990 to periodic reselection only on request of local party).

An attempt to remove control over the party manifesto from the hands of the leaders was not implemented but the adoption of these changes was instrumental in the split from Labour of the so-called 'Gang of Four' who proceeded to set up the rival Social Democratic Party (Roy Jenkins, Shirley Williams, David Owen and William Rodgers).

Modifications

The second successive electoral defeat for the Labour Party in 1983 prompted the party leadership to reassert its authority over the left and prepare further organisational changes that had an impact on the leaders, MPs, the Party Conference, the power of the trade unions, party constituencies, and policy-making. The party would lose two further general elections in 1987 and 1992 before these organisational reforms confirmed the strength of a leadership that rejected 'Old Left' policies in favour of a broader electoral appeal to all classes and finally abandoned socialism.

New Labour and policy-making

After becoming leader of the Labour Party, Tony Blair secured structural reforms on policy-making and the role of Conference with the acceptance of the 1997 document 'Partnerships in Power', which introduced a rolling programme of policy-making through Policy Commissions reporting to a National Policy Forum and the Conference. The official objective of this programme was to broaden the base of policy-making in the party by involving the rank and file at the initiation stage. This would also head off the public policy clashes at Conference which had been a feature of Labour's past. This may have occurred, but critics of this process now claim that Conference has become sanitised rather like the pre-reformed Conservative Conferences which had little power. Real policy-making power in the Labour Party, they said was still held by those at the top even after these changes and the party still retains a top down, rather than a bottom up structure. McKenzie's thesis on power distribution in the two parties is still therefore relevant. Both parties have adopted policy-making forums in a move to democratise their policy structures – the Conservatives to give more power to Conference, Labour to reduce conflicts at Conference. Paradoxically both efforts can be seen as attempts by the leaderships to better manage the rank and file.

The Labour leader

FACTFILE

- **The traditional method of selecting a Labour Party leader until 1981 had been by a ballot of MPs, largely similar to the Conservative process. In democratising the procedure the party set up an Electoral College with an initial vote split: 40 per cent trade unions, 30 per cent Parliamentary Party and 30 per cent constituency parties.**

- **After the selection of Margaret Beckett as deputy leader in 1992, the 1993 Annual Conference altered the proportionate share of the vote to one third for each constituent part, which had the effect of reducing the power of the trade unions in the selection process.**

- **The introduction of the one member one vote principle (OMOV) removed the trade union block vote in leadership elections. Now individual trade unionists could vote on an equal footing with Labour MPs, Euro MPs and constituency members of the Labour Party.**

- **This new system was effectively used for the first time in 1994 with the selection of Tony Blair as new Labour leader and John Prescott as his deputy.**

The governments of Tony Blair

The democratisation of the Labour Party internally began by Kinnock and continued by Smith and finally Blair helped Labour succeed in winning the 1997 and 2001 general elections. It is probable that New Labour could win a third successive election victory mirroring the successes of the Conservative Party before the new millennium.

By modernising the party (changing the mechanism for leadership elections, altering the block vote and Clause IV, introducing OMOV, consulting members through policy forums, and reducing dependence of trade union finance by attracting support from businesses) Tony Blair has moved the party to an acceptance of many of the policies of the previous Conservative governments. Whether this amounts to an acceptance of a new so called 'neo-liberal agenda' is debatable. What was noticeable was the adoption by Tony Blair of the ideas of *John Macmurray (1961)* and *Amitai Etzioni (1995),* called communitarianism or ethical socialism. Now New Labour would emphasise community involvement instead of equality, a stakeholding society midway between state provision and the free market. These 'third way' ideas helped in the re-election of the Labour Party after 18 years in opposition. Such ideas are equally attractive to left Conservatives as to right Socialists – terms which begin to lose their meaning as we enter the twenty-first century. Labour has thus become a non-ideological catch-all party.

Groups within the Labour Party

The Labour Party has its share of groups or factions reflecting divisions along a left continuum (hard, centre or soft) now translated as modernisers and traditionalists. Typical of those on the far left is Labour Briefing which is critical of the current leadership and was linked with the Target Labour Government Group of the early 1980s. Another hard left group is the Campaign Group opposed to the current modernising tendencies of the Labour leadership. Right-wing groups include Labour 2000 founded in late 1995 which presses for more modernising policies and accepts many of the Conservative reforms on unemployment and competitive tendering.

Questions

1 How does socialism in the Labour Party differ from the ideas of communitarianism?

2 Briefly summarise Tony Blair's changes to the Labour Party.

3 Why did Labour return to power in 1997 after 18 years in opposition?

Liberal Democrats

The Liberal Democrat Party was formed out of a merger of the new Social Democratic Party and the traditional Liberal party in 1988. Prior to this merger the Liberal party had represented **the third** force in British politics after its last period in office in 1922. A number of reasons are advanced for the Liberal decline since that time. They include:

- **A failure to adapt** to changing social, political and economic situations.

- **The Labour Party** proved more attractive to the working-class vote.

- **A series of damaging splits** destroyed the parliamentary strength of the party.

Although the Liberals (Liberal Democrats) have suffered exclusion from political power since the 1920s (because of the electoral system), they have always had minority representation at Westminster and a healthier presence in local government. Part of their attraction in local government has always been their philosophic emphasis on people's rights, local participation and decentralisation of political power.

Ideology

The modern ideas of the Liberal Democrats – a belief in a free market, but a state controlled economy, civil rights and a written constitution, environmental protection, devolution of political power, a reformed parliamentary and electoral system – can be traced to the old Liberal Party ideology. This was made up of a coalition of beliefs ranging from an individualistic attachment to laissez-faire economics and a suspicion of state power, to a trust in democratic politics with reformed parliamentary institutions.

After New Labour adopted much of this programme and moved to the centre-ground the Liberal Democrats lost some of their distinctive ideology. Charles Kennedy the current leader has sought to re-establish a separate place besides New Labour in a kind of centre-left coalition. Tactical voting and this new position helped the Liberal Democrats to a record 52 MPs at the 2001 general election. Kennedy ambitiously claimed that his party was now the official opposition to New Labour in the face of a divided Conservative party. Only time will tell if there is to be a realignment on British politics this new century with the Liberal Democrats becoming a major player again in the political system.

Minor parties

There are a considerable number of minor parties in Britain including the politically serious Celtic parties (Scottish and Welsh Nationalists), Northern Irish and Green Party. Other parties exist on the political **'fringe'** or **extremes**. Some belong to the 'fun' side of politics – where they participate in elections to publicise their causes.

All minor parties suffer from the effects of the 'first past the post' electoral system at Westminster as do the Liberal Democrats. Obviously the Scottish National Party and the Plaid Cymru (Welsh Nationalists) are in a league of their own attracting sizeable support within their own countries. The SNP is less supportive of devolution and favours independence for Scotland. Plaid Cymru is now more united around the issue of the survival of the Welsh language than on a separate state for Wales.

Summary

1   The late nineties and the millennium have seen a reversal in the fortunes of the two main British political parties if not in the party system.

2   The Labour Party (or New Labour) responded to a long period in opposition by ideological and organisational reforms, and Tony Blair succeeded in becoming Prime Minister after emphasising 'modernist' ideas which changed Clause IV of the Labour constitution, once regarded as the central platform of that party's commitment to socialism. The party now appeals to all classes rather than the working class alone – a recognition of the changed social structure of Britain, and the fact that the party is no longer dependent on its old electoral base.

3   The failure of the Conservative Party at the 2001 general election and the replacement of William Hague by Iain Duncan Smith as leader could signify that the party is facing a long period in opposition. The party remains disunited and has yet to return to its previous electoral strength.

4   The Liberal Democrats have increased their parliamentary representation despite the electoral system and can claim a bigger share in politics as a result.

Sample question and answers

A2 Level question

1 Discuss the part played by the political parties in British politics.

Political parties perform a number of functions within the British political system. Possibly the most important function is representation, followed by participation, articulation, communication, electoral choice and the process of governing.

Parties are voluntary organisations that represent the views of the electorate to the government. By providing party manifestos they set out to the voter their policy plans should their MPs be elected. Most democratic states operate a system of indirect democracy whereby Members of Parliament represent all the electorate's wishes, irrespective of which party supported them. As a representative the party MP is not tied to any particular interest – a problem that has in the past affected the Labour Party. But the duty of the representative (working through the party) is to carry the concerns of the electorate into the public policy arena. Parties are therefore playing a valuable role here; if we imagine a political system without parties then we will be more aware of this function.

Parties help the participative function of democracy in a number of ways. They encourage people to participate in local and national politics either as passive helpers or active members. Again, without the activity of political parties it would be difficult to find people willing to participate in politics at all. Even in a developed political democracy like Britain, political apathy between general elections is high. Those that are encouraged to join find the party provides a vehicle for political recruitment to office. In local councils the political parties provide the members that run the machine, independent candidates having all but disappeared at this level. Participation in local politics is often a recruiting and training ground for national political office, therefore its importance cannot be overstressed.

In a democracy it is difficult for individuals to articulate their demands to policy makers. Joining a political party gives this opportunity. Although Robert McKenzie claimed correctly that more people were engaged in pressure group activity than political parties – the two complement each other. If pressure group activity has taken members away from political parties, many others will see the political importance of their actions and return to influence the parties.

The communication function of political parties revolves around the internal structures and memberships. Although the modern Conservative and Labour Parties may suffer from what Robert Michells called 'the Iron Law of Oligarchy', whereby an unrepresentative oligarchy or elite evidently control the party, eventually the leadership of political parties must be responsive to their membership's views. There have been recent trends towards internal democratisation in both the Conservative and Labour Parties making the leaderships more aware of rank and file interests. Party leaders who ignore party opinion, whether in Parliament or the wider party, often find themselves challenged.

It is fairly obvious that without the political parties there would be little electoral choice for the electorate. By placing themselves before the electorate, governing and opposition parties hope to secure re-election/election with a mandate from the people to govern. The difficulty in the British system centres on the electoral mechanism of first past the post, which offers a real either/or choice to the voters which results in one of two main parties winning. The British system therefore gives more electoral choice to supporters of the two main parties (Conservative and Labour) and less choice to those who support the Liberal Democrats or other minor parties. Electorally, the voter has a wide choice; legislatively, two main parties dominate Parliament in either a two party or dominant party parliamentary system.

The governing function is also essential to democratic politics. Parties provide the mechanism whereby legislatures can function. Majority parties in the British system are usually guaranteed control over the House of Commons; one virtue of the present electoral system is the avoidance of weak governments. When in office the party is able to implement its programme. The electorate are aware of the consequences of a Conservative or Labour administration. Although the electoral system usually produces alternation in government and therefore healthy renewal, if the electorate so choose one party can be dominant with long runs in office. From 1979 until 1997 the Conservative Party remained in office for this reason eventually being replaced by the New Labour Party. The success of Tony Blair in winning a second term in the 2001 election has again raised questions about the efficacy of the electoral system in delivering alternating party government.

Theoretical approaches

The analysis of pressure groups is approached from the general perspective of **pluralism**. This is an attempt to conceptualise a democratic political system as a constellation or grouping of separate interests impacting on each other. Within the construct there will be **equal** influence with policy makers in a two way process of inputs and outputs. This is often called a systems model of politics.

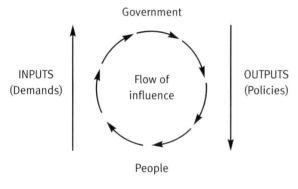

A systems model of politics

Within the systems perspective we can identify **five interrelated models** of group activity:

1 group politics;

2 collective action;

3 sectional;

4 neo-corporatist;

5 neo-liberal.

Group politics

A pure pluralist approach, this emphasises the importance of group behaviour for influence with policy makers. Large numbers of groups exist within a political culture, which is constantly changing. Governments listen to the views of all individual groups but inevitably larger, more powerful groups have more influence. Some check on this system exists as group pressures are counteracted by others – **countervailing power**.

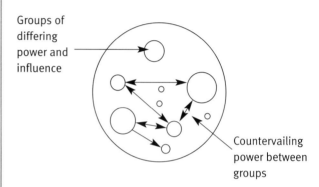

Groups of differing power and influence

Countervailing power between groups

A group politics view of the state

Collective action

This model is similar to the above except it emphasises why people join groups. People have policy influence collectively, not as individuals, and will join groups if the benefits gained from membership are greater than the costs. The problem for some exclusive groups is that **improvements** in policies go to **all** the public, not selectively to group members, but this is inevitable in democracies.

Sectional

Here groups are seen as influencing the policy agenda for their own ends. Sometimes referred to as elite pluralism because one section, or a **combination** of powerful **interests**, concentrates on advancing their interests at the expense of the wider community. The leaderships of these organisations also benefit more than the memberships.

Neo-corporatist

Pure corporatism existed in political states where industrial interests (business and labour organisations) combined in policy formulation with the government, as in Germany and Italy in the thirties and forties. A variation on this arrangement was said to exist during the Labour governments of

Harold Wilson and James Callaghan when the **Trades Union Congress** and **Confederation of British Industry** worked closely over industrial policy in a tripartite (three way) relationship.

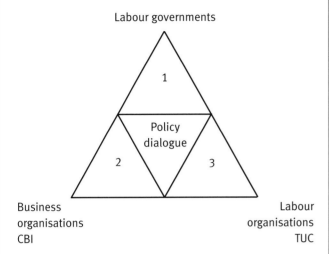

A neo-corporatist view of the state

Neo-liberal

This view places parliamentary representation above the importance of groups which are tolerated in the political system. Associated with Margaret Thatcher's Conservative governments of 1979 to 1990 when trade unions were excluded from close governmental relationships in industrial policy for **ideological** reasons. This government preferred to keep open a two-way dialogue with business interests in a dual relationship.

Evaluation of theoretical approaches

All theoretical approaches have a contribution to make to our understanding of group politics. Pluralism is clearly the overriding perspective derived from classic American writers who tended to adopt a functionalist view of the democratic state (*Easton 1953, Dahl 1961*).

Of the models within pluralism, the neo-corporatist view is now historical and is unlikely to be repeated with the new Labour government. Under Tony Blair's leadership the New Labour Party has begun the process of distancing itself from the trade unions. John Major continued a Conservative policy of neutrality or **holding the ring** towards groups which were regarded as too sectional for the public interest but could not be ignored.

Classifications and comparisons

There are two important differences between a pressure group and a political party:

1 **Existence** Groups exist for more **specific** purposes than a political party. A party is **all-embracing** in its policy-making, appealing to the general public. A group, usually having fewer resources, will be preoccupied with one area of public policy although this will have wider implications. The League Against Cruel Sports is an established organisation (71 years old) fighting to extend the protection of laws over domestic animals to wildlife. Although a **single issue** group in this sense, its activities stretch beyond opposition to the hunting of wildlife to include conservation of species and ownership of over 2,000 acres of sanctuary land.

For a political party to be so narrowly focused is clearly an electoral liability; the organisation is seeking to maximise its appeal. Both the Labour and Liberal Democratic Parties have suffered in the past from voter identification (helped by the media) with narrow or **sectional** interests. The Liberal Democrats are electorally strong in English local government, being the second party behind Labour since the 1995 local elections, and have been identified in the past as the party of community politics. The Labour Party (which began life as a form of organised labour pressure group) has in the 85 years of its existence been closely identified with trade unions and radical causes. The transition to a party of government has not been easy.

2 **Objectives** Pressure groups and political parties can be further differentiated in terms of their objectives. Groups are seeking **influence** with policy makers; parties exist to acquire and hold

political **power**. For a political party the most frustrating aspect of opposition is the inability to achieve its policies whilst presenting itself as a government in waiting. A pressure group does not concern itself with elections and political campaigns (except to influence the parties' policies) and will operate with whichever party is in power. During the eighties the Green lobby had remarkable success in changing party attitudes to the environment and this was reflected in the party manifestos at the 1997 general election.

Types of group

Early attempts to analyse pressure group activity produced confusing classifications. There are two basic types of group: **sectional** and **cause**. Sectional groups exist to protect one section of the population; in this sense they are **partial** to their memberships (*Duverger 1966*). They are found mainly in the economic sphere of society representing the interests of professionals, organised labour, civic and other groups.

```
1   Industrial Commercial
        Institute of Directors
        Building Societies Association

2   Employee Labour Organisations
        Trades Union Congress
        Unison

3   Professional
        Royal Institute of British Architects
        The Law Society

4   Civic
        County Councils Association

5   Other
        Royal Automobile Club
```

Examples of sectional groups

Cause groups exist to advance (**promote**) an idea, set of values or beliefs. They are not exclusive and draw their memberships from a wide sympathetic public. Typical groups in this category would operate in the areas of the environment, welfare, animal rights and civil liberties.

```
1   Environment
        World Wide Fund for Nature
        Greenpeace

2   Welfare
        National Society for Prevention of Cruelty to
            Children
        Age Concern

3   Animal Rights
        League Against Cruel Sports
        Royal Society for Prevention of Cruelty to Animals

4   Civil Liberties
        Liberty
        Charter 88
```

Example of cause groups

Resources

Although the two categories of sectional and cause overlap and **hybrid groups** belong equally to both, there are fairly clear distinctions between them. In terms of **resources** sectional groups have the financial edge because of fee-paying subscriptions from memberships. Organisations like trade unions are usually well resourced with large centralised head office staffs offering a range of services to their members. Smaller, less powerful cause groups have to rely on public donations and fewer staff but can sometimes be equally effective. The single issue group CLEAR (Campaign for Lead Free Air, 1981–83), founded with a grant from business, was successful in convincing policy makers of the need to reduce lead in petrol. Operation Black Vote (2001) has succeeded in raising awareness of the lack of ethnic minority representation in Parliament from its small East London office.

Influence

In terms of **influence**, groups are further distinguished by the possession of **insider** or **outsider** status (*Grant 1993*). Insider groups have most influence with government because they offer expertise essential to the implementation of policy. According to *Finer (1968)*, much of this influence is traded in an anonymous empire of officials and contacts with group representatives. Studies of the National Farmers Union have shown how the agricultural industry secured preferential policies by being on the inside.

Outsider groups are usually less influential with government as they offer little **expertise** or **trade off** in return for policy influence. The Campaign For Nuclear Disarmament, a major protest group in the sixties and seventies, never entered the 'closed' world of influence. For ideological reasons the objectives of this group were never compatible with the defence and nuclear policies of a Conservative government. Indeed, CND was regarded as a Labour pressure group partly because of the pacifism still remaining in that party and because Socialists took an active part in unilateral peace campaigns. In the eighties and nineties CND still found plenty of environmental issues to protest against like the transportation of nuclear waste. And after the announcement of the bombing campaign against Afghanistan in October 2001 by the US and British governments in retaliation for the terrorist destruction of the New York World Trade Centre, CND were quick to join other pacifist organisations and anti-war groups in a lobby of Parliament and Downing Street.

Although CND remains an 'ideological' outsider, there are examples of groups gradually acquiring insider status as they become more acceptable to government. Certain cause groups – The Howard League For Penal Reform is one example – have achieved **respectability** and will be in regular contact with policy makers where their interests are affected. In a study of change in pressure group politics, *Baggot* (*1995*) showed a gradual trend by government to consult with outsider groups more frequently than in the past, removing to some extent the disadvantages facing these types of group.

Membership and representation

Sectional and cause groups have different memberships although clearly they are not mutually exclusive. Considerable numbers of motorists are members of the motoring organisations (Automobile Association, Royal Automobile Club), but will be involved in other employment or professional groups in their daily lives. Groups will seek to maximise their strengths wherever possible, occasionally enticing members from other rival organisations. Apart from the increased financial resources larger memberships bring, numbers are important to groups for two reasons:

1 The amount of **leverage** or influence over policy makers is usually greater with large memberships.

2 Membership is the key to **representativeness** – the ability to show the government that a group speaks for as many of the people as it claims to represent.

The strength of many professional groups is based on the notion that they represent their total profession. The old professions of law and medicine (Law Society, British Medical Association) have more influence with

policy makers than the newer profession of teaching which is divided between various groups (Association of Teachers and Lecturers, National Union of Teachers, Professional Association of Teachers, Association of Masters and Mistresses).

Many cause groups seeking influence can claim larger **potential** than **actual** memberships. In the campaign to 'clean up' public broadcasting and violence in the media, the National Viewers and Listeners Association (founded by Mary Whitehouse) could claim to represent a large silent majority of dissatisfied viewers and listeners in its consultations with the BBC. Similar claims could be made by the British field Sports Society in its fight against John McFall's Wild Mammals Protection Bill of March 1995.

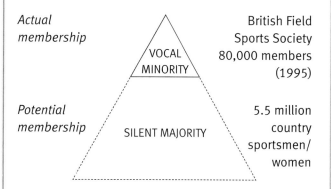

Actual membership — VOCAL MINORITY — British Field Sports Society 80,000 members (1995)

Potential membership — SILENT MAJORITY — 5.5 million country sportsmen/ women

Groups representativeness.
The example of the British Field Sports Society

Questions

1 What was tripartism?

2 Give one difference between a pressure group and a political party

3 Why do insider groups have more influence with government?

Influencing policy makers

The policy debate

Influencing the public policy debate demands different strategies and techniques depending on the type of group involved. Before a group can move to influence government opinion, it must first concentrate on **raising awareness** with the public. According to *McCulloch* (*1988*) an issue attention cycle must be negotiated before governments act on a problem. Once a matter is placed in the **public agenda**, groups will endeavour to keep it there until policy is enacted, changed or protected.

Campaigning

Many insider groups use **quiet** campaigns behind the scenes with government ministers and officials, which rarely attract media or public attention. Cause groups are traditionally associated with protests and demonstrations in attempts to get their message across – often a sign of desperation and a signal that they have little insider influence. The Campaign for Nuclear Disarmament raised public awareness of the dangers of nuclear war despite years of public demonstrations. Some groups had more influence on public policy because their ideas were more compatible with government. Improvements in the environment fall into this category.

The passing of the Criminal Justice and Public Order Act 1994 gave the police additional powers to control public protests and demonstrations: the new charge of aggravated trespass could be used particularly against road protesters and hunt saboteurs. Extensive media coverage of demonstrations throughout the nineties against the road building programme, the export of live animals and other emotive issues again brought into focus the problem of anti-parliamentary activity. **Direct action** protests and demonstrations can result in unintentional violence, or anti-political activity. By their very nature they are a challenge to parliamentary representation and the established machinery or protest. During 2000 the high cost of fuel in Britain in comparison with other European countries led to a series of direct action protests by hauliers and a transport lobby opposed to government taxation on petrol and diesel. After declaring an emergency situation to get fuel supplies moving again Tony Blair faced-off the protesters in his most crucial test of governing to date. The issue failed to make much impact on the 2001 general election precisely because some concessions to the lowering of the tax were made before the event thus diffusing the situation.

Access points

There are many access or influence points in the political system (after public opinion) which provide an opening for pressure groups to affect policy-making. The most important are: • European Union • executive and administration • local government • Parliament • political parties.

European Union

The European Union and its institutions (The Council of Ministers, European Parliament and European Commission) are increasingly targeted by national pressure groups attempting to influence legislation affecting their interests. Often this **lobbying** will be

FACTFILE

- **The most successful example of a pressure group in the late nineties placing a matter on the public policy agenda was the single issue group, the Snowdrop Campaign, of 1996 to 1997.**

- **In the short space of one year this group's objectives went from protest to legislation from March 1996 to February 1997 when the Firearms (Amendment) Act was passed.**

- **Formed to achieve the abolition of handguns after the tragedy of the Dunblane massacre on 13 March 1996, the group managed to carry public opinion after a publicised media campaign to bring pressure on the Conservative government and politicians.**

- **The remarkable point about the group was how they convinced John Major's government to ban handguns above .22 calibre. Although Labour pledged not to make an issue of this policy in the 1997 general election Tony Blair completed a total handgun ban after becoming Prime Minister.**

directed at British ministers, MPs and civil servants in a consultation process before laws are made or after it is discovered that **EU Directives** are impacting on their interests. Three examples of British interests which have been affected by European legislation are:

1 agriculture;

2 road haulage;

3 fisheries and fishing.

In agriculture, the National Farmers Union have shown their negotiating strength by securing reasonable treatment in the allocation of grants from the Common Agricultural Policy. The road haulage industry was less than successful in resisting the imposition from Europe of the extra costs of tachometers to vehicles restricting journey times in the interests of health and safety. British fishing has suffered natural decline reflected in negotiations with Europe. European fishing quotas have been resented by a weak industry that regards the granting of access to British waters as a betrayal of their interests.

Executive and administration

Pressure groups are able to exert direct influence on government through contacts with ministers and officials. Although we have seen that insider groups have the advantage in the **consultation process**, many outsider groups will be contacted should the

Study and Revise AS and A2 Level Government and Politics

government so wish. **Generalised contacts** between group representatives and ministers occur in the numerous standing advisory committees (over 1000 in 1998) set up by government in most policy areas. Groups will also be represented, by government invitation, in the work carried out by royal commissions, tribunals and inquiries.

It is now accepted practice for government to consult with group representatives in an affected policy area before contemplating legislation. This **institutionalised** arrangement works because:

1 groups have the opportunity to influence legislation and

2 government gains the cooperation and expertise of interests essential to the successful implementation of policy.

Without this contact or dialogue, policy would be unworkable and the **expertise** possessed by some groups could be used against the government. Margaret Thatcher was able to resist the National Union of Mineworkers **sanction** in the strikes of 1983, but her successor John Major had less success with education. The introduction of tests for school pupils under the National Curriculum was initially opposed by the teaching unions who refused to cooperate with the scheme. After a prolonged dispute, the Department For Education agreed to modify the procedures and John Patten, the minister responsible, was replaced by the more conciliatory Gillian Shephard.

The closest contact between a government and groups occurs in the **clientele relationship** established in the policy communities of the civil service (or Whitehall). Officials in each main spending department (Education, Health, Work and Pensions, Home Office) regularly consult their 'client' groups; representatives, whose opinions, expertise and contacts are essential for the smooth implementation of policy.

Local government

In the United Kingdom, local authorities and unitary authorities (counties and district councils) are the main providers of localised services. Two features make them very dependent on central government:

1 Most of their financial resource comes from the centre.

2 Their statutory powers are derived from Parliament.

This has implications for pressure groups at the local level – their activity will be directed at the way authorities implement central policies. Of the many contentious issues found in local and community politics, **land use** probably arouses the most interest, and will serve as a good example of the activity of such groups.

The Environment Minister Nicholas Ridley referred to the NIMBY syndrome (Not In My Back Yard) as signifying the opposition to development found in the British countryside. People opposed to developments

Government departments

A clientele relationship

quickly form local **direct action** groups and are prepared to take on planners, central government inspectors, local officials and councillors. Typical areas where groups are active include:

- The road programme – building of bypasses around villages removes heavy traffic but destroys important farming land.

- Waste disposal – sites are needed for the disposal of domestic and industrial waste, but few people welcome them.

- Major national construction projects – these are needed for the economy but resisted because they affect the character of local communities.

The nineties and the millennium were a particularly active time for land and environmental groups of all kinds protesting against what they claimed were dangerous developments.

The construction of the Channel Tunnel aroused considerable group interest. Kent villages threatened by blight from the first proposed Channel route successfully lobbied Members of Parliament from their own constituencies. The final route for the rail link avoided these communities but was imposed on others, a classic illustration of the land use dilemma. Other protests included action by 'tree people' who refused to leave trees in the designated route of the proposed Newbury Bypass road and the despolation of the first GM (Genetically modified) field crop trials which spread to supermarkets selling produce of this type. Neither of these protests were successful although they placed these matters on to the public policy agenda.

Parliament

Both Houses of Parliament (House of Commons and House of Lords) are targeted by groups seeking to influence **legislation**. Groups can employ the services of professional lobby organisations but traditionally make direct approaches themselves. This is particularly evident in the procedure surrounding the introduction of **private members' bills,** when interests target Members of Parliament with prearranged legislative detail. Although not as legislatively strong as members of the American Congress, British Members of Parliament and peers can speak in debates, table amendments to bills, raise questions with ministers, take part in committee proceedings and generally advance the cause of groups. For every issue or cause, sympathetic Members of Parliament or peers will be found supporting and advancing or opposing and obstructing the matter; a clear example of countervailing pressure.

CHECKLIST

✓ John McFall's unsuccessful Wild Mammals (Protection) Bill (1995) was written by the League Against Cruel Sports. Changes made to this bill (removing the hunting clauses) allowed it to be brought forward by Alan Meale in January 1996. The subsequent bill passed both Houses of Parliament and was enacted as the Wild Mammals (Protection) Act in February 1996.

✓ Austin Mitchell's Home Buyers Bill, enacted in 1984, was produced largely by the Consumers' Association intent on breaking the Law Society's monopoly of house conveyancing.

✓ Both bills illustrate that it is easier to change the particulars (the politics of detail) rather than the overall policy direction (the politics of issues) which is set by a government.

Political parties

Certain pressure groups have close relationships with political parties and most groups attempt to influence party policy if they can. The most publicised links exist between the Labour Party and the trade unions and the Conservative Party and business. The Liberal Democrats try to avoid open identification with any one section, for fear of damaging their centrist image.

Heavy financial dependence on the trade unions was electorally disadvantageous to Labour in all previous general elections and the party is seeking to modify this. After the Nolan Committee Inquiry into Standards in Public Life (1995) Tony Blair made it clear that he would seek a new financial relationship with the unions. The removal of the sponsorship link whereby individual unions help the electoral expenses of candidates would:

1 demonstrate publicly that the Labour Party is not controlled by extra-parliamentary unions;

2 keep the main financial link through donations from unions and other sources;

3 put pressure on the Conservative Party and their financial sources;

4 keep the trade unions at arm's length over policy matters.

Although the Labour–union connection receives most publicity in terms of **policy influence**, it is equally important to note that business organisations have substantial 'behind the scenes' influence over the Conservative Party. Financially, both major parties are dependent on donations from their respective interests and although they govern for the democratic majority, they tend to focus on their own group constituencies.

Questions

1 What does the term direct action politics mean?

2 Which access point do you consider the most important and why?

3 Why is the clientele relationship important?

4 Give one example of a local group in your area and say what its aims are.

Groups and democracy

Sectional and community interest

Pressure groups are an essential ingredient in democratic politics complementing the activity of political parties in a pluralist society. If citizens have rights to be heard by government and participate in policy-making, then pressure groups help this process (*Finer 1968*).

The problem for government is striking the right balance between granting access to sectional representation and protecting the interest of the community, assuming the two are different. There are two basic positions on this dilemma:

- The equilibrium theory describes pressure groups as a valuable asset to society. In a **pure pluralist** system the interests of the minority (the section) are balanced or held in equilibrium against the majority (the public) interest.

- The conspiracy theory, or **elite pluralism**, claims pressure groups are a danger to democratic society. Powerful interests dominate the lobbying process and secure favourable policies from government.

Both the above positions oversimplify the world of pressure group politics. The public interest is difficult to define and there will be occasions when it will coincide with the sectional since groups cover the vast majority of the population in some form or another. In the case of the fuel protests of 2000/01 transport hauliers blockaded the oil refineries preventing fuel reaching the filling stations. Clearly the government decided the public interest was being disrupted by the actions of a minority and decided to act lest the whole country be brought to a permanent standstill.

Clearly some groups are more influential with government than others but there is a tendency for a balance to be re-established. Organised labour was influential with the governments of Harold Wilson and James Callaghan and business interests with the governments of Margaret Thatcher and John Major. Tony Blair has managed to strike a balance between business and trade union interests preferring a middle way where neither group will dominate the attention of government.

Changing group influence

Public sector groups – teachers, nurses, the police, doctors – and trade unions generally **lost influence** with Conservative governments mainly for ideological reasons, whilst financial and business interests enjoyed close contacts.

Alienation from the traditional party and group system (especially by the young) is said to be a contributory factor in the rise of new social movements intent on challenging the economic and social order (*Hallsworth 1994*). Some of these groups represent new interests; Alarm UK was founded in 1995 by Emma Must to coordinate the activity of 300 local road action groups. Others are a reworking of the traditional, rather than radical departures from the old interests. Now there is an annual anti-capitalist protest in London coinciding with world protests against the G8 wealthy countries summits and globalisation. Unfortunately these demonstrations have a tendency to produce hostile reactions and bad publicity for the causes they are championing.

It is possible to see a parallel between the activities of protest movements of the sixties and seventies, when the emotive issues were the Vietnam War, nuclear weapons and minority rights, and the new cause groups. Rising affluence and declining class identities (*Inglehart 1977*), coupled with the break-up of the Soviet Union and ending of the Cold War, may have refocused issues for new generations. In the late nineties and at the millennium, groups at the forefront of protest were concentrating on animal rights, roadbuilding, wildlife protection, atmospheric pollution, citizens' rights and capitalist consumerism among others.

Groups and the Blair Governments

The Blair governments of 1997 and 2001 have faced a number of direct action protest as a result of changes in the political agenda and the tendency for interests to take to the streets. The fuel protests, the Countryside Alliance demonstrations, opponents of university top-up fees and opposition to the war in Iraq all produced problems for the government. Fuel protesters achieved a change in the duty on petrol; the Countryside Alliance managed to confuse the issue on foxhunting; and opponents of university top-up fees continued their fight after the Higher Education Bill passed the House of Commons on a severely reduced government majority of 28, down from 161 in March 2004. Pressure against British involvement in the war on Iraq lead to the establishment of the Hutton Enquiry, which reported in 2004, and the resignations of both Robin Cook and Claire Short from the Cabinet.

On another level, the Blair government has demonstrated a commitment to 'inclusive politics' or a 'big tent' strategy in pressure group politics. This has given minority groups like Stonewall (gay rights) some policy influence which was denied them under the previous Conservative governments. But other powerful interests like trade unions have been kept at arm's length.

Summary

1 **Pressure groups are a well established feature of the British political system.**

2 **They complement political party organisation and play an important part in the representation process guaranteeing participation in policy-making to a wide number of interests.**

3 **Because they are considered essential to the working of a democratic state, discussion of groups inevitably involves an examination of some theoretical approaches to political systems.**

4 **This is one area where you must keep up to date with the changes in issues reaching the public agenda through the influence of groups.**

5 **A selection of issues of group concern in the late nineties and at the millennium included constitutional reform, export of live animals, opposition to field sports, individual rights, road building protests, environmental protection and anti-nuclear activity. These are likely to remain topical beyond the year 2002.**

Sample question and answer

AS Level question

1 How do pressure groups influence policy-making?

This question focuses on the specific policy-making role of groups and demands an understanding of parliamentary processes. Material for the answer could include:

1 *A discussion of the access points between groups, the executive and administration.*

2 *How groups influence legislative detail, particularly through private members' bills.*

3 *The tendency for insider groups to form clientele relationships with government departments.*

4 *Discussion of the formalised consultation process that now occurs as standard practice between groups and government.*

5 *The removal of certain public sector and trade union groups from close policy influence since the eighties.*

PREVIEW

In this chapter you will revise:

- **The part played by political opinion polls in the democratic process.**

- **The use of referendums and their relationship to the electoral system.**

- **Arguments for and against retaining the present British electoral system.**

- **The merits of alternative electoral systems.**

Political opinion polls

Political opinion polls are designed to test public opinion on any number of issues and are an obvious measure of a government's popularity. Although they may not influence the Prime Minister in choice of general election date (Margaret Thatcher was said to have paid more attention to local government election results), they are considered important enough for the political parties to commission their own polls from the major polling organisations Gallup, National Opinion Polls (NOP), Harris, Market and Opinion Research International (MORI) and International Communications and Marketing (ICM) (the top five). The results of these polls often appear in the newspapers or on television and are a major source of information for the electorate.

FACTFILE

- **The media also conduct their own opinion polls sometimes in conjunction with the top five polling organisations. Newspapers, radio, BBC Television and Independent Television, make the effort during general election campaigns particularly.**

- **University academic research use their own opinion poll data for analysis and comment on electoral trends. The two most prominent surveys are carried out by BES (The British Election Study) and CREST (The Centre for Research into Elections And Social Trends).**

Types of political opinion polls

There are six types of political opinion poll, which place questions before a representative sample of the electorate, covering the following areas:

1 **Suitability to govern** Here the attempt is made to ascertain people's opinions on who would make the **best Prime Minister, leader, or party** for

government. In the 1992 general election John Major was consistently more popular than both Neil Kinnock and Paddy Ashdown (*Crewe 1992*). Under Neil Kinnock both the Labour Party and its leader were unpopular (1983–92). Under John Smith (1992–94), the Labour leader and the party recovered popularity. Tony Blair reversed this trend in the 1997 general election when for the first time in decades a Labour leader was more popular than a Conservative leader. This pattern was repeated in the 2001 general election against William Hague, Tony Blair's leadership of the New Labour government being assessed as the more popular.

2 **Issue questions** Issue questions concentrate on voters' opinions on which party has the **best policies**. Typical questions focus on inflation and prices, defence, the National Health Service, education, and law and order. Since **issue** or **instrumental voting** is now considered a more important factor in voter preference, it is to be expected that parties are anxious to discover which issues are advantageous and which electorally damaging. In the 1997 general election (New) Labour led on traditional social issues like education and the NHS and overtook the Conservatives on taxation, inflation and defence. Other issues like the general state of the economy may have been overtaken in voters' minds with the perception of 'sleaze' in the Conservative Party. In 2001 the Conservatives made the mistake of concentrating on Europe as a major campaign issue. Both the 2001 analyses by BES and CREST showed that the electorate preferred the National Health Service, education and tax as the major issues. Labour led on the first two issues.

3 **Voting intention** Polls on voting intention are taken throughout a general election campaign and are probably the most important political polls. First used in the general election of 1945, they are not strictly speaking opinion polls but surveys on **intended voting behaviour** and they do not predict the outcome of the general election. As snapshots of public opinion, they must be used with care for there is the tendency to freeze frame events at a particular time, which may or may not be a good guide to the actual election result (*Game 1994*). The polling organisations have a mixed record on the degree of accuracy and predictability of the winning party in these sorts of poll. In 1987 they were accurate in selecting the Conservative Party. In 1992 most polls made a classic error by predicting a Labour win. Improvements in polling techniques (secret ballots, telephone polling,

discounting refusals) enabled the polling organisations to salvage their reputations in the 1997 general election. In 2001 there was less fluctuation in poll results with ICM coming closest to the final verdict, which gave Labour 42 per cent of the vote against the Conservatives 33 per cent and the Liberal Democrats 19 per cent. The accuracy of the ICM prediction could relate to the fact that they conducted 7,000 interviews during the campaign giving them a very large representative sample of raw data on which to work.

4 **Actual vote**   Polls on votes cast or actual voting behaviour, usually called **exit polls**, are carried out shortly after people leave the polling centre. As people have secretly recorded their vote they are less inhibited in replying to pollsters' questions of how they voted. For this reason alone, exit polls usually have a better record of predictability of the potential election winner. In the 1997 general election, exit polls for both BBC TV and ITN predicted a Labour lead well below the final figure of 179 seats (*Butler and Kavanagh 1997*).

5 **Longitudinal studies**   Longitudinal studies are a common sociological method of obtaining detailed information over a period of time using the same group of respondents and returning to interview them at fixed periods. They can provide valuable insights into changing attitudes and opinions and are particularly useful for studying fluctuations in political views. As **panel polls** they are used throughout a general election campaign and thicken up the information detailing last minute vote switching, late decisions, party and leader preference and general voter volatility. The big five polling organisations have the resources to carry out these polls, which are time consuming, expensive and difficult to run. Despite that their record is more accurate than the one-off forecast polls and has a lasting relevance (*Kavanagh 1992*). The British Election Study 2001 used this method in wave sampling before, during and after the campaign. In 2002 they will return to the same respondents for interviews one year after the general election (*Billinghurst 2001*).

6 **Constituency opinions**   Individual constituency polls endeavour to break down the national electorate into more quantifiable measures of public opinion. Often carried out by or on behalf of the political parties, they sometimes concentrate on opinions in marginal seats where results are not a foregone conclusion. In 1997 local polls were also held in two controversial seats affected by the sleaze factor: Neil Hamilton's in Tatton and Piers Merchant's in Beckenham. The publication of

these and other local polls can have an effect on those voting tactically. In this sense they are performing a service by informing people of the likely impact of their vote. However the accuracy of these polls may not be reliable if carried out by volunteers who lack the resources of the polling organisations.

CHECKLIST

✓ **For validity reasons opinion polls must survey statistically significant numbers to reach quantifiable results. Sample sizes vary from 1,000 adults (the most typical) to 5,000, although polling organisations have reached 10,000 in extraordinary circumstances.**

✓ **Large samples of population are not necessarily more accurate, but they do allow the achievement of a representative cross section of the electorate based on quotas of age, gender, ethnicity or class.**

✓ **Sampling errors of between plus and minus 3 per cent generally reduce the larger the sample, although these figures are regarded as acceptable in the polling industry.**

✓ ***Butler and Kavanagh (1997)* draw attention to the 'spiral of silence' of Conservative supporters which made some pollsters doubt the size of the Labour lead in 1997. This may have been a feature in 2001 also where the overwhelming popularity of New Labour discouraged Conservatives from public protestations of support.**

✓ **Other problems in opinion poll sampling which are difficult to allow for include under-registration of voters, late swings and undecided voters. *Kavanagh (1992)* first raised the possibility that embarrassed publics gave politically correct answers for fear of offence.**

✓ **Clearly it is difficult for pollsters to account for every eventuality even with improved methodologies – there will always be refusals or 'shy' voters.**

Influence of the polls

The publication of opinion poll results may have unintended consequences on the electorate. Psephologists (those who study elections) have long been aware of this problem although there is very little empirical evidence supporting generally held circumstantial views (*Denver 1989*). In 1967 the **Speaker's Conference on Electoral Reform** recommended that the results of political opinion polls should not be published in the three days before an election. The Wilson Labour government rejected this suggestion because it was not convinced that voters were particularly influenced by the polls. Academic opinion is now divided on poll influence. Some claim a **negative impact** as polls influence the level of abstention or apathy. If polls predict a substantial win for one party, does this reduce voter turnout from those who feel powerless to influence the outcome? **Positively**, supporters of polls say they promote a higher turnout by stimulating interest in the general election. The may also act as an aid to those contemplating tactical voting by providing information on the state of the parties. Two particular political opinion poll effects have been noticed.

Repulsion

Opinion polls may have a **repulsion or underdog effect** by causing different types of voting behaviour to that intended. Voters might decide to remain at home instead of casting their vote for a party that is clearly going to win (according to the polls), conscious that they have little or no effect on the outcome. Alternatively, voters may decide to switch support throughout the campaign to a party that appears to be doing less well in the polls. Both these 'boomerang' effects probably have most influence on sympathy voters, the uncommitted or the alienated. Last minute switching of vote to the Conservatives occurred in the 1992 general election (*Crewe 1992*). Again in 1997 there was a great deal of vote 'churning' right up until election day; the polls' prediction of a Labour win (correct that time) could have produced Conservative votes.

Attraction

A widely believed idea is that opinion polls have a bandwagon or **attraction effect**. People like to be associated with winning parties; they may feel they do not want to waste their vote on a loser. Climbing on the bandwagon of a party which the polls predict as the most likely winner is a more satisfying form of political activity as it increases the eventuality of that fact occurring. Again, as with the boomerang effect, certain types of voter influenced by a bandwagon might be at the periphery of politics as uncommitted voters, floaters, detached or semi-detached. Alternatively, they could be strongly committed to a party that just happens to be in the lead according to opinion poll survey evidence. Since there are only a handful of serious contentious parties with a chance in a general election, this is bound to occur with millions of voters.

Comment

There are many theories of voting behaviour pointing to increased voter volatility in the nineties. If the effects of opinion polls on the vote are computed in addition, it is not difficult to see why predictions of party success in general elections cannot be made with any scientific certainty. The rational voter may exist, but if any one of the effects associated with opinion polls occurred, poll results would be consistently wrong. Up to 1987 opinion poll results were consistent in their accuracy – an impressive record considering the difficulties in sampling public opinion (*Eatwell 1993*). Predictions of a Labour win in the 1992 general election were hopelessly wrong and damaged the credibility of the polling organisations. The methodological corrections made to market research techniques enabled the organisations to get it right in the 1997 and 2001 general elections making 1992 appear as an exception.

Questions

1   Name the six types of political opinion poll.

2   Why did the 1967 Speaker's Conference recommend that opinion poll results be banned from publication three days before an election?

3   How have opinion poll organisations corrected market research technology since the disastrous events of 1992?

Tactical voting

The growth in support for the Liberal Democratic, Scottish and Welsh Nationalist Parties in England, Wales and Scotland, alongside traditional attachments to the Conservative and Labour Parties, introduces a bewildering choice for the voter in general and local elections. For many, to exercise that choice is to vote tactically, voting for a candidate who is most likely to defeat their least favoured party. Tactical voting in general elections has increased according to evidence from 1992, 1997 and 2001.

The question of the **power of opinion polls** as an influence on voter preference is more complex. Voters in safe seats (where a one party majority is secure) have little choice if they do not accept the winning candidate. This is precisely where tactical voting becomes important, for such people can choose to give their vote to a party that could unseat the safe incumbent, preventing the division of opposition votes. Alternatively, those in marginal seats are

targeted by the political parties because the vote is more evenly balanced and tactical voting could remove a particular candidate. In the 1997 general election the Observer newspaper published a comprehensive list of 200 seats where tactical voting could unseat sitting Conservative MPs. Again in 2001 an ICM/Observer poll predicted that tactical voting would hurt the Conservatives. This may have been the case but according to *Kellner (2001)* the evidence is patchy except in a few seats. Internet communications and the advice of the Labour-supporting musician celebrity Billy Bragg, for example, had some effect in Dorset South won back from the Conservatives with Liberal Democratic support. But it is difficult to be precise about the effects such information (based on opinion polls) has on the electorate. The Liberal Democrats' increase to 46 seats in 1997 from 20 in 1992 owed something to tactical voting. Yet this did not have a marked effect on the outcome and may have been worth only 25–35 seats to Labour or Liberal Democrats within a Labour majority of 179 (*Budge, Crewe, McKay and Newton (1998)*). In 2001 the Liberal Democrats increased their seats by eight up to 52, but how important a part did tactical voting play in this? *Kellner (2001)* thinks it did help the party convert wafer thin majorities into solid victories and Labour supporters reciprocated Liberal Democrat support by helping that party in its fight against the Conservatives.

Local political information on the strength of the respective party support is also provided by constituency opinion polls, but there were fewer of these in 2001. The majority of tactical voters in marginal seats are relying on national opinion poll results to gain a snapshot of their local situation which, however, may be very different. This raises the problem that national opinion polls may be distorting the democratic process rather than adding to democracy.

Opinion polls and democracy

Publication of political opinion poll results is defended on the grounds that they aid democracy. Despite shortcomings, they keep the electorate informed on the opinions of others and they provide some opportunity for the expression of public views between elections. Polls designed to test opinion on particular policies may also be useful to government in establishing people's attitudes or responses to them.

The main drawback of opinion polls from a democratic viewpoint is that they can work to the advantage of the government and the disadvantage of the opposition. Although not a decisive influence on choice of election dates, Prime Ministers obviously seek to avoid (if they can) going to the country when unpopular. Governments could also be assisted by opinion polls ascertaining majority opinion on particular issues which can feed back into policy changes or adjustments, although the weight of evidence is to the contrary. Margaret Thatcher persisted with the introduction of the Community Charge or Poll Tax as a reformed system of local government finance in 1990 despite warnings from Michael Heseltine and other ministers that it would be unpopular. Had this been tested in an opinion poll beforehand, the government would have been better informed of the level of public disquiet surrounding this particular policy change.

Referendums

The government can ascertain public opinion more directly by the use of referendums – questions to the electorate on a specific issue demanding a positive or negative response. Since electorate opinions cannot be separated by issue – voting in general elections is not item by item, but taking or leaving a whole programme – it could be argued that referendums have a place in a representative democracy. Unfortunately for supporters of this idea, there is no constitutional provision for the holding of referendums in Britain even though few have been held to date. Referendums are therefore sufficiently rare to be regarded as foreign to the British constitution, primarily on the grounds that an indirect parliamentary democracy cannot function by constant appeals to the electorate over the heads of its representatives. It is instructive to examine referendums from the three perspectives of representativeness, executive dominance and constitutional implications.

Representativeness

It is difficult enough to ascertain public opinion on single issues; clearly there are items in a governing party's manifesto that supporters find objectionable. Despite that, British parliamentary democracy relies on a thin concept of the **mandate**. There is a tie between the electorate and the majority party elected to govern and this is generally accepted by all the mainstream political parties. However, the mandate is not binding – governments do not have to implement programmes laid before the electorate in manifestos. It is implied that they will have flexibility or room for manoeuvre pragmatically responding to events as they unfold.

On this weak form of the mandate it would be possible to allow occasional referendums even if they breach the idea of parliamentary sovereignty. Some form of constitutional safeguard is offered to the people by a referendum exercise in popular sovereignty taking power back to the people (*Bogdanor 1991*).

If the strong form of the mandate idea – that once elected a government is obligated to carry out policies laid before the electorate and voted on in general elections – is more acceptable to the political left, it is no surprise that most of the referendums held in Britain to date have been under Labour governments. Either the tradition of direct democracy is stronger in the Labour Party or the referendums held were a response to difficult constitutional questions requiring bottom up agreements to change in the status quo. The 1998 referendum in Northern Ireland was an attempt to settle the problem of the constitutional position of the province – by the establishment of a New Northern Ireland Assembly. The 1975 referendum on continued membership of the EEC helped a divided Labour Cabinet (under Harold Wilson) avoid a damaging split by allowing executive dissent a public voice. In a similar vein, the 1998 referendums in Wales and Scotland on the question of devolution for those countries also went some way to head off separatist demands by conceding a Scottish Parliament and Welsh Assembly. The Blair New Labour government was able to fulfil its manifesto pledge in this area (the strong form of the mandate).

Executive dominance

Although the executive supports the weak idea of the mandate for reasons of expediency, it is not keen to consult the electorate again between general elections. John Major rejected a referendum for Britain in 1992 on the ratification of the terms of the Maastricht Treaty after the first Danish referendum on the issue. The Maastricht Treaty was subsequently ratified by the British government after passing the House of Commons (indirect representation), but not after a referendum consulting the people (direct representation). It is interesting that both the Conservative and Labour Parties opposed referendums on Maastricht even though the leaders did not rule out using them in the future. John Smith, the Labour leader to 1994, promised a referendum on electoral change after rejecting the 1993 Plant Commission Report on Electoral Reform. This promise was reiterated by his successor, Tony Blair, after his election as Prime Minister in 1997.

Executive dominance of referendums is also evident in the design and mechanism of securing the vote. Since a common criticism of British parliamentary

democracy is the lack of public debate on many policy issues, it could be said that the public are unprepared for complex constitutional debates and cannot therefore formalise opinions on any issue. This would be a major problem in any referendum on proposals for Britain to join the EURO – the single European currency. Tony Blair included this promise as one of the pledges in the Labour Party Manifesto of 2001, and a referendum is expected in the current parliament, but it could be fudged or delayed as the issue divides the electorate and cuts across parties. The Blair government would have to overcome cynicism and lack of information about the EURO by fire brigade exercises in political education. In the 1975 EEC referendum all households were supplied with pro- and anti-EEC statements before the poll, but was this enough? In the run up to the poll, additional publicity through the media was given to the respective arguments but the pro-lobby outspent the anti-lobby.

There remains the problem of the design of the survey and questionnaire. Many complex political issues cannot be reduced to a simple Yes/No response; leading questions suggesting the merits of one answer over another must be avoided. In the 1979 referendum on Welsh and Scottish devolution, Nationalists criticised the insistence on a **qualified majority** of 40 per cent to be in favour of the proposals before the Wales Act 1978 and Scotland Act 1978 could be implemented. In the 1998 referendums qualified majority voting was replaced by the simple majority requirement. In the 1999 referendum over an elected mayor for London the question was far easier to understand even if only 34 per cent of those eligible to vote subsequently turned out on May 4 2000 when the election was finally held.

FACTFILE

- **The British referendums held to date have all had a national or constitutional significance for the United Kingdom.**

- **It is obviously possible to design referendums having a social or moral focus, but these have been avoided as matters best dealt with by traditional representation.**

- **If more contentious referendums were held taking matters out of Parliament, parliamentary sovereignty and the role of MPs would be further undermined. In the one exception to this rule, West Wales is allowed a local referendum on Sunday opening of public houses every 10 years.**

The electoral system

The British simple plurality system

The British electoral system is a **simple plurality** or first past the post system (FPTP). It has many virtues and few drawbacks in the sense that no electoral system is perfect – some are simply more proportional than others.

The system is called 'simple plurality' because the winner needs more votes than any other single candidate but not more votes than all the other candidates – in fact it is rare for this to happen. Voting is a simple matter; voters place a cross against their preferred candidate and the one with the most votes wins.

Tony Blair Labour Party	**X**
Iain Duncan Smith Conservative Party	
Charles Kennedy Liberal Democrats	
John Swinney Scottish Nationalists	

The British simple plurality system ballot slip (a hypothetical example – the leaders of the parties do not all stand in a single constituency)

Comment

The **advantages** claimed for the present British electoral system include:

- **Simplicity**   It is easy to understand and simple to operate. The voter knows which party will form the government, and there is no behind the scenes manoeuvring as with coalitions.

- **Strong government**   The system enables a single party to dominate Parliament and then form a government. This government in turn can claim a mandate for its policies and avoid damaging pacts or coalitions which can weaken an executive.

- **Representativeness**   Electors have an MP to lobby who comes from a reasonably small, single member constituency. This ensures that MPs represent the views of all their constituents even if they did not support the MP (*Watts 1994*).

The **weaknesses** in the present system have attracted most attention, particularly from the Liberal Democrats and smaller parties who suffer disproportionately from it. At the outset it is worth remembering that until the 1920s, when the Liberals were eclipsed by the Labour Party under the existing electoral system, that party did not champion electoral reform. The main drawbacks in the simple plurality system are:

- **Proportionality**   One test of electoral systems is that they should produce MPs in a legislature roughly proportionate to the vote they receive. This matching does not occur in the British system. In a British constituency the candidate with the most votes is not necessarily the most popular. If there are only two candidates the winner must get a majority (over 50 per cent) but with the more usual situation of three or more, the winner may need just over one third of the vote to get elected. This can mean that more voted against the winner than for – and it certainly means that up to 70 per cent of votes cast in a single constituency are wasted. Those votes that supported other candidates are lost (not counted) and those surplus votes for the winner are also unnecessary (superfluous).

Because votes are wasted in this way, there is no proportional link between the total votes cast for each party nationally and the final number of seats (MPs) achieved in the House of Commons. Smaller parties therefore suffer a **disproportional representation** in the allocation of seats, in what is called the electoral system effect. The figures for the 2001 general election illustrate well the problem for the Liberal Democrats who won eight per cent of total seats with 19 per cent of the popular vote.

	Seats in Commons (MPs)	Percentage of national vote	Percentage of Commons seats
Conservative	166	33	26
Labour	413	42	64
Liberal Democrats	52	19	8
Others	30	6.5	2

Disproportional representation for the Liberal Democrats' 2001 general election result

- **Minority government**   Although strictly speaking British government is majoritarian with usually a workable majority in the House of Commons from a national electorate viewpoint, many governments are elected on a minority of the popular vote. Since 1945 no government has in fact won more than 50 per cent of the popular vote. Even Labour's landslide win in 2001 was based on 42 per cent of the popular vote.

- **Over-representation of one party** Although the independent Boundary Commission reviews electoral districts every 10 to 15 years to ensure constituencies do not become disproportionate in terms of electors, there was evidence that the electoral map of Britain produced two nations – a predominantly Conservative South and a Labour North. This partly resulted from the concentration of Labour votes in the North where votes were wasted in safe seats. Conservative strength in the South was more evenly spread thus producing more southern MPs disproportionately (*Rooker 1992*). From 1997 this situation corrected itself as the election was fought on new boundaries affecting 500 constituencies. Labour gained nationally out of the new total of 659 MPs.

- **Maintenance of adversarial politics** The present electoral system helps to maintain the artificiality of two party politics resting on an adversarial system. Each major party is encouraged by its electoral prize and stranglehold on power to present politics in an oppositional form (*Finer 1975*). This in turn is encouraged by the existence of safe seats (approximately 70 per cent) which permanently return Labour or Conservative MPs to the House of Commons. Even marginal seats, which have the potential to produce a change of government by small swings, play into the hands of the two party system because the electoral system gives everything to the winner. The argument for a reformed voting system is even stronger on marginality grounds, for a small group of the electorate have a significance out of proportion to their number.

Electoral reform

Mainly because of the problems of disproportionality and unfairness in the British simple plurality system, since the 1970s discussion of reform has become almost a permanent feature of the political system increasing as either Labour or Liberal Democratic parties felt more disadvantaged. In 1996 with the Conservative government into its seventeenth year of consecutive administration, pressure for change accelerated. As the 1997 general election approached, there were those within the Labour Party who felt 'one last push' would carry them into government under the simple plurality system. Equally, there were those who felt Labour would again become dependent on Liberal Democratic support (as in 1976–79) in any future hung Parliament, suggesting that the price of this support could be a promise to reform the system. This fear evaporated as Labour became the government in 1997 on a record

landslide eclipsing its result in 1945. A similar result in 2001 pushed electoral reform into the background although New Labour examined numerous alternative systems in its pledge to replace the existing Westminster system after a referendum.

Questions

1. Why were referendums regarded as foreign to the British constitution?

2. Explain the concept of the mandate.

3. What is the importance of tactical voting?

4. What are the two main drawbacks to the British simple plurality (FPTP) electoral system?

Alternative voting systems

We have seen some of the values considered necessary in democratic electoral systems: **proportionality, strong government, representativeness** and **electoral choice**. Most electoral systems, including the British present system, embody these values, but no one system has a monopoly of all. In suggesting replacements two types of system are examined: **majority systems** that give good majorities in constituencies and **proportional systems** that ensure a proportional link between numbers of representatives and the popular vote. The following are the more important:

- **(AV) Alternative vote system (majority)** This would be the easiest form to introduce in place of the existing British system. The main difference to first past the post would be greater electoral choice placing candidates in preference order. The system was first suggested in 1910 and again by the Labour government of 1931.

Tony Blair Labour party	1
Iain Duncan Smith Conservative Party	4
Charles Kennedy Liberal Democrats	2
John Swinney Scottish Nationalists	3

An alternative vote ballot paper

Votes are initially distributed according to first preferences – any candidate receiving more than 50 per cent is elected. If no MP emerges on the first round, then second preferences are used to build up other candidates to the required number. Although this system does not give proportional representation, it is easy to understand and ensures MPs have majority constituency support. It is used in Australia for federal elections to the House of Representatives and in State Parliament elections.

- **(PL) Party list system (proportional)** Party list or list systems are proportional in the sense that votes are apportioned to party lists according to the share of the vote received. The electorate vote for a party (not candidates) and seats are allocated according to lists supplied by the parties. This system is used in Israel, Belgium, Finland, Sweden and in European Union parliamentary elections outside Britain. Its main drawback is that electorates have little choice in the selection of party candidates – but its MPs are proportionately related to the actual vote.

Labour Party	
Conservative Party	
Liberal Democratic Party	
Scottish National Party	
Welsh National Party	**✗**

A party list ballot paper

- **(STV) Single transferable vote system (proportional)** This system is more complex than the others examined so far. Larger constituencies are involved with a number of MPs selected by respective parties. Voters express preferences (as in the alternative vote) but votes are distributed according to a formula.

The Droop formula for working out which candidates are elected is:

$$\frac{\text{number of votes cast}}{\text{number of seats} + 1} + 1$$

To be elected, candidates must pass the quota. Surplus votes are then redistributed according to voter preferences 1, 2, 3, etc. A process of redistribution of votes from those who passed the quota to the less successful continues until all seats are filled. Apart from complexity, the main disadvantage with this system relates to the larger constituencies needed which could mean that MPs become more remote. This is partially offset by a greater number of MPs in each constituency and the proportionality of the system. It is used in the Australian Senate, the Republic of Ireland and Malta.

Iain Duncan Smith Conservative Party	6
Charles Kennedy Liberal Democratic Party	2
Gordon Brown Labour Party	8
Kenneth Clarke Conservative Party	7
Simon Hughes Liberal Democratic Party	3
Jack Straw Labour Party	4
Ann Widdecombe Conservative Party	1
Dafydd Wigley Welsh National Party	5
John Swinney Scottish National Party	9

A single transferable vote ballot paper

- **(AMS) Additional member system (hybrid)** Some alternative voting systems are hybrid – a mix of both majority and proportional systems. The most cited example is that used in Germany (formerly West Germany), which was introduced after 1945. Here two systems are used, with voters having two votes. The first is expressed for a candidate under simple plurality, the second for a party list. Those elected by simple plurality get seats, the remaining seat allocation for each party being filled on a proportional basis according to their share of the vote. This system balances the disadvantages of simple plurality with the advantages of a proportional system.

The future

The prospects for reform of the British electoral system seemed a real possibility with the election of the Labour government of 1997. Tony Blair promised a referendum on the voting system in the Labour manifesto after an independent electoral commission had examined the proportional alternatives to our present simple plurality system. The Jenkins Commission (1998) recommended the AV Plus (Alternative Vote) system. Of the five systems examined by Jenkins (AV, SV, STV, AMS and First Past the Post), the SV model was recommended for Westminster elections by the Labour Plant Commission in 1993. The promise to hold a referendum on electoral reform before 2000 was not implemented partly because of opposition with the

Labour leadership. Although New Labour introduced reforms to the other UK electoral systems it remains to be seen if it will change the FPTP elections to the Westminster Parliament. Having won a second election in 2001, Labour appear to have lost enthusiasm for this kind of reform. The result is that Britain now has a number of different electoral systems in operation. Versions of AMS are used for elections for the Scottish Parliament and Welsh Assembly, a European List System is used in the Euro-Elections, the Northern Ireland Assembly was elected in 1998 under STV and the Mayor for London elected under a version of AMS.

Tony Blair and electoral reform

In 2004, the prospects for electoral reform of the first past the post system of electing MPs to the Westminster Parliament looked increasingly remote. The issue has now moved down the political agenda and is unlikely to become current again unless the Liberal Democrats can force the issue by substantially increasing their share of the vote from the 18.3 per cent (52 seats) achieved in the 2001 general election.

It is possible that increased tactical voting at the next election (expected by 2005) will increase the Liberal Democrat share of the vote but it is doubtful if it will be enough to 'break the mould' of two-party politics. With both Labour and the Conservatives opposed to electoral reform, the future of British politics looks set to remain in the dominant party model.

Summary

1. Although British political opinion polls do not generally have a good record, various changes have been made to polling methodologies to improve their accuracy and they are now an essential ingredient in a representative democratic system fulfilling useful functions.

2. Referendums are a form of opinion poll on specific issues that have implications for parliamentary sovereignty. The question of British membership of the EURO still remains to be settled by referendum.

3. The strengths and weaknesses of the British electoral system are well documented. The question of electoral reform is still on the political agenda with the election of the second Blair government in 2001.

Sample question and answer

AS Level question

1 Do referendums give too much power to groups outside Parliament?

This question demands an understanding of the constitutional position of referendums. Carefully show how referendums relate to the sovereignty of the people argument and in effect bypass Parliament. You should be able to describe parliamentary sovereignty and its relationship to referendums. Develop the point about the power of pressure groups who would openly campaign on referendum issues. As there have been seven referendums in the United Kingdom, there are few examples of pressure group referenda campaigns.

You could focus on the 1975 EEC referendum campaigns of both pro- and anti-EEC groups. Such a campaign is likely to be repeated over the promised referendum on European Monetary Union which could be held in 2002 or 2003. Make some evaluation of the increased power pressure groups might gain from campaigning in possible future referendums and compare with the role of political parties. Since political parties focus on election campaigns where issues are less specific, it is possible they would lose influence in these areas. This is a debatable point and you should be prepared to argue a case for or against.

Traditional theories of electoral behaviour

Social class

Early approaches to the study of electoral choice concentrated mainly on the idea that voters aligned themselves to political parties largely on social class lines (class alignment) (*Butler and Stokes 1974*). As the Labour and Conservative Parties had dominated British politics in the post-war period 1945–70, so the majority of the electorate perceived of themselves as either working or middle class. The Labour Party attracted the working-class vote and the Conservative Party the middle-class vote. A basic problem was to explain the success of the Conservative Party in winning general elections if a majority of the electorate (approximately 60 per cent) were working class; if the vote followed class patterns there should be more Labour governments.

Two factors were considered important:

1 **Party attachment**   Class membership is related to party attachment and identity. During the fifties and sixties the majority of the electorate **strongly identified** with one of the two main parties (*Kavanagh 1990*). This strong **partisan self-image** aligned the electorate behind the Labour or Conservative Party (partisan alignment) and produced fairly consistent general election results

(*Butler and Stokes 1974*). Each party could count on a 'hard vote' (as there were few floating voters) and the certainty of their own reliable class constituencies.

2 **Deviant voters**   Class voting never followed neat patterns; there were always **deviant** voters prepared to support parties outside their class for a variety of reasons (cross-class voting).

Deviant voters fell into two categories:

- **working-class Tories** who voted Conservative and

- **middle-class radicals** who voted Labour.

Complex sociological reasons were given as explanations for this behaviour which took voters from their traditional parties.

Working-class Tories

Two explanations for working-class Conservative voting behaviour came from *McKenzie and Silver (1968)*.

1 Working-class Tories voted on **deferential** grounds – they deferred to the Conservative Party because in their opinion it was superior to and better able to govern than the Labour Party.

2 Those who did not fit this category were **secular** voters. They chose the Conservative Party for practical reasons.

Parkin (1968) and *Jessop (1974)* advanced a more controversial theory. For them, working-class Conservative voting was explained by socialisation into Conservative and middle class values. As the **dominant value system** of British society was held to be predominantly conservative, so a large section of the working class would be influenced to vote for the party that embodied those ideas.

A final traditional explanation for working-class Conservative support came from *Butler and Rose (1960)*. They suggested that as living standards rose, a greater number of working-class voters experienced a middle-class lifestyle which propelled them towards

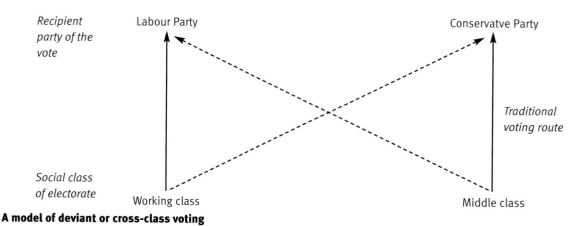

A model of deviant or cross-class voting

the Conservative Party. This causal link between living standards and party preference (**embourgeoisement theory**) has never been totally discredited and was one of the reasons why the governments of Margaret Thatcher were so successful in attracting working class support.

Middle-class radicals

Two factors have always supported middle-class Labour voting:

1 **Occupation**   Those in public sector service employment (teaching, social work, nursing) are drawn to the Labour Party because it is perceived as more concerned with social welfare spending than the Conservative Party (*Parkin 1968*).

2 **Intellect**   Intellectually certain middle-class voters see no class contradiction in supporting the Labour Party; the ideas of Conservatism are not attractive. The middle-class image of the Parliamentary Labour Party would also prove attractive as many first generation professionals remember the socialising influences of a working-class background.

FACTFILE

- **A feature linked to the traditional pattern of voting behaviour was the existence of a fairly stable two-party system.**

- **The Conservative and Labour Parties dominated politics throughout the fifties and sixties attracting the major share of the vote. During these years both parties secured an average vote of 87.5 per cent, leaving little room for the Liberal Party as a third force.**

- **Dominance by the two major parties of the electoral system fitted well with the theories of class and partisan alignment and political socialisation. The majority of the electorate were said to be socialised by family background into supporting either the Conservative or Labour Parties.**

Political socialisation

Family background plays a major part in the formation of political attitudes. According to *Butler and Stokes (1974)* there is a strong correlation between the political ideas of parents and those their children will eventually adopt. Tracking this **causal link** showed how family origin conditioned educational and occupational choice. Those who had economically secure family backgrounds and a good education tended to support the Conservative Party. Labour

Party supporters were drawn predominantly from those with less secure family and educational achievements.

These ideas connected **short** and **long** term social factors in a framework of voting behaviour and showed how a person's life experience – beginning with childhood — impacted on electoral choice. *Butler and Stokes (1974)* concentrated on the influences of housing, schooling and occupation. In their framework, *Rose and McAllister (1990)* included the influence of political values and party images.

Interpreting the vote

Explanations of voting behaviour have become more complex since the 1970s for the following reasons;

1 The tie between the electorate and the two main political parties has declined (**partisan dealignment**).

2 The specific class attachment to the Conservative and Labour Parties has weakened (**class dealignment**).

3 Voter **volatility** has increased to the point at which it is no longer accurate to talk about a competitive two party system. Three main parties, Conservative, Labour and Liberal Democrats compete for the vote, even if the simple majority system of election produces strong single party government.

Social, political and other factors have a bearing on electoral choice and these must be examined to complement the above features.

Social variables

The main social variables influencing political attitudes and the vote are: **age, gender, religion, ethnicity and class**. In the 2001 general election the Labour Party led the Conservatives in most of these categories, confirming long term volatility rather than conformity in the electorate.

Age

The connection between age and voting is subject to conflicting interpretations. It was generally accepted that the tendency to vote Conservative increased with age. Ageing is usually linked to the acquisition of more material prosperity and a general satisfaction with status quo. This conditions political outlooks which reflect in greater Conservative support. In the 2001 general election, Conservative support was weaker than Labour in every category except the 65 plus age group.

Butler and Stokes (1974) rejected the theory of **senescence** (literally, growing old) – of voters moving to the political right as they aged – as too simplistic. They noticed a tendency for the vote to be **immunised** or **conserved** against change in political attitudes. Literally, this would imply voters remaining with the party of their first choice with loyalty increasing as they grew older. The problem with this explanation is that if the young 'conserved' their vote (and they are more radical than the old), the electorate would be gradually radicalised, over the generations.

Gender

Women are not more Conservative than men, and this is not greatly significant in electoral terms. *Crewe* (*1985*) claimed that sex differences in the vote were of slight importance to the outcome of elections. This was supported by *Dunleavy and Husbands* (*1985*) who placed an estimate of five per cent difference between the sexes in terms of the vote.

In the 1960s and 1970s the gender gap between men and women voters favoured the Conservative Party. During the next decade its beneficial effects for Conservatism disappeared, only to resurface in the first general election of the nineties, 1992. By the 1997 general election it was impossible to detect a meaningful gender difference in the electorate although Labour had a slight lead (*Curtice 1997*). This pattern was repeated in 2001 with only women in the 55+ age group likely to vote Conservative. In the 2001 election 118 women were elected (95 Labour, 14 Conservative, 5 Liberal Democrat and 4 other) representing 18 per cent of the total of 659 MPs.

Religion

The connection between held religious attitudes and beliefs and party preference has received little attention from psephologists. There is sociological evidence of a decline in religious practice (**secularisation**), but it is difficult to tie this to political behaviour. Compared to Europe (France, Germany, and Italy, for example) the traditional link between religious and political attitudes in Britain is weak. The notable exception to this is **Northern Ireland** where Catholics support republican or socialist parties (Sinn Fein or SDLP) and Protestants support parties seeking to keep the United Kingdom link (Ulster Unionists).

Historically Labour received support from Non-conformists (Wesleyans and Presbyterians) in Wales and Scotland and it is still the dominant party in those regions. Catholics in England have supported the more radical Labour and Liberal Democratic Parties, whilst church-going Anglicans were said to lean towards the Conservative Party. The expression 'the Church of England is the Tory Party at prayer' links the established Church with the oldest political party, but there was never any institutional connection.

Ethnicity

Ninety per cent of the ethnic minority vote goes predominantly to the Labour Party for a variety of reasons. Labour are regarded as being more **sympathetic** to the interests of African/Caribbean, Asian and other ethnic groups partly because of their **attitude** to race relations. Of the race relations legislation passed to date, the laws controlling immigration (the Immigration Acts) have been enacted by Conservative governments. Those promoting race relations in the host society (the Race Relations Acts) have been passed by Labour governments.

Labour support is strong across the whole social spectrum of the black vote and connects with social class and party identification (*Layton-Henry 1992*). Voting Labour is often seen as a way of conforming to the predominantly working class position experienced by ethnic minority groups in general (**expressive voting**). One could expect therefore that those groups that have moved up the social class scale to turn towards conservatism. In the 2001 election all groups in the upper class categories AB voted preponderantly Conservative.

Although Labour again secured the support of the majority of this group in 2001, ethnic minorities are under-represented in the House of Commons with approximately one per cent of the House (12 Labour MPs) being returned in the general election. This might be reflected in the studies which show an increased apathy and reluctance to vote for any political parties by young British Asians (*Lee 1997*).

Class

Social class-based changes in electoral behaviour were first picked up in studies of the 1979 general election and tracked in all subsequent elections. Two writers, *Sarlvik and Crew* (*1983*), were instrumental in developing the related theories of partisan and class dealignment mentioned earlier.

- **Partisan dealignment** describes the general declining commitment to the main political parties as the electorate becomes more instrumental in the use of its vote. The two main parties' share of the vote declined from a 90 per cent average to a 75 per cent average from the 1970s to the 1990s.

- **Class dealignment** referred to the specific reductions in class-based voting for the Conservative and Labour parties, among the middle class and working class respectively. From the 1970s to 2000 middle class support for the

Conservative Party has declined from a four-fifths to a three-fifths share of the vote. Labour's share of the working class vote over the same period has fallen from two-thirds to less than a half. The results of the 1997 and 2001 general elections do not dispute this trend but according to *Curtice (2001)* voters are changing their behaviour because the choices on offer from the parties have changed. This is particularly the case with the shift from old to new Labour.

CHECKLIST

✓ **The main consequence of dealignment is the increase in electoral volatility as voter loyalty to the main political parties declines. Voters are more willing to switch from major to minor parties with the Liberal Democrats being the main beneficiaries. According to *Denver (1993)*, switching between Conservative and Labour is less common. This has repercussions for the appeal of the parties during election campaigns, as some floating voters are willing to be influenced. Such behaviour over the long term relates to how elections are fought and the political appeal of the parties during the campaign itself.**

✓ **The causes of dealignment are linked to the effects of the changing social structure and class society. Middle class political detachment from the Conservative Party is partially explained by the emergence of a new middle class or 'salariat' (*Wright 1976*). These middle class radicals work in public sector professions (teaching, social work and the civil service) and felt the insecurity of occupations dependent on public expenditure. In the 1997 general election these lower middle class or C1s swung heavily to Labour, a pattern repeated in 2001.**

✓ **Apart from the traditional explanations of working class Tory voting behaviour, the fall in support for the Labour Party is also explained by the fragmentation of that class. According to *Crewe (1985b)*, a new working class had emerged by the end of the seventies willing to support the radical programmes of Margaret Thatcher. This new class was predominantly more prosperous than the traditional working class and there were important differences in housing tenure, employment patterns, locality and disposable incomes, that affected the vote.**

The significance of these divisions of working class support was also heightened by occupational changes resulting in the decline of manual employment, traditionally important for the Labour vote. *Ivor Crewe*'s conclusions that dealignment had damaged the Labour Party were based on the **British Election Studies** of the 1979, 1983 and 1987 general elections. Labour faced the prospect of becoming a sectional party representing a shrinking fragment of the working class. The traditional working class were still Labour, but the new working class had no interest in socialist policies or a Labour government.

Ivor Crewe's pessimistic views of the effects of dealignment on the Labour Party were not shared by *Heath, Jowell and Curtice (1985 and 1987)*. They argued that the effects of dealignment had been exaggerated – the decline in Labour support since the 1960s was part of a **trendless fluctuation** of events rather than the result of any dramatic change in voting behaviour. The Labour Party could regain some of its lost working class support because class was still an important factor in the makeup of electoral choice.

The results of the 1997 and 2001 general elections showed that Labour could regain lost ground among the skilled working class voters (the C2s). These had supported the Conservative Party in the long run of election victories from 1979, and were regarded as an important target for any party.

Questions

1 Explain the deferential vote.

2 How does family background influence the vote?

3 Why did explanations of voting behaviour become more complex after the 1970s?

Political variables

Political variables influencing the vote are generally regarded as those not totally affected by social long term factors. The main ones are: issue or judgemental voting, political perceptions and the impact of electoral campaigns. All presuppose a rational model of voting behaviour which was rejected by traditional writers as too complex.

Issue or judgemental voting

The first identification of issue or judgemental voting was made by the sociologists *Himmelweit, Humphreys and Jaeger (1985)*. They suggested that electoral choice should be understood as the **deliberate** selection of parties, not as the product of long term political socialisation. In this **consumer** model of voting, the electorate decide on the relative merits of the parties largely on the issues. Traditionally in voter preference surveys the Labour Party does well on the issues of the welfare state, health and education; the Conservative Party on taxation, defence, and law and order. In 1997 Labour outperformed the Conservatives on all these issues, overcoming voter concerns which had kept them out of power for 18 years.

A party can therefore do well on the issues in the minds of the electorate but still lose elections. In 1987 Labour was ahead of the Conservative party on the main issues (jobs, health and education) but lost the election (*Crewe 1987*). Again in the 1992 general election, Labour did well in raising its issue profile — but the Conservatives still won. In the 2001 election voters preferred the Conservative Party on Europe and tax, yet Labour won the election *(Billinghurst 2001)*. The most important issues in this election were the National Health Service, education, Europe and tax; only the first two gave Labour a lead.

Political perceptions

Electoral perceptions of the political parties are an important influence on the vote (*Heath, Jowell and Curtice 1985*). Within these perceptions long term factors (political memory) and short term factors (reacting to government policies) will play a part. In the 1960s it was argued that the electorate were largely ignorant of the different ideologies of the respective parties – one reason why *Butler and Stokes (1974)* felt the complexity of issue voting could not replace class voting.

Although the electorate are ill-informed about politics, they are aware of what the parties stand for. Awareness of the **Labour Party** as **left** or **soft** and the **Conservative Party** as **right** or **hard** colours opinions. Before 1997 the electorate preferred Labour policies on welfarism and Conservative policies on the economy, but the higher priority on economic issues did not affect the outcome. After the 2001 election New Labour had successfully blurred these divisions. By moving to the centre stage it was no longer possible to predict what the party stood for in the minds of the electorate.

As the electorate become more **volatile** and **dealigned**, general elections have become tests of competence to govern rather than arguments between competing ideologies (socialism versus capitalism). Public confidence in a party's ability to govern or 'deliver the goods' is a crucially important winning factor. During the seventies the Labour opposition image was of a divided party, incompetent to govern or manage the economy. Conservative general election wins under **Margaret Thatcher** were based largely on economic **feel good** factors which had been absent in the early nineties. Using an econometric model, *Sanders (1993)* found a strong correlation between interest and inflation rates and continuous support for the Conservative Party. It is interesting that in the 1997 general election economic prosperity failed to attract votes to the Conservatives dogged by charges of sleaze and splits over Europe.

The impact of election campaigns

There are two different interpretations of the impact of election campaigns on voter attitudes:

1 The **traditional** sixties view of election campaigns was that they had little effect on the voter. This **neutral** view fitted well with the idea of a stable electorate bound by long term class loyalties to two main political parties. Relatively short term election campaigns would not affect the outcome.

2 The **modern** view of the impact of electioneering on electoral choice coincides with the rise of realignment and a more volatile electorate. If more voters are detached from the political parties (**floating voters**) or are undecided, short term factors like party performance in election campaigns will be **influential**. Since a considerable amount of vote switching, or 'churning', goes on during the campaign, more importance is attached to media presentation and 'packaging' of the respective parties. During the 1992 general election campaign, vote switching favoured the Conservative Party. It was estimated that 11.1 million voters changed their minds with an extra 3.2 million votes for the Conservatives against a loss of 1.81 million – a net gain of 1.39 million; enough to win the election. From the 1997 and 2001 elections the emphasis in campaigning in all parties was placed on 'spin', 'soundbites' and carefully managed political meetings. Labour measured the impact of its own campaign through focus groups which told it what its supporters were thinking.

Other variables

Regions

Geographical variations in the vote have long been a feature of British electoral politics. Support for the political parties varies from region to region even within social classes. A manual worker in the South-West of England is twice as likely to vote Conservative as one in Wales. From the late seventies a regional variation in the vote between the North and South of England (**the North–South divide**) became a regular feature of general elections.

FACTFILE

- **Writers at Essex University produced an explanation for the rout of Conservatism in 1997.**

- **This 'Essex Model' extrapolated economic influences on the vote overlain by political factors. Economic mismanagement and voters' perceptions of it, of what used to be called 'the feelgood factor', contributed to the Conservative defeat.**

- **The recession effects of the early nineties were still being felt by voters in 1997 – Blair's fronting of a New Labour government with 'neo liberal' policies tipped the balance away from a divided Conservative Party. (*Budge, Crewe, McKay and Newton 1998*)**

The North of England, Scotland and Wales became predominantly Labour whilst the South moved towards the Conservatives. **Social class** differences between the regions partially explain this effect with Labour working class votes concentrated in the North, Wales and Scotland. Another explanation offered by *Johnson and Pattie* (*1992*), concentrates on **economic factors**. They claim that regional vote variations follow the general patterns of economic development – areas of decline have moved towards Labour, those of prosperity towards the Conservatives.

A locality or neighbourhood influence on the vote was first documented by *Denver* (*1993*). The type of neighbourhood (working class/middle class) in which you live could condition electoral choice with Labour predominating in urban centres and Conservatives in rural or shire areas. *Peele* (*1995*) thought that locality acted as an independent variable on the vote partially explaining volatility. Critics of these theories argue that address is not a significant factor in the makeup of electoral choice. The results of the 1997 general election confirm some of these trends. The Conservatives lost all representation in Wales and Scotland (supporting the English party charge) and virtually all the urban areas and suffered inroads by Labour into its traditional strongholds in the south of England. Reversing an earlier truism, Labour was a more national party than the Conservatives – its support was spread more evenly and geographically across Britain, it broke out of its traditional working class localities and appealed to a wider class cross section of the population. In the 2001 general election Labour increased its strength in the London suburbs which had previously been Conservative strongholds before 1997. Paradoxically Labour's

share of the vote fell in many of its old strongholds in the North, Midlands, Scotland and Wales as the party swung towards the middle class breaking out of its old working class base.

The media

Election campaigns are largely fought in the media, with television playing a primary role closely followed by the press. If voting behaviour is the result of a complex mix of attitudes and values, then relatively short term media election campaigns are not going to be influential with 'hard' **loyal** voters. The greatest impact of television and press reporting of politics is on 'soft' or **floating** voters unattached to parties, but it is difficult to unpick the influences.

Academic research in this area is divided between sociological theories of media influence now augmented by political theories – reinforcement theory confirms political beliefs – agenda setting theory helps set beliefs – framing theory helps focus beliefs and direct effects theory directly conditions attitudes. (*Budge, Crewe, McKay and Newton 1998*)

The effect of the print media (newspapers) on voting behaviour is therefore problematic although it is thought to be stronger than the electronic media (TV and radio) (*Norris 1996*). In the 1992 general election Labour faced a generally hostile press but this did not greatly affect the outcome; the party was unpopular (*Heath, Jowell and Curtice 1994*). In the 1997 general election the majority of newspapers (tabloid and broadsheet) switched from Conservative to Labour endorsement. Tony Blair made a concerted effort to secure the backing of Rupert Murdoch's Sun and Times which together with the Express (owned by the New Labour peer Lord Hollick), Mirror, Guardian and Independent gave him an advantage in print media never before experienced by a Labour leader. It is important to focus also on the popularity of New Labour and the unpopularity of the Conservatives before conceding too much influence to this fact. A similar situation arose in the 2001 election with the red-tops or mass market Sun and Mirror newspapers heavily endorsing Tony Blair, together with the broadsheets, Guardian and Times. The Telegraph and Mail remained supporters of William Hague and the Independent refused to endorse any party.

Television reporting of politics is more politically balanced because of statutory controls and the public appear to accept this. *Trenaman and McQuail* (*1961*) claimed that television exposure during election campaigns was educational and it did not appear to condition political attitudes or the vote, even though people were informed of issues in the campaign. This was confirmed by later studies of media consumption which demonstrated that people tended to filter or screen political messages they were not receptive to (*Seymour-Ure 1974*). Although TV broadcasts may have favoured the Conservatives in 1997, this did not affect the result (*Golding and Deacon, 1997*). A downturn in turnout in the 2001 election may be connected to voter fatigue over the long three week campaign and growing disillusionment with politics. Certainly there is evidence that voters regard elections as a television turnoff particularly in the commercial sector which relies on advertising for revenue. The one contest that would have aroused the voters would have been a head to head debate between Tony Blair and William Hague mirroring the confrontation between George W Bush and Al Gore in the United States election of 2000. Unfortunately New Labour rejected the idea.

Sectoral voting

In a model of voting behaviour, *Dunleavy* (*1979*) explained voter preference by sectoral analysis. The Conservative electorate inhabited the **private** sector and the Labour electorate the **public**. Access to and consumption of education, transport, housing and employment varied from one sector to the other. The public utilised state provision of services; the private supplied their own. These were the conditioning factors in electoral choice. They conveniently fitted the Conservative ideology of **individualism** and the Labour ideology of **collectivism**.

Such a theory is now outdated as New Labour have deliberately moved away from collectivist ideology. By winning two elections, 1997 and 2001, on a centrist platform Tony Blair showed how aware he was of changes in class perceptions, ideologies and detachment of the average voter.

Questions

1 Why are issues important to the vote?

2 Do election campaigns influence the vote?

3 How important is the media to a political party's electoral fortunes?

The 2001 general election

The result of the 2001 general election was groundbreaking in many ways. Tony Blair became the first Labour Prime Minister to win a second consecutive term. Not since the days of Harold Wilson in the sixties had the same Labour leader returned to Downing Street. Another important factor in this result was the decline of voting. Turnout at just 59 per cent was the lowest at any election since 1918, a worrying

feature for British democracy and the first past the post electoral system.

	Total Number of Votes	MPs elected	Share of vote %
Labour	10,740,168	413	42
Conservatives	8,352,845	166	33
Liberal Democrat	4,815,249	52	19
Other	–	30	6.5

The 2001 general election result

The outcome of the 2001 general election with a second new Labour government was expected but the reduction in Labour's majority to 167 and the increase in Liberal Democratic seats to 52 was a surprise. Part of the explanation for this result lay in the boundary changes of 1997 which affected 500 constituencies and were still helping Labour.

According to *Peter Kellner (2001)* four factors served to deliver Tony Blair his second landslide.

1 The Conservatives continued to lose ground among the important middle class groups who matter most in battleground seats.

2 New Labour MPs defending seats did better than expected and may have benefited from incumbency.

3 Tactical voting hurt the Conservatives more than Labour as Liberal Democrats helped to dislodge William Hague's party.

4 The electoral system does not now give a close relationship between seats gained and votes cast. Labour achieved a 64 per cent share of House of Commons seats for only 42 per cent share of the vote.

John Curtice (2001) added academic analysis to this picture by noting that trends that first appeared in 1997 were expanded in 2001. First, the old left/right, Labour/Conservative division appears to have declined as Labour moves to the right. Second, a large minority of the electorate no longer bother to vote with turnout falling to 59 per cent. And third, the FPTP (first past the post) voting system may not now be capable of delivering alternate governments of differing political persuasion. The upshot of all this is that for the Conservatives to win the next election they would have to win at least 12 per cent more votes than Labour to secure a majority. A task made doubly difficult by the bias in the electoral system in Labour's favour.

Problems for the Conservatives

Even with the election of Iain Duncan Smith as new leader in 2001 the prospects for the Conservative Party do not look promising. If New Labour continue to attract the middle class vote it will be difficult for the Conservatives to achieve power in the future. The movement of Labour to the right and the continuance of Conservative economic policies also presents problems of presentation for the old party of the right. The Conservatives have got to reconstruct their electoral base and widen their appeal otherwise they risk repeating Labour's experience of long opposition in the seventies, eighties and nineties.

Problems for Labour and democracy

An increasingly apathetic electorate (turnout in the 2001 general election fell below 60% for the first time in a modern election) has posed problems for the Labour government and British democracy generally.

In March 2004 it was reported that the government were thinking of introducing compulsory postal voting in an effort to solve this problem. The Conservatives and other opponents are sceptical that such a measure will serve to reattach the electorate to the political system. The Electoral Commission (2004) suggested the lowering of the voting age to 16 would help political participation. Others are less convinced.

Apart from changing the first past the post system (which in itself could be a cause of apathy), the following ideas have all been floated as ways of increasing citizen participation in politics:

- Longer polling days, giving voters more time.

- Greater use of postal voting, which in experiments has increased turnout.

- More ballot stations in shopping malls and other places. Again successful where experimented with.

- Internet and text voting (so-called e-voting) is problematic as some people do not have access to computers or mobile phones.

Summary

1 Traditional studies of voting behaviour tended to focus on fairly simple social determinants of electoral choice, for example social class and political socialisation (family background and life experience).

2 Modern studies include the impact of secondary influences on the vote – political issues, instrumental or judgemental attitudes and changes in the social structure.

3 Although the long term trends in British voting behaviour since the sixties have been towards greater volatility or changeability in the electorate, this has not produced significant alternation in governments. Both major parties have had long spells in government, Labour with a broken run 1964/79 and the Conservatives from 1979 to 1997. Now Labour has achieved two successive spells in office from 1997 to 2001 and beyond.

4 This highlights a problem in psephology, that of extrapolating from the short to the long term. Studies of general elections are snapshots of political behaviour at any point in time. They are not predictions of future behaviour. The idea that politically people do not behave in rational predictable ways is still valid.

Sample questions and answers

AS Level questions

1 Define floating voters.
2 Why are floating voters important?

1 • *Define floating – uncommitted voters.*
   • *Look at their characteristics, explain why they float. Give reasons – volatility, apathy, disenchantment with government, policy appeal of other parties.*
   • *Most do not float between Conservative and Labour parties. Give reasons.*
2 • *Explain why they are important, provide the key to winning elections.*

- *Link with the idea of growing volatility in electorate, so becoming more numerous.*
- *Examine issues that cause voters to switch allegiance.*
- *Distinguish between long and short term factors affecting the vote.*
- *Describe Labour Party attempts to broaden appeal away from working class traditional support towards middle class.*
- *Look at Conservative government's 'feel good' factors and policies designed to attract and keep working class votes.*

Structures

The structure of local government in England and Wales at the end of the nineties is still essentially a **two-tier** system based on counties (the top tier) and districts (the lower tier). This broad division between two levels of local authority is an historical survival pre-dating the **1972 Local Government Act**, the first serious attempt to reform the structure. This Act was in turn partially based on the proposals contained in the Redcliffe–Maud Report of 1968.

The two-tier system of local government

Maud wanted to see a reduction in the 1,200 local authorities in England and Wales, which would be replaced by 61 large **unitary authorities** responsible for all services. In addition to this single tier system, recommendations were made for the establishment of eight **provincial councils** based on provinces of equal size. These were generally seen as a step towards regional government and possibly the beginning of a devolved system of power. These last proposals (the most radical) were not acted upon, implementation being left to the Conservative government of Edward Heath 1970–74. This government decided to implement a two tier system based on counties and districts, further subdivided between metropolitan and non-metropolitan areas. The **1972 Local Government Act** introduced 47 shire counties and six metropolitan counties providing major services, together with 333 rural (shire) districts and 34 metropolitan districts in England and Wales. London was separately organised from 1963 (London Government Act) into 33 borough councils and a Greater London Council. This system was further modified with the passing of the **1985 Local Government Act** which removed the Greater London

FACTFILE

The Redcliffe–Maud Commission was charged with examining the structure of local government with a view to making recommendations for its improvement. It was highly critical of the structures prevailing at that time, particularly:

- **Boundaries**
  Local government areas did not fit the pattern of life and work in modern Britain.

- **Division of responsibilities**
  The existing split in the delivery of services between local authorities led to fragmentation and division of responsibility which in turn made proper strategic planning impossible and uneconomic.

- **Population and resources**
  There was great disparity between population and resources. Some authorities served populations of 50,000, others up to 1 million. Functions were allocated along lines that made little administrative sense.

- **Size**
  Many local authorities were too small to function efficiently lacking qualified staffs and resources.

- **Local democracy and relations with central government**
  Possibly the most important findings of the Maud Commission (which would have far reaching effects with the Conservative governments of the eighties) were the criticisms relating to local democracy and central–local relationships.

The effects of the structural defects existing in local government were:

- **The public perceived local government as irrelevant, with a consequent increase in apathy.**

- **Central government ministers were reluctant to expand the powers of existing local authorities because of the inefficiencies in the system.**

Council and the metropolitan counties on the grounds of inefficiency. The removal of the Labour dominated Greater London Council and metropolitan counties paved the way for the introduction of a single-tier system providing all local authority services, which would become more influential into the nineties.

Source: The Association of County Councils

	FIRST TIER MAIN AUTHORITY Major services	SECOND TIER LOWER AUTHORITY Local services
47 Shire councils	✓	
333 Rural shire districts		✓
36 Metropolitan districts	✓	
33 London boroughs	✓	

The structure of local government 1985–95 (England and Wales)

Problems in the two-tier system

The changes introduced into the local government structure by the 1985 Local Government Act did not remove the problems which were inherent in the system. Although the functions of the Greater London Council and metropolitan counties were transferred to what in effect was a unitary (single) tier in those areas – and to separate agencies or boards (*Stewart 1995*) – the rest of the country was still administered locally through a complex mix of county, district and parish councils. For a variety of reasons (political and administrative) the central Conservative government were by 1992 anxious to move to a single-tier system (paradoxically rejected in 1972 by the same party) which would prove easier to control. Critics pointed to a number of remaining problems in the structure:

- From the perspective of local democracy (understanding local politics) the system was confusing.

- The provision of major services (education, housing, social services) from two levels of local authority made unnecessary fragmentations in what ought to be a 'seamless robe' or blanket covering the populace.

- Resources in terms of personnel and administration were partially duplicated by separate county and district councils serving the same area.

Politically, the Conservative government was anxious to see greater financial controls placed over local councils, and the removal of Labour dominance in much of local government. The abolition of the Greater London Council and the six metropolitan councils was seen by some critics as an attempt to remove Labour Party influence (Labour was the dominant party in those authorities) in what became oppositional authorities promoting **municipal socialism**. A further final change was the more radical attempt made to alter the culture of local government by the introduction of private business methods and outside contracting – in effect moving local authorities to **enabling** rather than **providing** authorities (*Isaac-Henry 1993*).

This ethos continued into the New Labour governments of 1997 and 2001 but with greater emphasis on community involvement and citizenship participation in the work of local authorities.

Review of unitary structures

Bowing to pressure from shire county representatives and other groups, central government agreed in March 1995 to reopen the whole question of the future of county councils threatened with abolition. In the review consultation process to December 1995

CHECKLIST

✓ To move local authorities in the direction of a single unitary tier system, the Conservative central government passed the Local Government Act 1992 and introduced a complex two and a half year review of existing structures.

✓ A Local Government Commission for England was established (absorbing the old Local Government Boundary Commission for England) under the chairmanship of Sir John Banham, later replaced by Sir David Cooksey from 1995.

✓ The original recommendations of the commission were for the establishment of 50 new unitary authorities (providing all services) with the dismantling of only seven out of 39 shire counties.

✓ By leaving the existing two tier county and district structures intact for the majority of the population the commission was creating a new three tier system across England and Wales but 'never in one area' (*Duvall 1995*).

the Secretary of State for the Environment, John Gummer, examined unitary plans for all the 39 English counties and agreed that with the exception of **Avon, Cleveland and Humberside** all other county councils would remain, even if in an altered format. In some counties large towns or districts were naturally hived off to form their own unitary authority, as with Milton Keynes' removal from Buckinghamshire. Both Buckinghamshire and Bedfordshire demonstrated that resourceful counties had influence with the Secretary of State by successfully removing the threat of abolition. Buckinghamshire (the last Conservative controlled county council in England and Wales at the 1993 council elections) had the support of former Cabinet Ministers Lord Carrington and Sir Ian Gilmour, and Bedfordshire was supported by Lord Pym with private backbench lobbying in both counties (*Arnold-Forster 1995*).

Evaluation of the new system

The introduction of what in effect is a 'hybrid' system of local government (a mix of two-tier and single-tier) has had a mixed reception. The intention of central government was to produce smaller authorities with average populations of 150,000 to 250,000 with regard to **local interests** and **efficient local government**. Early indications were that smaller unitary authorities would be less likely to provide full services, although in the words of *Sir John Banham*

(*1995*) larger authorities could 'take in each other's washing'. The Association of County Councils was critical of the costs of reorganisation and claimed that the hybrid system would be more expensive to run. In **Cleveland**, which was replaced in April 1996 by four successor unitaries (Hartlepool, Redcar and Cleveland, Middlesborough and Stockton-on-Tees), four new Directors of Education and Directors of Social Services, to take one example, added 25 per cent to salary costs (*Association of County Councils Briefing 1995*).

In the strongest academic criticism of the new structure *John Stewart*, Professor of Local Government and Director of the Institute of Local Government Studies (Inlogov), University of Birmingham, and *George Jones*, Professor of Government at the London School of Economics (*1995*), claimed the new system was an unnecessary mess. In their eyes the Banham Commission decisions were hard to justify on the grounds of consistency. By the end of 1998, according to *Copus (2001)* the whole system had become a patchwork of unitary and two tier structures with unitary authorities co-existing alongside counties, districts and London boroughs. By 2000 this was further complicated by the addition of an elected Mayor for London (Ken Livingstone) and a new Greater London Authority (GLA). There appears to be little uniformity in this structure and the Blair government since 1997 has concentrated on internal efficiency, democracy and citizen accountability rather than return again to this problem.

Managing local authorities

The committee system

The internal structures of local authorities bring together councillors (elected representatives) and officials (appointed professionals) in a policy-making and management system. Policy decisions of councils are based on a committee system with full council meetings as the ultimate authority. Management matters do not usually occupy a great deal of councillors' time (*Young and Rao 1993*). In practice (and this pattern has hardly changed) meetings of a full council handle reports or minutes from the various committees and sub-committees. Some are accepted with little debate; others arouse party political controversy and are returned to committees or sub-committees for amendment. Eventually policy-making votes are taken in full council which is dominated by the ruling political party – the one with most councillors.

Policy-making and committees

Although councils have a free hand in the structures of their committee systems, they generally reflect the departmental nature in the organisation of council work (*Hutt 1990*). Chief officers (responsible for the management and implementation of policy in their departments) report upwards to their respective committees and sub-committees, which make recommendations to a Policy and Resources Committee (since 1972) before final policy recommendations to the full council. As with central government bureaucracy, departmental rivalry (**departmentalism**) pervades this structure as officers seek to advance the interests of their departments over others. Coordination of these disparate committees is also a problem as councils seek to establish a **corporate identity**. Two reports drew attention to these problems: the Maud Report 1967 and the Bains Report 1972.

FACTFILE

- **The Maud Management Report 1967** The Maud Committee on Management in Local Government Report (1967) made radical suggestions to overcome problems of coordination and policy-making. Its main recommendations were:

  1 reductions in the number of committees to improve efficiency;

  2 establishment of a Management Board to assist coordination;

  3 clear separation of the respective duties of elected councillors and appointed officers.

  Although these proposals were not generally acted upon, they paved the way for the adoption of better management practices in local authorities after the publication of the Bains Report.

- **The Bains Report (1972)** The Bains Committee were expressly tasked with finding better management structures for the reformed two tier system of local government introduced by the 1972 Local Government Act. The report's main recommendations (1972) were for the creation of a Policy and Resources Committee interposed between the various council committees and full council meetings. In addition a chief executive position would be created, responsible for a senior management team following a corporate management policy. This procedure was the general pattern of management followed in most local authorities until the late nineties.

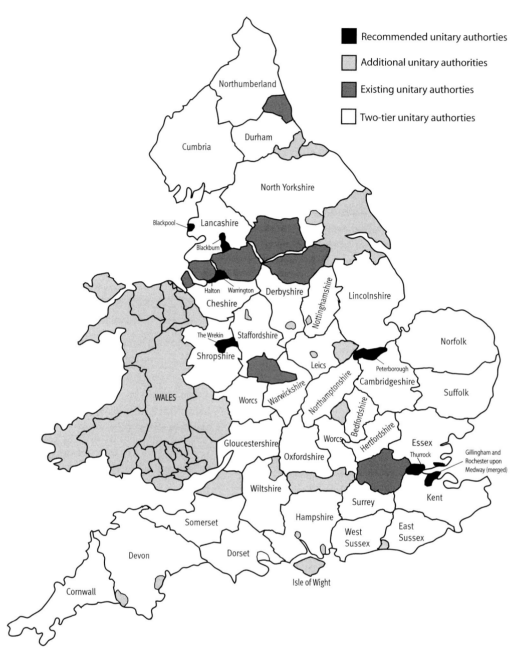

Legend:
- ■ Recommended unitary authorties
- ▫ Additional unitary authorities
- ▩ Existing unitary authorties
- ☐ Two-tier unitary authorties

Northumberland, Cumbria, Durham, North Yorkshire, Blackpool, Lancashire, Blackburn, Halton, Warrington, Derbyshire, Nottinghamshire, Lincolnshire, Cheshire, The Wrekin, Staffordshire, Shropshire, Leics, Norfolk, Peterborough, Cambridgeshire, Suffolk, WALES, Worcs, Warwickshire, Northamptonshire, Bedfordshire, Gloucestershire, Worcs, Hertfordshire, Essex, Thurrock, Gillingham and Rochester upon Medway (merged), Oxfordshire, Wiltshire, Surrey, Kent, Somerset, Hampshire, West Sussex, East Sussex, Devon, Dorset, Isle of Wight, Cornwall

Map based upon Ordnance Survey mapping with the permission of the Controller of Her Majesty's Stationery Office, © Crown copyright, Licence No 100019872.

	FIRST TIER MAIN AUTHORITY		SECOND TIER LOWER AUTHORITY
	England	Wales	England
County (shire) councils	✓		
Rural (shire) districts			✓
Unitary authorities	✓		
Unitary authorities		✓	
Metropolitan districts	✓		✓
London boroughs	✓		
Greater London Authority and London Mayor	✓		✓

The structure of local government (England and Wales) from 1997 and 2000.

The Cabinet system and changes to the committee structure

Following the Local Government Act 2000 many authorities restructured their organisations around a Cabinet system with a revised committee structure. Typical of this new structure for an upper tier authority is that introduced by Buckinghamshire County Council in 2001. Under the Buckinghamshire County Council Constitution the full Council elects the Leader of the Cabinet who in turn selects his/her deputy and Cabinet of seven other councillors. The Leader of the Cabinet is also Leader of the Council and his role includes the functions of leading the development of Council, policy and resource allocation, chairing the Cabinet, responsibility for Council services and budget planning, and representing the council externally. In all this he is assisted by a Chief Officer of Paid Services, together with a number of strategic managers representing the areas of resources that are in the Cabinet, namely Community, Resources, Adult Care, Schools, Children and Young People and Planning and Transportation. The main committee of the council is the Overview and Scrutiny Committee with sub-committees for Environment, Personal Care, Lifelong Learning, Partnership and Corporate Performance. In this structure we can find echoes of both the Maud and Bains Reports, and the preference for the executive leader and cabinet model. Other models put forward in the Act included the directly elected mayor and cabinet and the mayor and council manager.

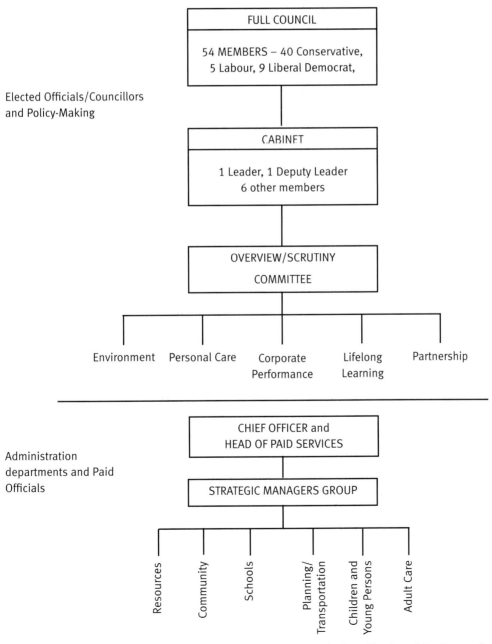

BUCKINGHAMSHIRE COUNTY COUNCIL

Elected Officials/Councillors and Policy-Making

FULL COUNCIL

54 MEMBERS – 40 Conservative, 5 Labour, 9 Liberal Democrat,

CABINET

1 Leader, 1 Deputy Leader 6 other members

OVERVIEW/SCRUTINY COMMITTEE

Environment   Personal Care   Corporate Performance   Lifelong Learning   Partnership

Administration departments and Paid Officials

CHIEF OFFICER and HEAD OF PAID SERVICES

STRATEGIC MANAGERS GROUP

Resources   Community   Schools   Planning/ Transportation   Children and Young Persons   Adult Care

The committee and departmental structure (after reorganisation 2001) of Buckinghamshire County Council

1 Give two problems in the two-tier system of local government.

2 What was the main objective of the Banham Commission 1992?

3 On what grounds did Professor John Stewart and George Jones criticise the unitary system?

4 Give one problem of the committee system in local government.

Councillor–officer relationships

Apart from a central government input, policy-making in local government reflects a compromise between councillors and their officials. The **orthodox view** of the relationship between elected councillors and paid officials is that policy-making (or the political role) rests with councillors and the administrative role with officials. Yet policy and administration (as with central government) are very closely connected. Council staffs are **professionals**; councillors are **amateurs**. Departmental senior staff advise council and are bound to influence decisions.

Policy identification

If policy-making in local government jointly involves both councillors and officers (the Bains Committee felt it should), then officials can be publicly identified with council politics. Alternatively, it could be argued that officials and councillors formed an **elite** government in their own interests (*Stoker 1991*). This view is in turn countered by the idea of competing centres of power (**pluralism**) within the administrative and policy structures of local authorities. On this level there are too many other interests to be dominated by a single elite.

Policy disputes

The emphasis on management and policy implementation in local councils has produced a breakdown in some councils of the traditional trust between officers and councillors (**mutuality**). This was first noticed during the governments of Margaret Thatcher 1979–1990 as 'conviction' Conservatives entered local councils determined to implement central philosophies. Urban socialists, for their part, were determined to oppose central government policies also (*Gyford 1985*). *Laffin and Young* (*1990*) first pointed to the difficulties faced by councillors required to implement policies of which they personally disapproved.

Increasingly, radical politicians of both Conservative and Labour persuasion have taken a greater interest in the implementation of policy in addition to its initiation. **Partisan conduct** is said to reach considerable numbers of councillors as they place party interests above representational work. This manifests itself in the attendance of officials at party group meetings and the acceptance of councillor participation in the management practices of local councils (*Young and Davies 1990*). This is a continuing problem in local government organisations to which both councillors and officers have had to adapt. The new structures introduced after the Local Government Act 2000 partially addressed this problem.

Democracy in local government

The local democracy argument has always featured in defences of the system of local government in England and Wales. Local councils and councillors as elected representatives are seen as an essential part of the democratic process, even if interest in their work is low by international standards. The Banham Committee Report (1994) emphasised the importance of local democracy in the drive to smaller unitary authorities, but did not tackle the question of the British electoral system which is held by some as partially responsible for local apathy (*Rallings and Thrasher 1994*). Equally, there is said to be no absolute correlation between the size of a local authority and increased interest in local affairs (*Newton 1982*).

Participation

The generally held belief is that local government should be accessible and close to the people it serves. If people are to be encouraged to **participate**, local government boundaries should reflect local community feelings. Part of the reason why counties like Humberside have disappeared in the Banham Review (the Local Government Commission for England was directed by government to consult all the people in the affected counties) was presumably because local opinion sought the removal of a remote (and unnecessary) authority created in 1972. The people of Kingston upon Hull, the East Riding of Yorkshire, North Lincolnshire and North East Lincolnshire – from 1996 recreated as four unitary councils – never lost their attachment and feelings of identity with the smaller units.

Developing the ideas of attachment to localities, *Gyford* (*1991*) draws attention to three dimensions of local involvement:

1 **Participative** – the involvement of the local electorate in council decisions.

2 **Consultative** – where local authorities make an effort to establish what local people want.

3 Informative – a relationship where local councils endeavour to keep their citizens informed of local services in the most convenient ways possible.

Participation became a feature of the Blair government's modernising agenda for local government after 1997. Seeking to establish ever closer ties between communities and the local authority services provided, they set out their plans in the document 'Local Democracy and Community Leadership' in 1997. A number of ideas were put forward for local authorities to adopt to bring closer citizen involvement, including citizen juries, focus groups, community forums and local referendums. Councils are beginning to put these mechanisms into place but by 2001 and 2002 many had yet to do so.

Political impacts

Local government is now totally dominated by national politics. There clearly is a Conservative, Labour or Liberal Democratic way of running councils (**politicisation**) and local electorates' perceptions of councillor value have been taken over by national political concepts (**nationalisation**). It is difficult to put a precise date on these developments; *Gyford, Leach and Game* (*1989*) have tracked national party political involvement in local councils and demonstrated how the national Conservative and Labour Parties came to dominate local politics after 1945. Some consequences of this are:

■ **Many councillors** are returned unopposed in local elections. (All councillors serve four year terms. County councils have whole elections; districts elect by thirds.)

■ **Local apathy** is strong – the Widdicombe Report (1986) found turnout in British local elections at between 20 per cent and 60 per cent at the bottom end of international league tables.

■ **Local voting** behaviour focuses more on national issues than local, although there is contradictory evidence for this.

The arguments

The arguments against party politics in local government now seem dated if only because of the activities of radical right and left councils since the eighties. The dependence on party labels for electoral success discourages those not standing on a party ticket. The quality of candidates for local office may be lessened by this reduction of recruitment area. The relational problem concerns the conduct of council business. The argument that party political considerations should not be allowed to affect administrative detail is clearly over. With the changing cultures of councils, the impact of the current unitary

reforms and development of the 'enabling' concept, the debate has moved on. Now the **positive attributes** of party involvement in council business (defining local issues clearly for the electorate, greater participation through encouragement to get involved, the advantage of party discipline giving coherence to the programme) are joined in structural debate over a **revival or decay** of local government and what 'business' it is in (*Isaac-Henry 1993*).

Central-local relations

The constitutional position

Local government is a form of **self-government** in the sense that local authorities are given considerable independence from the centre. Relationships between these two levels of government (both impacting on the citizen) traditionally involved a delicate balance between control and independence; partnership and separation. Controls fall into three areas – **parliamentary, judicial** and **executive** although local authorities do not have three sets of controllers.

Parliamentary control

The powers of local authorities are conferred by parliamentary statutes emanating from central government. Councils therefore work within the broad general framework of central government policy. They do not legislate except in the sense of local by-laws which are also subject to executive controls.

Judicial control

Judicial control over local government is not as significant as in the early nineteenth century because of the development of central control. The courts can rule local authority power as being beyond its statutory remit or '*ultra vires*'. In 1981 the courts rejected the GLC's argument for subsidising public transport in the 'Fares Fair' case. They can also decide whether matters are within the competence of a local authority.

Executive control

Executive or administrative control over local government is substantial and covers all the activities of council work.

The theoretical position

As the functions of local government have changed, so the traditional relationship between the centre and localities has had to adapt. Under a unitary form of central government, local authorities cannot be completely independent units administering services irrespective of the policy dictates of the majority party in government. On the other hand, local government

CHECKLIST

The following are the more important executive controls over local government.

✓ **Controls over service provision** to maintain standards in, for example, education, child protection and social services. This embraces reserve or default power to supply services if local councils refuse and includes an inspection power over education and children's services.

✓ **Control over local government officials** Under the Local Government Act 1972 central government laid a broad duty over local councils to employ certain officials including Chief Education Officers and Directors of Social Services. Some of these appointments have detailed ministerial control over the types of people that can be employed. The Department of Social Security approves the qualifications of Directors of Social Services and the Home Secretary approved the appointment of Chief Constables when police authorities were under the control of local government. (They are now run as separate autonomous combined authorities.)

✓ **Ministerial approval** Local authorities require ministerial approval for a long list of functions including development planning, compulsory purchase orders and settlement of dispute between individuals and councils.

✓ **Financial control** The financial controls over local government are now quite significant and include expenditure capping, council tax regulation and standard spending assessments, all designed to bring council tax spending within central government plans for public expenditure. In addition, control over spending and value for money is examined by the Audit Commission established by the Local Government Finance Act 1984 to replace the traditional district auditor system.

enshrines important principles of local democracy and does not simply act as an agent of central government. These various positions find expression in theoretical models that place a differing emphasis on local power (**localism**) in its relationship to central authority (**centralism**). We can identify four models in the theory of the central–local relationship.

1 **Oppositional view** Many councils (mainly, but not entirely, Labour led) saw the growth of central government powers over local government as reducing local autonomy, particularly in the fields of education and social service provision. This attitude produced a deterioration in the relationship between the Department of the Environment and many councils. In April 1995 some councils were prepared to set illegal budgets because central government refused to finance in full the teachers' pay settlement that year. Councils were told to make administrative cost savings to find the money.

2 **Partnership view** The traditional picture of central–local relations is as a partnership with each side bringing different skills to the table. The Redcliffe–Maud Report of 1968 clearly defined central government responsibilities as focusing on provision of a standardised service, or where decisions could only be taken at the national level. Local government was best suited to provide services (like education) where the level of local opinion was important even if this should be done within a framework of national policy-making.

3 **Power-dependence view** This position tends to focus on the central–local relationship as one of consultation. Each level of government has its own power base which it can use in negotiation with the other side. Central government is not all powerful and local government is not powerless; they are mutually dependent on each other. A good example of this relationship is provided by the annual meetings of the Consultative Council on Local Government Finance (first established by the Labour government of 1975) which brings together the Secretary of State for the Environment and leaders of the counties, districts and metropolitan authorities in discussions of future council spending settlements.

4 **Agency view** Despite the above comments some writers feel that central–local relations today are characterised by an agency relationship where local authorities carry out functions entirely controlled and financed by central government (*Isaac-Henry 1993*). Under the Conservative governments to 1997 the trend for local government to act as an agent of central government became more marked, particularly in the areas of finance, functions and roles.

- **Finance** Central government controls over finance have increased with the replacement of the community charge by the **council tax** in 1993. **Standard spending assessments** (SSAs) have been introduced as the basis for the calculation of local authority grants. Finally, **capping** (since 1991) has been used to restrict the amount local councils can raise by the council tax. These three features – plus the activity of the Audit Commission – are devices now restraining local government finance and overspending.

- **Functions**   Possibly the biggest single change affecting the function of local councils was the introduction of market forces techniques into the supply of services. The free market was seen as the most efficient way of serving the customer. The 1988 Local Government Act introduced the practice of **compulsory competitive tendering** (CCT) which places a duty on local councils to allow outside contractors (in some cases council direct labour organisations can be considered) to bid for the provision of services in a competitive manner. Here the intention was to achieve two things: a) drive down council costs by purchasing the cheapest service and b) treat the elector as a consumer buying services that provided the best value for money. CCT was replaced in January 2001 by the Best Value programme as part of New Labour's modernising initiative. Although the compulsory element to involve private sector deliverers of local services was removed councils were still obligated to secure the most economic and efficient way of providing these services. And the fact that central controls have increased rather than decreased has lead commentators to conclude that Best Value reinforces the agency viewpoint *(Copus 2001)*.

- **Role**   The overall role of local government was reduced under the Conservative governments of Margaret Thatcher and John Major. Where services could not be contracted out, as with education, social services and housing, attempts have been made to break up the bureaucratic nature of local authority provision. Local government monopoly in educational provision has been broken into by the introduction of local management of schools allowing direct control over budgets and by opt-outs (grant maintained schools) allowing independence from local government control. The effects of this one change forced some councils to drastically reduce their headquarters educational staffs as services have been amalgamated. The 1988 Housing Act further reduced local government freedom in council housing adding to the right to buy scheme allowing tenants to purchase local authority housing. This Act specifically introduced the idea for the first time that local authorities should be enablers of housing rather than

providers by allowing private sector landlord competition into the municipal housing market *(Gray and Jenkins 1994)*.

Questions

1 Explain the terms 'Conviction Conservative' and 'Urban Socialist'.

2 Briefly describe the local democracy argument.

3 Give one consequence of party politics in local councils.

4 Briefly, what is New Labour thinking on local government?

The future

Since the election of the first Labour government in 1997 many changes in local government have been introduced. Labour remains committed to the unitary structures but is slowly overhauling local authority management to keep the distinctions between policy and its implementation. New Labour originally promised referendums in the localities to test the popularity of the introduction of elected English regional assemblies and although eight appointed Regional Development Agencies (RDAs) were set up in 1999, this pledge had not been implemented by late 2001. Labour is not yet convinced that there is a demand for popularly elected English regional councils although it conceded the argument for Scottish and Welsh separate assemblies. The election of the London Mayor and Greater London Authority was partially a response to bottom up demands for more public participation in the governance of London which had been removed with the abolition of the Greater London Council by Margaret Thatcher. New Labour also has plans which include the creation of elected mayors with executive powers in other English cities after referendums to test these ideas. It remains to be seen if the second Blair government will find the legislative time or political will to carry out these and other reforms.

Since 1998 the Labour Government has designated the most efficient local authorities as 'beacon councils'. These are meant to act as models to the rest and are rewarded with additional funds. One further development under New Labour has been the establishment of 'cabinet' systems of control in many local councils, recommended in the 1998 White Paper 'Modern Local Government: In Touch with the People'.

Developments and the second Blair government

Criticisms have been raised against the council tax system of local taxation. A current review of local government finance is expected to recommend changing to a hybrid system based on property values and incomes. This could be introduced after the next general election in 2005.

The local mayors system has not been a success for the government. By 2003 only 12 out of 30 areas had voted for an elected mayor and the Labour Party lost in over half the contests. This may have influenced Tony Blair in his decision to re-admit Ken Livingstone to the Labour Party so he could seek re-election as

London Mayor in May 2004 as the official Labour candidate. This development represented a U-turn on the part of Tony Blair who initially opposed Livingstone's election in 2000.

Regional Assemblies have yet to be introduced and the first referendums are due to be held in 2004. There appears little public enthusiasm for yet another change to the already complex structures of English local government.

Summary

1. **The study of local government (traditionally from a public administration perspective) is now over-complex because of the numerous structural reforms that have been implemented in the last decades.**

2. **The effect of these reforms arising out of the Conservative government's review of local government continued to be felt throughout the late 1990s.**

3. **Substantial changes have also been introduced into the traditional central–local relationship** **(now moving back to an agency model) and in the ethos of local government as a provider of the sub-national services to local populations.**

4. **In keeping with Conservative market thinking, the attempt (as with the civil service) was to move local authorities towards enabling arrangements whereby they controlled services bought in from private contractors.**

5. **Some of these features have continued with New Labour, from 1997 and 2001, which has its own modernising agenda for local government.**

Sample question and answer

A2 Level question

1   Is there any pattern to local government structural reform?

There has never been a time when local government has not been subject to some degree of change in the powers delegated to it, the structures within which it operates or the overall pattern of financing. From the nineteenth century to the present, local government has been subject to a bewildering series of changes which developed a subordinate system of government acting on the citizen at the local level. Central government concentrated on national administration and was content for most of the first half of this century to leave local decisions affecting people to locally elected councils to administer. Education, housing, environmental protection, social care and other immediate services were delivered by local governments to citizens within recognisable boundaries of counties or districts.

As population pressures on resources grew, so local councils became more dependent on central government grants to assist locally raised revenues (rates). Inevitably governments of both Labour and Conservative persuasions would have to tackle problems of resources, needs and structures against changes in consumption patterns, living and working arrangements. The first governments in the modern period to tackle these problems were the Labour governments of Harold Wilson in the 1960s.

The Wilson government of 1964–66 faced the problem of irrationality in the various structures of local government (counties, county boroughs, rural districts, urban districts) which had not been reformed structurally since its inception in the 1880s. By setting up the Redcliffe–Maud Commission (1966–69) Harold Wilson hoped to find a rational solution to the problem of duplication, confusion and inefficiency in the administration of local government services, caused by population changes, transportation developments and increasing demand. Although the government accepted Maud's recommendations for a single tier unitary system as the most efficient form possible (including the proposal for regional reorganisation), it was left to the incoming Edward Heath Conservative government of 1974 to implement any accepted changes.

Cont.

The basic structure of a two-tier system that is still in existence (in modified form) has its origins in the adaptations made by the Heath government to the Maud proposals of 1969. This government introduced the first major structural change to local government with the Local Government Act 1972 bringing in a two-tier system based on counties and districts. London government had previously been reformed with the London Government Act 1963 setting up a Greater London Council and 32 London borough councils sharing services with education in the centre run by an Inner London Education Authority. These London councils (mainly Labour dominated) would be abolished in 1986 by another Conservative government following more right wing principles than those adopted by the Heath government.

Throughout the second Labour administration of Harold Wilson 1974–76 and that of James Callaghan 1976–79 relations between central and local government continued in the traditional partnership pattern with regular consultation between the two sides. For example, the Consultative Council on Local Government Finance was established in 1975 bringing together for the first time central government ministers in direct talks with local government representatives. However, by the end of this period the Labour government had begun to restrict local spending by reducing the levels of rate support grants from 1974. This in turn paved the way for the considerable changes that would be introduced by Margaret Thatcher and her radical reforming Conservative government.

The government of Margaret Thatcher (1979–90) adopted a radically different perspective to local government from its Labour predecessors. It had a mandate to overhaul the rates system of local finance and was also determined to continue the restrictions placed over local government spending in line with its general drive to restrict public expenditure. The rates as a form of local taxation badly in need of reform had been examined by the Layfield Committee in 1977 who suggested their replacement by a local income tax. This proposal was not acted upon – instead a community charge (or poll tax) was introduced in 1986. The object of this new charge was to spread the cost equally on all users of local government services in line with New Right Conservative thinking irrespective of incomes or situation.

Other changes introduced into the local government dimension by the Conservative government (it has been estimated that approximately 124 Acts of Parliament passed during the 1980s had some effect on local government) included the abolition of the Greater London Council and the metropolitan counties in 1986, in effect establishing single tier authorities in those areas. Although these councils did duplicate some of the work taken on by the lower tiers and were removed because they were seen as an unnecessary burden on local government finance, critics have linked this action to the philosophical position taken by Margaret Thatcher that these councils were oppositional to her overall policies because they were invariably controlled by the Labour Party. There is evidence to show that the GLC and metropolitan counties were led by new 'urban socialists' determined to use local government as a challenge to the dominance of a radical Conservative government at the centre. Some of the policies of these councils were therefore seen as extravagant and responsible for the high costs of running councils in those areas.

Following a radical programme of 'conviction' politics, Margaret Thatcher began the process of altering the role of local government away from provider to enabler of services within the passage of various Acts. The Local Government Planning and Land Act 1980 began the process of compulsory competitive tendering (CCT) and market testing, whereby local authorities were obliged to contract out certain services including highway repair, grounds maintenance, catering provision and cleaning services. From the early eighties council tenants were given the right to buy council houses and the Housing Act of 1988 reduced further the role of local government housing by encouraging the activities of Housing Action Trusts. The last major service of local government, education, was also radically altered by the Education Act 1989. Now schools were encouraged to operate in a market for services by being allowed to opt out of local authority control through local management; the ultimate intention being to secure the opting out of all schools from local authority control.

The Major government from 1990 further adapted and redefined many of the above changes impacting on local government. Possibly the most significant reform was the removal of the unpopular community charge in April 1993 and its replacement by a more acceptable council tax

Cont.

Sample question and answer *cont.*

based on ability to pay. In addition, John Major continued with the capping arrangements introduced to control council spending together with standard spending assessments which restricted the level of grants paid by central government to the councils.

The final reform introduced by the Major government with implications through 1996 and 1997 was the passing of the Local Government Act 1992. This Act established the Local Government Commission for England under the chairmanship of Sir John Banham (Sir David Cooksey from 1995) charged with examining the existing shire county system of local government. Its main recommendation was the creation of 50 new unitary authorities but keeping the majority of existing counties. This 'hybrid' system has attracted its own critics who do not see how it solves the structural problems still remaining in local

government. As the Banham Commission responded to local opinion by surveying all those affected, it cannot be charged with being unresponsive to the local democracy argument.

Local government has given the appearance of being continuously reformed throughout the eighties and nineties because Conservative governments have tackled long overdue problems in finance, structure and central–local relations. If a date had to be found when local government ceased to be purely 'administrative' and became 'political', one would choose 1979 with the election victory of Margaret Thatcher and her new brand of Conservatism. This government (for ideological reasons) was determined to change the face of local government from the traditional decentralised partnership arrangement towards centralised agency status. The Labour government from 1997 has continued reforming local government.

In this chapter you will revise:

- The impact and influence of membership of the European Union on British political life.
- The effects of European Union membership on parliamentary and political sovereignty.
- How the European debate has divided the Conservative and Labour Parties.
- The constitutional implications of Britain's continued membership of the European Union.

- **Supranational** – the process whereby European institutions are created over and above the institutions of the nation states with powers that are superior to those of each constituent country.
- **Intergovernmental** – a Europe based on a system of confederal institutions whereby each constituent member state is able to veto policy that is contrary to their national interests.
- **Deepening** – the passing of European Acts which take the European Union closer down the road of integration to a federal or supranational structure.
- **Widening** – expanding membership of the European Union to include the poorer industrial countries of Europe which increases problems of economic, political and social integration.
- **EMU** – European Monetary Union of the 15 member states of the EU. Process began on 1st January 1999 and those states accepting will circulate the EURO currency from 2002. National currencies will be withdrawn.

Development of the European Union

The origins of the European Economic Community (EEC) – the term European Union (EU) was not adopted until after the passing of the Treaty on European Union, or Maastricht Treaty, in 1992 – lie in the post-war economic arrangements primarily agreed between Germany and France in the Schuman Plan of 1950. Although British Prime Minister Winston Churchill was instrumental in floating the idea of a United States of Europe as early as 1946, both Labour and Conservative governments kept Britain out of European arrangements because of commitments to the Commonwealth and a special relationship with the United States. As a result, the six European powers (France, Germany, Italy, Belgium, The Netherlands and Luxembourg) established the **first supranational institution**, the European Coal and Steel Community (ECSC), in 1952. This was closely followed by the creation of the European Atomic Energy Community (EURATOM) and the European Economic Community (EEC) in 1958. The primary objective of these early organisations (established by separate treaties of Rome and merged in 1967) was economic – to bring about increases in trade by the abolition of barriers and customs duties and the free movement of goods in a common market. The secondary objective was political – a hope that these trading nations would move towards a closer union as they transferred powers of regulation to the supranational EEC (*Geddes 1993*). It was this factor that successive British governments found objectionable.

British attitudes to Europe

Apart from opposition to the EEC for reasons of trade, successive British governments were opposed to membership on the grounds that **national sovereignty** would be damaged. By agreeing to join the EEC, countries were subjugating their Parliaments to the supranational organisations of the EEC. The British preferred to negotiate from the point of intergovernmentalism, maintaining state identities through the use of a veto in protection of national interests should that prove necessary. Fortunately the adoption of the 1966 Luxembourg Compromise introduced the idea of consensus or unanimity voting in place of qualified majority voting in the institutions of the EEC, which softened the effects of supranationalism taking it partly towards intergovernmentalism which was more acceptable.

After two unsuccessful attempts (1961 and 1967) Britain finally joined the EEC in 1973 under the Conservative government of Edward Heath, a committed European. By clinging to the intergovernmental idea, the British Conservative government of Edward Heath and Labour government of Harold Wilson (from 1974) were able to sell the idea of EEC membership to a sceptical public and the anti-Europeans. From this perspective the initial difficulties of British membership could be presented as worthwhile. They included:

1   High cost of subscription in the short term as a new member.

2   Loss of cheaper food sources from the Commonwealth as EEC tariffs were applied.

3   Less benefit from the Common Agricultural Policy (CAP) because British farming was efficient.

4 Acceptance of existing EEC regulations developed before Britain was a member.

On the important question of national sovereignty, the Heath government was able to claim that British sovereignty was not affected because ultimate sanction still rested with the Westminster Parliament rather than the EEC.

British membership of the EEC was popularly tested in a referendum by Edward Heath's successor, Harold Wilson, in 1975. By voting to stay in the Community (67 per cent were in favour) the British electorate helped Harold Wilson overcome difficulties in his own Cabinet and party over attitudes to the EEC. These would not be solved until opposition to Margaret Thatcher's Conservative government from 1979 convinced the Labour Party that the institutions of the EEC could keep socialism alive because the left played a significant role in the making of pro-Labour Community legislation.

Margaret Thatcher and relations with Europe

On one level Margaret Thatcher's attitudes to Europe damaged British relations with the EEC. Her insistence on securing a fairer British contribution to the whole EEC budget increased European opposition to her inside the Community. To some she was a 'little Englander', intent on securing the interests of the British nation state against the rest. Others saw her opposition to the Social Charter – she called it the 'Socialist Charter' – as signifying philosophical distance from the important social and labour relations protections fought for in Europe. (John Major would later sidestep the Social Charter in negotiations over Maastricht.) But it was opposition to the European Monetary System (EMS) that would contribute to her removal from the leadership of the Conservative Party. After being persuaded to accept full British membership of the EMS against her will in 1990, both her Chancellor, Nigel Lawson, and her Foreign Secretary, Sir Geoffrey Howe, resigned. Apparently neither could accept Margaret Thatcher's vision of a politically broader (wider) and shallower Europe (*Jones and Robins 1992*).

Questions

1 Name the three approaches facing the British government in relations with the EU.

2 What major factor kept successive British governments out of Europe?

3 How did the Heath government present the question of sovereignty to the public after joining the EEC?

4 Briefly summarise Margaret Thatcher's attitude to Europe.

Impact of Maastricht

Developments within the EEC during the 1980s proceeded on two fronts. Firstly, three new states were allowed to join, **widening** the Community: Greece in 1981 and Spain and Portugal in 1986. Secondly, Jacques Delors (President of the European Commission until 1994 when he was replaced by Jacques Santer) pushed the EEC into closer integration (**deepening**) by publicly declaring his intention that the EEC would develop along federal lines towards a single European currency and common foreign, economic and social policies by the end of the century. It is interesting that after he retired from office, Jacques Delors backtracked on this commitment by attacking the concept of closer European integration and the Maastricht Treaty itself (*Delors 1995*). Despite these comments, the passage of the Single European Act (SEA) of 1987 increased the commitment to economic integration and the Treaty on European Union (Maastricht Treaty) of 1992 took the process a stage further.

The European Union

Ratification of the Maastricht Treaty was a long, complicated process because of opposition to closer integration in all countries of the EEC. Referendums were held in France, Denmark and Ireland, but not in Britain which relied on executive endorsement through the House of Commons. John Major managed to secure a number of concessions in the treaty which helped him placate Euro-sceptical opponents in the Conservative Party. The final text of the treaty referred to 'closer union' rather than a federal arrangement; acceptance of the Social Chapter was removed by placing it in a separate protocol; Britain secured an 'opt-out' clause to the single European currency idea; and finally the **principle of subsidiarity** was conceded. This last concession, which meant that the Community would only take action if the member states could not achieve the objective on their own, was an important recognition of the growth of **elitism** in the European Union. It was claimed that the drive to further European integration was led by the political elites rather than the ordinary members of the constituent states (*Lynch 1993*). Subsidiarity, therefore, was seen as a basis for reducing the powers of the European institutions in favour of the separate countries and could be taken as part of an intergovernmental process.

Monetary union

Economic and monetary union (EMU) was possibly the most controversial aspect of the Maastricht Treaty and both Denmark and Britain were able to secure opt-out clauses until 1997. The plans for EMU call for the abolition of national currencies to be replaced by the **ECU or the EURO** (the name from 1996) and the establishment of a European Central Bank to regulate these currencies and decide interest rates.

CHECKLIST

The process of currency integration had three stages:

✓ **Stage one – set from 1990 when member states had to prepare for convergence of their economies. By 1995 some members were already experiencing difficulties in meeting the criteria.**

✓ **Stage two – from 1994 member states had to adopt common policies on interest rates, price stability and inflation. Again, Britain's leaving the Exchange Rate Mechanism in September 1992 (Black Wednesday) raised difficulties over this policy aspect.**

✓ **Stage three – the third and final stage began in 1996. By 1997 it was decided that the Euro would be introduced on 1st January 1999. Britain now under a Labour government would not join EMU in the first wave but Robin Cook the Foreign Secretary suggested it could be by 2002. Both French President Jacques Chirac and European Commission President Jacques Santer thought Britain would join the single currency at that time.**

European Union institutions

Decisions of the European Union are made in five basic institutions which reflect both **supranational** principles (no veto over decisions by member states) and **intergovernmental** arrangements (individual countries can have a veto if they perceive decisions to be against their state interests). The five institutions are the European Commission, the Council of Ministers, the European Council, the European Parliament and the European Court of Justice.

European Commission

The European Commission is the permanent executive body of the EU comprising 20 representatives or officials from the member states. It acts like a bureaucracy servicing the EU but has wider powers. Its main role is initiation of policy for European legislation and it tends to look at issues from a Europe-wide rather than narrow state perspective. It is often criticised for failing to respond to members' interests or having too much power. Commissioners are given responsibilities for particular policy areas – energy, transport, fisheries, science and agriculture are examples – and are expected to place the intergovernmental interest first. In the December 1995 meeting of the Commission Fisheries Committee negotiating national fish quotas, Britain had to abide by the qualified majority voting and needed the support of two other countries to change the proposals. The Commission spokesperson emphasised that the proposed drastic quota

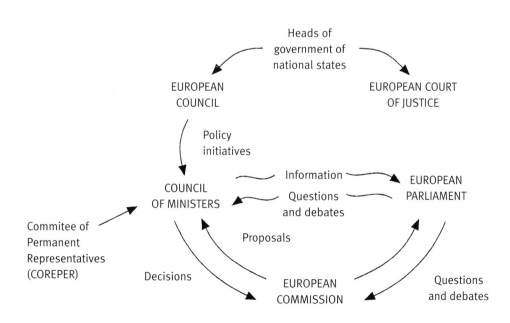

The institutions of the European Union

restrictions being imposed were in the best interest of all European fishermen and that Britain was not being singled out for special treatment (*Bates 1995*).

Council of Ministers

The main decision-making body of the EU is the Council of Ministers made up of ministers from the 15 member states. The Council meets in **different formations** (in effect separate councils) according to the policy under discussion, for example the Council of Economic and Finance Ministers brings together the ministers responsible for finance in the member states. Its main work comprises approval of Commission proposals and the issue of regulations and directives which are binding on all EU members. The voting procedure is a majority system which means member states cannot overrule decisions reached. The Councils are assisted in their deliberations by a Committee of Permanent Representatives (COREPER) which acts as a secretariat preparing papers and agenda. Occasionally decisions taken in COREPER are accepted by full council meetings with very little change.

European Council

European Council meetings bring together the heads of government of the separate member states to settle strategic decisions for the whole European Union. They are mainly used to break policy disputes in the EU or decide important new policy directions. The European Monetary System, the Single European Act and Treaty of the European Union (Maastricht) were all decided by heads of government meeting in council session in the country of the member state holding the EU presidency.

European Parliament

The European Parliament (EP) is not a Parliament in the strict legislative sense – the Commission initiates policy which is approved by the Council of Ministers – but it has certain basic powers. It can offer opinions on legislation, examine the work of the Commission and Council, influence the EU budget and theoretically dismiss the Commission. These original consultation powers have been supplemented since the Single European Act of 1987 and the Maastricht Treaty to include **cooperation procedure** (the ability to influence the Council of Ministers by greater involvement in procedure) and **co-decision powers** which give the EP the right to veto or reject legislation (*Nugent 1994*). The addition of these powers to the EP means a reassessment of its role from a weak institution to one of increasing influence. However, there are a number of problems associated with the institution.

Although the EP is the only other elected Parliament that could challenge the sovereignty of the Westminster national Parliament, its democratic representational credentials are not strong. British turnout in the 1994 European elections at 36 per cent was among the lowest in the EU. In the 1999 elections (members of the European Parliament, MEPs, serve five year terms) turnout fell to 24 per cent undermining claims to sovereignty even further. Public apathy, therefore, on the role of the EP and European institutions is high with the result that claims of a mandate for any particular vision of Europe are hard to substantiate. This argument could therefore be used to support a future Conservative or Labour referendum on the replacement of the pound by the Euro-currency.

European Court of Justice

The European Court of Justice is charged with the upholding and administration of EU laws. As all directives, decisions and laws in the EU are based on the written treaties of the EU, the European Court plays the primary role in interpreting the meanings of these treaties and their applicability to member states. European law is binding over member states and in this sense does not need enactment in the separate Parliaments. Citizens of member states are thus given rights and obligations without recourse to their own legislatures and can appeal directly to the European Court. The power of the European Court over national legislation contravening European law was demonstrated in the **Factortame Case** of 1990 whereby the Court ruled that sections of the British Merchant Fishing Act of 1988 were incompatible with European law. In March 1996 Spanish fishermen were granted leave by the Court to sue the British Government for £30 million for being excluded from British waters.

Parties and the European Debate

Labour

Tony Blair, Prime Minister from 1997, changed Labour attitudes to Europe. The Party passed through periods of pro- and anti-Europeanism. Some on the left saw the institutions of the European Union as a capitalist club offering little to the working classes of the member states. Others had a more pragmatic approach, particularly the modernisers. During the years of opposition to the Conservative governments of Margaret Thatcher and John Major 1979–97, there were those in the Labour party who looked to Europe for socialist support to oppose what they regarded as sectional policies harmful to the working class. The general election of 1997 presented Labour (under

Blair's strict leadership) with the opportunity to appear united on European policy against a divided and unpopular Conservative Party. Since becoming the government this unity has continued with Tony Blair taking the EU Presidency in the first half of 1998, attending the Amsterdam Summit, signing up to the Social Chapter and incorporating the European Convention on Human Rights into UK law as a Bill of Rights. The decision to join EMU has been pushed back beyond the first wave in 1999 and will be based on three decisions (according to the Labour manifesto). Firstly the cabinet and secondly Parliament would have to agree. Thirdly the electorate would have the final say in a referendum. After winning the 2001 general election Tony Blair gave the impression of moving towards Britain joining Euroland in his second term of office. The events of September 11 2001 – the terrorist destruction of the New York World Trade Center and the bombing of Afghanistan – pushed the timetable back. New Labour have declared that Britain will join the Euro when five economic criteria have been met. It is likely that a referendum on this issue will be held in 2002 or 2003 after the introduction of the single currency in France and Germany.

Conservatives and Liberal Democrats

The Liberal Democrats are united in their commitments to Europe – the Conservatives hopelessly divided. The replacement of John Major after his 1997 election defeat by the more Euro-sceptical William Hague signalled that of the remaining 165 MPs in the new Parliament the balance was towards the Euro-phobes or sceptics. After their defeat in 2001 the Conservatives replaced William Hague with the more Euro-sceptic Iain Duncan Smith as leader in preference to the Europhile Kenneth Clarke. Euro-enthusiasts wish for greater influence in Europe, either through intergovernmentalism or federalism, to secure the benefits of greater prosperity. Euro-sceptics are opposed to greater European integration – some are anti-marketeer nationalists, others fear for loss of British sovereignty. Pragmatists do not belong to either category – according to *Geddes* (*1993*), they are characterised by a common sense approach and accept membership of the EU as inevitable. These divisions helped the party lose the 1997 and 2001 general elections. By focusing narrowly on the European Single Currency the Conservatives misjudged the mood of the electorate who placed a higher priority on domestic issues like education and the National Health Service in 2001.

Sovereignty and federalism

According to *Bulmer* (*1994*), debates over British sovereignty centre on two aspects. Firstly, parliamentary sovereignty is the notion that the House of Commons has always had legislative primacy. This is now removed by European Union law and legislation. Secondly, there is the idea of national sovereignty, whereby the UK has the policy freedom to operate as it wishes. By joining the European Union, Britain has lost some of this exclusivity. Decisions are now taken in Brussels which have the potential to divide political parties in the foreseeable future. UK sovereignty was affected by both the Maastricht Treaty (1992) and the Treaty of Amsterdam (1997). Amsterdam was a further development along the road to monetary union and economic integration. By removing the qualification for a unanimous vote in all policy issues more power was given to the Union.

EU enlargement

Proposals to enlarge the European Union from 15 states to 28 were begun in 1998. These were ratified in the Treaty of Nice (2000) which included plans to admit the former states of Eastern Europe. The refusal of the Irish Republic to ratify the treaty through a referendum in 2001 made the issue of further enlargement more complex, and less certain. After a second referendum in 2002, the Irish people voted to accept the Nice proposals.

Changes to the structure of the EU continued throughout 2002, 2003 and 2004. It was agreed at the Copenhagen Council of 2002 to admit ten new states in 2004 and the two former eastern bloc countries, Bulgaria and Romania, in 2007. This would bring the total number of member states to 27. The enlarged EU will comprise the following states: France, Germany, Italy, Belgium, The Netherlands, Luxembourg, Britain, Ireland, Denmark, Greece, Spain, Portugal, Austria, Finland, Sweden, Cyprus, Czech Republic, Estonia, Hungary, Latvia, Lithuania, Malta, Poland, Slovakia, Slovenia, Bulgaria and Romania.

The European Constitution

A current major area of difficulty in Britain's relationship with the EU is the proposed new European Constitution. The draft constitution was discussed at the Brussels Intergovernmental Conference in December 2003 and again in Berlin in 2004. The British government failed to reach agreement particularly over the establishment of a public prosecutor and the surrender of control over internal taxation and no firm decisions were reached. Having been against it, the Labour government has now agreed to place the new constitution before the people in a referendum for final sanction. The other EU states are holding referendums and the Conservative and

Liberal Democrat opposition parties are also in favour. The Blair government appear at this time to be concerned that they might fail to win a majority for the proposals which could be a portent of the result on any future referendum on the Euro.

Evaluation of enlargement

The enlargement of the EU has implications for both the European Parliament and the Council of Ministers. The number of MEPs (Members of the European Parliament) will rise on enlargement from 626 members to a fixed maximum of 732. The Parliament will still retain its legislative, budgetary and supervisory powers and may become more effective with additional members. The Nice Treaty of 2002 extended the procedure of qualified majority voting in the Council of Ministers which will effectively prevent an impasse in the new 27-member council.

Questions

1 What is the role of COREPER?

2 Explain co-operation and co-decision.

3 What was the impact of the Factortame Case (1990)?

4 What is the basic difference between Euro-sceptics and Euro-enthusiasts (europhiles)?

5 How is British sovereignty affected by the EU?

Summary

1 **Membership of the European Union (formerly the European Economic Community) has had a profound effect on British political life in terms of external relations and foreign policy, political sovereignty and the impact on the internal cohesion of the political parties.**

2 **The movement towards European integration offers a number of options for the future direction of British governments: remain in the EU under present developing intergovernmental relationships (confederation), resist the drive towards a supranational Europe (federation), or move to a twin track variable geometry situation combining both approaches allowing a longer term period of adjustment.**

3 **Whichever position is ultimately taken, future governments will have to settle problems of monetary union in the shorter term and decide whether Britain remains at the centre or periphery of other European developments.**

Sample question and answer

A2 Level question

1 How does membership of the European Union affect the UK constitution?

Membership of the European Community (European Union) has had a marked impact on the British constitution and the practice of politics in the United Kingdom. As the British constitution is mainly prescriptive or informal without a single written or codified document, the act of joining a community with a descriptive constitution was bound to have repercussions over the political institutions and practices of Britain. Procedural changes in domestic laws have been imposed on the British bringing them into closer harmonisation with Europe. The constitutional implications arising from this have highlighted divisions within the major political parties and affected the working of the party system, the executive and Parliament.

The initial act of joining the European Community allied the British state to a written constitution through the Treaty of Rome for the first time in its long history. The British Parliament gave effect to the provisions of the Rome Treaty by passing the 1972 European Communities Act; this had two initial effects on the constitution – one parliamentary, the other legal.

Parliamentary sovereignty was affected by the need to apply legislation on its citizens originating from a separate sovereign Parliament (the European Parliament). There was no historical precedence for this dilution of legislative power of the British legislature. The House of Commons and House of Lords have now surrendered their claims to be the sole source of legislation for the British people. New interpretations of parliamentary sovereignty (and electoral sovereignty) were now needed to embrace this reality. Legislation from the European Parliament in effect breaches the principle that no Parliament can bind its successor. Clearly future governments will be bound by legislation from this source.

Cont.

The effects on the British legal system of membership of the European Union have added a new dimension to statute law. Now the judiciary must apply European statutes and provisions that affect the United Kingdom directly, through the courts. British freedom of action under the law has therefore been curtailed. Legally, British citizens are now subject to European Community regulations that are binding and enforced through the courts with appeal to the European Court. In cases of conflict between British domestic law and European Treaty provision, European regulations prevail. Subordination to the laws of the European Union has thus added a new dimension to the rule of law principle. Now traditional judicial review of executive action that is regarded as 'ultra vires' (beyond the powers given in statutes) also includes the European Court and judges taking decisions that affect the British executive. This has been demonstrated in a number of cases including the 1991 Factortame case, where sections of the British Merchant Fishing Act of 1988 were held in breach of European Community policies of free trade by the European Court.

Membership of the European Community was encouraged by successive British governments (although the Conservative Party was initially more enthusiastic) because of the benefits which flow from greater cooperation between the European member states. The initial 1972 European Communities Act has been supplemented by the signing of the Maastricht Treaty 1991 and the Single European Act of 1986, both of which have drawn Britain closer to the ideals of a United Europe. Although Britain achieved the principle of subsidiarity at Maastricht, she still gave up an element of national sovereignty under the Rome Treaty. By being a member of the EU, Britain voluntarily restricted the action of future governments which in itself placed limits over parliamentary sovereignty.

Although Britain has surrendered elements of national sovereignty to the European Union, it has the ultimate sanction of withdrawal from the Rome Treaty. The 1975 Referendum on the European Community gave the British people a choice on continuing membership. Formal safeguards include consultation over future changes in the structures of the EU. Margaret Thatcher was able to reduce Britain's contribution to the EU budget in 1979. Important new policy made in Brussels must have the consent of a British minister who is answerable to the government and Parliament. John Major and Douglas Hurd changed the wording in the Maastricht Treaty from a Federal Europe to one of a closer union, to satisfy both the Euro-enthusiast and Euro-sceptic wings of the Conservative Party rather than Parliament itself. As a last safeguard, the British Parliament has the ability to discuss draft regulations and express opinions through the House of Commons Select Committee on European Legislation.

There is little doubt that Britain's membership of the European Union has affected the constitution, but whether this threatens the political system is a matter for debate. Lord Denning's comment that British sovereignty was affected by European law which restricted the autonomy of the legal system was accurate. But by redefining the traditional concept of parliamentary sovereignty to embrace EU law, the constitution is altered rather than damaged. Adaptability has always been a feature of the constitution and membership of the EU can be seen against a background of adjustment to political reality.

Index